American Politics in the Heartland

Douglas Madsen
Arthur H. Miller
James A. Stimson

University of Iowa

KENDALL/HUNT PUBLISHING COMPANY
2460 Kerper Boulevard P.O. Box 539 Dubuque, Iowa 52004-0539

Copyright © 1990 by Kendall/Hunt Publishing Company

Library of Congress Catalog Card Number: 90–81650

ISBN 0–8403–5890–3

All rights reserved. No part of this publication may be reproduced, stored in a retrieval system, or transmitted, in any form or by any means, electronic, mechanical, photocopying, recording, or otherwise, without the prior written permission of the copyright owner.

Printed in the United States of America
10 9 8 7 6 5 4 3 2 1

Contents

Part 1. **The Public: Attitudes, Beliefs, and Polls, 1**

Chapter 1
Confidence in Government During the 1980s, **3**
Arthur H. Miller

Chapter 2
Understanding Public Opinion Polls, **29**
Kent L. Tedin

Chapter 3
America's Heartland: Examining the Midwestern Myth, **53**
Tami Buhr

Chapter 4
The Mood of the American Electorate, **81**
James A. Stimson

Part 2. **Elections and Their Consequences, 109**

Chapter 5
First in the Nation: Iowa and the Presidential Nomination Process, **111**
Peverill Squire

Chapter 6
Localism in Presidential Elections: The Home State Advantage, **129**
Michael S. Lewis-Beck and Tom W. Rice

Chapter 7
The Paradox of Ignorant Voters but Competent Electorate, **137**
James A. Stimson

Part 3. **The Actors in Washington: Congress, Presidents, Courts, and Bureaucrats, 155**

Chapter 8
Strategies for Building Coalitions in Congress: Majority Versus Minority Party Presidents, **157**
Cary R. Covington

Chapter 9
So Many Cases, So Little Time: Judges as Decision Makers, **175**
Timothy M. Hagle

Chapter 10
The Politics of Administration, **195**
Douglas Madsen

Part 4. **The Public Policy Outcome, 219**

Chapter 11
Inside Games, Outside Games, and the Common Defense: Congress and National Defense, **221**
James M. Lindsay

Chapter 12
Trade Policy: Government Action in the Face of International Commercial Rivalry, **245**
John A.C. Conybeare

Chapter 13
Agriculture Policy and Policy Making, **269**
G.R. Boynton

Part 1

The Public: Attitudes, Beliefs, and Polls

Chapter 1

Confidence in Government During the 1980s

Arthur H. Miller

The Iran-Contra arms scandal of 1986 reawakened concerns in the United States about confidence in government. Scandals such as Watergate and the Iran-Contra affair raise the spectre that those in the highest offices, including the president, do not govern by the rule of law and moral principle. Thus, it is reasonable to hypothesize that these events undermine public confidence in government and political institutions, or that they create doubts about the legitimacy of government actions.

The research goal of this report is twofold. First, we attempt to determine if a decline in political trust occurred as a response to the initial revelations of the Iran-Contra scandal. To answer this question we begin with an investigation of change in political confidence for the period from 1980–1988, attempting to determine if 1986 witnessed a resurgence of distrust that coincided with Iran-gate. Next, the extent and magnitude of the shifts in confidence during this period are examined for various social and political groups that help to control for possibly spurious effects. Lastly, we evaluate competing theoretical and empirical explanations previously offered for the level of, and change in, political trust that is observed for the 1980–1988 period.

Trends In Political Trust

Despite his anti-government rhetoric, Reagan's first term in office had demonstrated that an active executive could bring about political change and get things done. This demonstration of strong and effective leadership won not only high marks for Reagan personally, but it restored much of the confidence in government that citizens had lost during the previous decade and a half (Miller, 1983; Citrin and Green, 1986). What some had heralded as an "age of cynicism" appeared to end with Reagan's series of election victories (McElvaine, 1986).

Yet, within two years of his 1984 reelection, political trust declined significantly from where it was in 1984. Over the two years preceding the 1986 elections the percent saying they trusted the government in Washington to do what is right "always" or "most of the time" dropped from 44% to 38% (see Table 1.1). And an even larger decline occurred in the percentage of citizens believing that politicians "care what people like them think", down from 57% to 43%.

Some might argue that the reversal in public assessments of government and political leaders between 1984 and 1986 was relatively minor and no cause for concern. But, within the historical context of a presumably personally popular president, this expression of disenchantment was unexpected. As can be seen from Table 1.1, Reagan had made great strides in restoring confidence after it reached a historical low under the Carter administration in 1980. Unfortunately, those gains were short lived. Half of the gains in the perceived trustworthiness of government were lost between 1984 and 1986. During that same period the perceived responsiveness of public officials plummeted all the way to its historical low point of 1980 (see Table 1.1). Furthermore, the new loss of confidence in government which occurred between 1984 and 1986 continued on into 1988.

Early Effects of Iran-Contra

But why was the resurgence of trust so short-lived and the 1986 decline so severe? The seemingly obvious answer is because of the Iran-Contra scandal. After all, the 1986 Michigan post-election survey was conducted during the weeks when the initial leaks about the arms shipment to Iran were first appearing in the media. The decline in confidence could, hypothetically, thus reflect the substantially more negative evaluations of those respondents interviewed at a time when the seriousness of the Iran arms affair had become evident. The interviewing for the Michigan survey took place between November 5, 1986 and January 31, 1987. The NES is one of the few national surveys that still employs personal rather than telephone interviewing, thus it takes longer to complete the study than one done by phone.[1]

TABLE 1.1
Individual Confidence in Government Items and Trust Index, 1964-1988

QUESTION: How much of the time do you think you can trust the government in Washington to do what is right--just about always, most of the time, or only some of the time?

	1964	1968	1970	1972	1974	1976	1978	1980	1982	1984	1986	1988
None of the time*	0%	0%	0%	1%	1%	1%	4%	4%	2%	1%	2%	8%
Some of the time*	22	36	44	44	61	62	64	69	62	53	57	55
Most of the time	62	54	47	48	34	30	27	23	31	40	35	36
Always	14	7	7	5	3	3	3	2	2	4	3	4
Don't know	2	2	2	2	2	3	3	2	3	2	2	2
	100%	100%	100%	100%	100%	100%	100%	100%	100%	100%	100%	100%
(N)	(1445)	(1337)	(1497)	(2279)	(2499)	(2859)	(2288)	(1614)	(1401)	(1921)	(1081)	(1775)
PDI[a]	+55	+25	+9	+8	-26	-30	-39	-48	-31	-10	-21	-23

QUESTION: I don't think public officials care much what people like me think.

	1964	1968	1970	1972	1974	1976	1978	1980	1982	1984	1986	1988
Agree*	35%	43%	47%	49%	50%	51%	51%	52%	46%	42%	52%	56%
Disagree	62	55	50	49	46	44	45	44	49	57	43	42
Don't know	2	2	3	2	5	4	5	4	5	5	5	2
	100%	100%	100%	100%	100%	100%	100%	100%	100%	100%	100%	100%
(N)	(1557)	(1337)	(1502)	(2689)	(2505)	(2387)	(2281)	(1397)	(1418)	(2229)	(1082)	(1574)
PDI	+26	+12	+2	0	-4	-7	-6	-8	+3	+15	-9	-14

Trust Index[b]

	1964	1968	1970	1972	1974	1976	1978	1980	1982	1984	1986	1988
0 High	52%	40%	35%	35%	24%	21%	20%	14%	25%	31%	25%	24%
1 Medium	35	42	35	34	36	39	37	42	36	41	34	36
2 Low	13	18	31	32	40	40	43	43	40	27	41	40
	100%	100%	100%	100%	100%	100%	100%	100%	100%	100%	100%	100%
PDI	+39	+2	+4	+3	-16	-19	-23	-29	-15	+4	-16	-16

*Indicates cynical response.
[a] The Percentage Difference Index is calculated by subtracting the percentage giving a cynical response from the percentage giving a trusting response.
[b] The Trust Index combines the two confidence items by indicating the number of cynical responses given to both items: none, one or two. "Don't know's" on either of the two component items cause the index to be counted as "missing data."

Roughly 70% of the interviewing, however, had been completed by the end of November.

The initial revelations about the sale of arms to Iran began to appear in the media around mid-November. Reagan's first televised news conference where questions were raised about the issue occurred on November 19. But the early disclosures were marked by confusion, the lack of specifics and Reagan's attempt to deemphasize the importance of the issue. In the face of increasing pressure to do something about the emerging crisis, Reagan finally acted. On Tuesday, November 25 Vice Admiral John Poindexter, the President's national security adviser resigned and Lieut. Col. Oliver North, a National Security Council staff member, who was later to emerge as the major operative in the scandal, was relieved of his duties by Reagan. By the end of November, amidst continuing revelations, a series of investigations were begun on the President's instructions.

The net impact of all these developments on public opinion was clearly demonstrated in a poll conducted by the New York Times/CBS news during the first week in December. The poll showed that Reagan's overall public approval rating had declined from 67% at the beginning of November to 46%, the most precipitous one-month drop ever recorded by a public opinion poll measuring Presidential popularity (New York Times, December 7, 1986, p.E1).

To test for the possibility that the 1986 decline in political trust was a response to the Iran-arms scandal we divided the NES respondents into two sets, those interviewed before and after the November 25th dismissal of Poindexter and North.[2] As demonstrated by the

TABLE 1.2
Trust Index Before and After 1986 Iran-Contra Disclosures for Total Sample, Democrats, Independents and Republicans[a]

Trust	Before November 25				After November 25			
	Total	Dem	Indep	Rep	Total	Dem	Indep	Rep
High	25%	19%	23%	35%	25%	19%	16%	38%
Medium	34	34	29	37	33	33	37	35
Low	40	47	48	28	41	48	47	27
	100%	100%	100%	100%	100%	100%	100%	100%
(N)	(685)	(324)	(87)	(258)	(331)	(174)	(39)	(112)
PDI	−15	−28	−25	+7	−16	−29	−31	+11

[a] Only pure Independents are separated from the partisans; those that lean one way or the other are included with the appropriate set of partisans.

Trust Index presented in Table 1.2, we found virtually no difference in the level of confidence for these two sets of respondents.[3]

Of course the aggregate stability in trust for the two subsamples may have resulted from counterbalancing trends among partisan groups. Republicans may have rallied in support of their President thus expressing increased trust, and Democrats may have become more negative and lost confidence, while Independents remained unchanged for lack of a partisan predisposition. But, again the evidence failed to substantiate the hypothesis. As Table 1.2 reveals, Republicans interviewed later did express slightly more confidence, but Democrats were unchanged while Independents became more distrusting. These differences by time of interview and partisanship were so slight, however, as to be statistically insignificant. Moreover, the before/after differences are greatest for those categories where the number of respondents are smallest, thus suggesting no more than sampling fluctuation. In short, most of the decline in confidence came prior to the full effect that could eventually be expected from Iran-Contra.

Splitting the sample by time of interview did reveal, however, a significant drop in Presidential approval, thereby coinciding with the trend reported by the Times/CBS poll. The decline, as indicated by the NES subsamples, was from 67% approving to 59%,[4] and occurred for all partisan groups, although it was slightly greater among Republicans and Independents than for Democrats.

The fact that Presidential approval dropped immediately as the Iran-Contra scandal began to unfold, whereas trust did not, has important substantive and methodological implications. Firstly, it helps to validate the measure of political trust (the NES trust measures have been criticized by Mueller and Jukam, 1977). If the trust measure responded as quickly to changing events as Presidential popularity, it could hardly provide a valid indicator for deep seated evaluations of political authorities and institutions more generally. Secondly, and perhaps most importantly, it helps to solidify the argument that trust in government was on the decline even before the Iran-arms scandal had begun to have a major effect on public opinion. This suggests that the 1980–84 recovery in trust was tentative, never fully crystallized, nor based on an enduring solution to the problems that were the root cause of the previous long-term decline in trust.

How Widespread Was The Decline?

Alternatively, the fact that Democrats were more distrusting than Republicans in 1986 (see Table 1.2), suggests the possibility that the decline from 1984 may have occurred only among Democrats. If the drop in confidence was evident only among the supporters of the out-of-power party, it would be less politically significant. But, the trends in political trust among partisan subgroups, summarized in Figure 1.1, reveal a widespread decline that cut across party lines. However, while trust declined for both Democrats and Republicans, the magnitude of the shift toward a more negative image of government varied across the partisan groups. The smallest downturn, not surprisingly, appeared among Republicans. Yet, the fact that there was a significant decline for Republicans is noteworthy, as it indicates that the Reagan/Bush administration was in trouble even among its own constituents, and that the discontent reflected more than mere party conflict.

As in the case of partisanship, the correlations between demographic variables and political trust have not been consistent over the years. Moreover, since the social characteristics of a population change very slowly demographic variables cannot help explain sizable attitudinal shifts, like those observed for trust between 1980 and 1988. Nevertheless, comparing the relative magnitude of change for different demographic groups is instructive, as it indicates which groups were most sensitive to those factors causing distrust. After all, we would draw different conclusions if trust were declining only among the "have-nots" in society. Like the earlier rise in trust, the 1984–86 decline was in fact a widespread phenomenon evident in nearly all social categories but with varying rates of change. Some of the most dramatic declines came among blacks (Howell, 1988), the least well educated and those with the lowest income (see Table 1.3).

The rapid decline in trust among the disadvantaged does not appear to be simply a reflection of self interest, however, as confidence also fell, albeit less quickly, among the most affluent and better educated people in the country (see Table 1.3). Nevertheless, despite a decline in trust, those in the upper 20% of the income scale and college educated people were the only groups to remain predominantly positive toward government since the Republicans regained the White House in 1980. Moreover, the difference in levels of trust for the highest and lowest education and income groups in 1986 and 1988 represent the sharpest class related polarization in attitudes toward

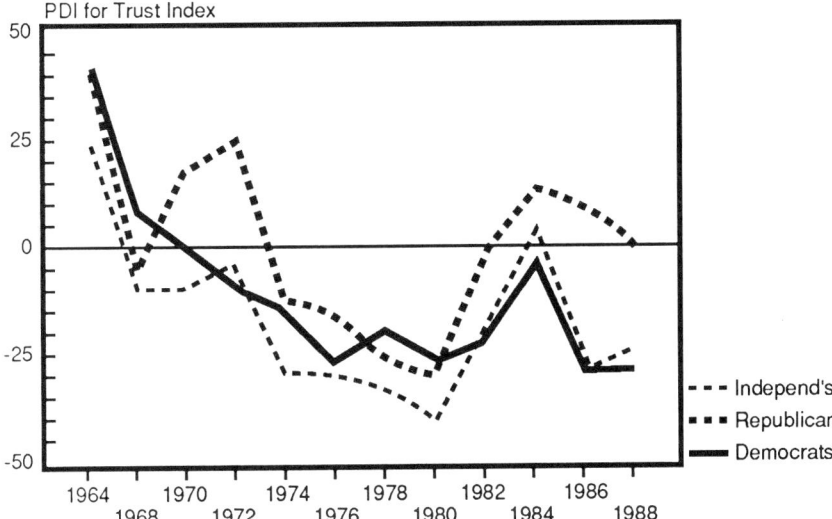

Figure 1.1. Political Trust by Partisanship

government that has occurred since the early seventies. The substantial income related differences in the levels of trust for 1986 and 1988 suggest that economic factors may have played an important role in the recent shifts.

While a majority of affluent Americans remained positive in their evaluations of government toward the end of the eighties, the young, another group politically significant for the future hopes of the Republican party, had again lost confidence. In the 1984 election campaign, Reagan made special appeals to the young people in America. The youngest generation was targeted by Republican strategists as the group that could eventually propel their party into majority status. The Trust PDI figures in Table 1.3 for the younger age groups in 1984 suggest that they did indeed respond very favorably to the Reagan appeals. Those under the age of 40 were predominantly positive toward government and political authorities that year, whereas a majority of those over 40 were negative. But, the disillusionment that set in after 1984 was felt most strongly among the young, and by 1986 they again were predominantly negative just as their elders.

In summary, the decline in confidence that occurred between 1984 and 1988 was as pervasive as the improvement that had appeared in the previous four years. Nevertheless, because of different rates of change for various social groups, by the end of 1988 only

TABLE 1.3
Trends in Political Trust by Demographic Categories

	1964	1968	1970	1972	1974	1976	1978	1980	1982	1984	1986	1988
Race												
Whites	+44	+23	+10	+11	+12	+17	−22	−28	−13	+7	−10	−12
Blacks	+24	+16	−33	−38	−53	−43	−28	−35	−31	−16	−49	−40
Education												
Grade School	+21	+9	−22	−24	−43	−44	−43	−46	−39	−21	−46	−44
High School	+52	+29	+14	+11	−15	−19	−27	−29	−14	0	−12	−19
Some College	+60	+26	+25	+30	+16	−8	−14	−19	−14	+10	−14	−9
College	+65	+43	+39	+27	+18	+14	+6	−20	+14	+9	+11	+9
Income												
Lowest 20%	+2	+6	−23	−18	−35	−36	−33	−40	−36	−14	−36	−43
Middle 20%	+36	+18	−3	+8	−5	−15	−20	−30	−22	+3	−14	−17
Highest 20%	+59	+40	+29	+24	−1	0	−11	−22	+1	+17	+4	+7
Age												
18–29	+50	+31	+12	+11	−3	−14	−14	−28	−13	+9	−13	−17
30–39	+48	+34	+11	+8	−9	−18	−18	−27	−12	+14	−1	−16
40–49	+40	+25	+13	+10	−10	−9	−23	−27	−18	−3	−15	−11
50–59	+39	+21	+1	−12	−21	−17	−22	−31	−11	−2	−9	−5
60+	+20	+2	+15	−7	−28	−32	−41	−34	−19	−4	−16	−25

Republicans, the college educated and wealthy people remained predominantly positive in their evaluations of government and political authorities. All other major groups had once again become overwhelmingly cynical.

Explaining Political Distrust

If this widespread decline in confidence was not the result of Irangate, how do we explain it? A number of possible general explanations, frequently referred to in the Political Science literature on trust, stem from an academic debate between Citrin and Miller (1974). The major issues of that exchange revolved around the question of whether confidence in government reflected the popularity and style of the President and incumbent administration, as argued by Citrin, or represented a more profound discontent with the inability of political leaders to formulate policies that effectively and equitably solved social problems, as Miller contended. Three alternative theoretical explanations emerged from the Miller/Citrin dialogue and subsequent academic research. Briefly stated, the first involves the popular appeal of the person currently in the White House. The second focuses on the visible performance of the incumbent administration, that is, its ability to solve problems, especially those of an economic nature. The third explanation incorporates public satisfaction or dissatisfaction with the policies and programs implemented by the national government. Which theory most effectively and accurately explains the shifts in trust during the 1980-88 period is an empirical question, to which we now turn.

Presidential Popularity

In the American system of government, the President is the most visible political leader in the entire country. It is reasonable to hypothesize, therefore, that the popularity of the President may have a substantial effect on the confidence that citizens express in government and political authorities conceived more generally. Indeed, this is exactly the argument that Citrin (1974) employed to explain the decline in political trust which occurred from the mid-sixties to the early seventies. More recently Citrin and Green (1986) attributed the 1980-84 improvement in trust to Reagan's popular persona, rather than government performance or policies.

On the surface the argument appears convincing. A series of personally unpopular Presidents (Nixon, Ford and Carter) led to the deterioration of respect, not only for the presidency, but for all politicians and the political institutions they represent. Reagan, a very charismatic and charming person, comes into office and the confidence people have in the political system is restored. On closer inspection, the theory has a number of problems. Neither in the long nor short-run does Presidential popularity adequately account for change in political trust (the longitudinal correlation between presidential popularity and trust is only .10). For example, during the economic recession of 1982, Reagan's personal popularity, as measured by a 0–100 thermometer rating scale, was lower than Jimmy Carter's had been two years earlier, yet trust increased. Similarly, between 1984 and 1986 Reagan's average thermometer rating rose, while trust plummeted (see Figure 1.2).

Presidential job approval, frequently used as another measure of popularity, on the other hand was more strongly associated with trust (a longitudinal correlation of .5). This stronger relationship, however, appears to reflect public assessments of how well the President is dealing with policy, rather than a response to his personal popularity. Moreover, despite the stronger correlation, Presidential approval and trust frequently fail to co-vary. For example, between 1980 and 1984 the population trend for Presidential approval and trust were parallel, both improving. But, when confidence fell two years later, Reagan's approval rating actually rose slightly (see Figure 1.2). Similar contradictory trends were also evident among partisan subgroups.[5] In short, the association between Presidential popularity and trust is at best inconsistent, thereby contradicting Citrin's theory.

The absence of consistent trends for trust and Presidential popularity has important implications. To discover otherwise would raise serious questions about the validity of the trust index as an indicator of attitudes more profound than the evaluation of the incumbent President. Furthermore, it would be normatively disquieting to find that public opinion regarding how right and proper government actions are, or how responsive politicians are to their constituents, reflects nothing more than Presidential charisma.

Previous research suggests, however, that citizens primarily judge politicians on individual qualities relevant to the conduct of office, such as competence and integrity, rather than superficial traits like charisma and personal appeal (Page, 1978; Shabad and Andersen, 1979; Miller et al., 1986; Kinder 1986). Indeed, in examining the

Confidence in Government During the 1980s   13

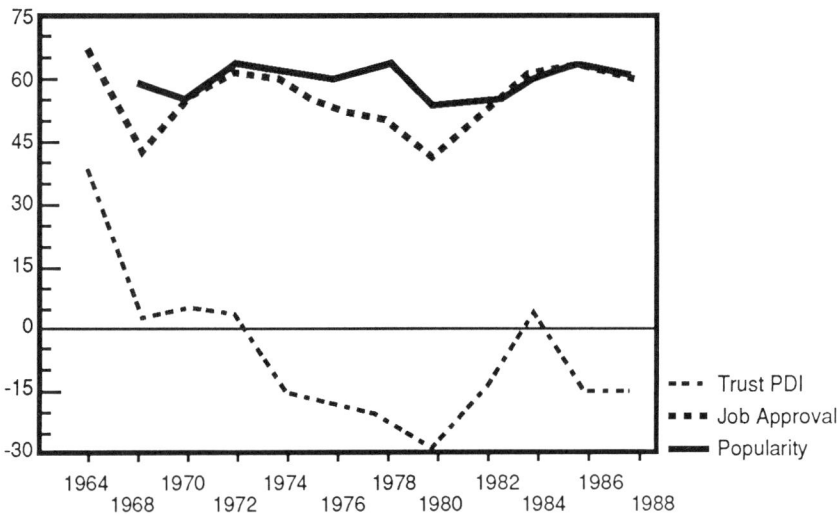

Notes for Figure 1.2
Trends in Presidential Popularity, Job Approval and Trust 1964–1988

	1964	1968	1970	1972	1974	1976
Popularity[a]	—	60	57	65	63	61
Job Approval[b]	69	43	57	62	60	53
Trust PDI	+39	+2	+4	+3	−16	−19

	1978	1980	1982	1984	1986	1988
Popularity[a]	64	56	55	61	63	61
Job Approval[b]	50	41	51	63	64	60
Trust PDI	−23	−29	−15	+4	−16	−16

aPopularity was measured with the mean NES thermometer rating. The scale ranges from 0–100 degrees. Zero indicates the most negative feelings toward the President, 50 is neutral and 100 is the most favorable rating. No measure was availabe in 1964.
bEntries are the percent of population approving of how the incumbent is handling the job of the President. NES data are used for the years 1974 and 1980–1986. Gallup data are used for the other years. Missing data are excluded from the calculations.

Figure 1.2. Trends in Presidential Popularity, Job Approval and Trust 1964–1988

relationship between trust and the incumbent president's persona, Citrin and Green (1986, p.446) rightly conclude that, "people may lose confidence in government because its top leaders are perceived as immoral, incompetent or both."

During the period of 1980-88 the relative impact of public judgments regarding the President's competence and morality on political trust changed. Carter's honesty and integrity were unquestionable, but he was not perceived as a strong and effective leader.[6] It is popularly believed that Reagan won the election in 1980 because he offered more effective leadership. However, contrary to what the mass media often suggest, upon entering the presidency Reagan was not perceived by the public as a person of exceptional moral character or competence (in 1980 only 18% of the public said that "moral" and 15% said "strong leader" described him "extremely well"). But, over the course of his first term in office, his performance earned him an improved public image. By 1984, "moral" and "strong leader" were seen as fitting him "extremely well" by roughly one-third of the NES respondents (34 and 30 percent respectively). Given that these judgments were significantly related to trust in government (see Table 1.4), it is reasonable to conclude that Carter's perceived lack of competence contributed significantly to the crisis of confidence in 1980, and that Reagan's public image of strong leadership influenced the rise of trust from 1980 to 1984.

With the easing of economic problems in 1984, the public's assessment of the President's character began to shift in focus from leadership, to concerns about morality and compassion for others. In 1984 Reagan's perceived strength of leadership contributed more strongly to political trust than did his moral integrity (as indicated by regression coefficients of .15 and .09 respectively in Table 1.4). But, by 1986 concerns about morality and compassion had increased in importance and the impact these concerns were having on confidence equaled that found for assessments of leadership.

Reagan was not perceived as someone who was "compassionate" and concerned about people. Only 18% of the public in 1984 and 16% in 1986 thought that "compassionate" described him "extremely well". Furthermore, Reagan's lack of concern for ordinary people was significantly related to political distrust in both those years, as was also true for Bush in 1988. Indeed, a multivariate analysis which included the three trait assessments of Reagan (Bush in 1988) as a "strong leader", "moral" or "compassionate" person, demonstrates that all three dimensions of presidential character con-

TABLE 1.4
Regressions Predicting Trust Index From Presidential Character Traits[a]

Traits	1980	1982	1984		1986		1988[c]	
Moral	.12*	.11*	.09*	.06	.18*	.11*	.15*	.13*
Strong Leader	.09*	.14*	.15*	.12*	.19*	.13*	.12*	.11*
Compassionate[b]	—	—	—	.11*	—	.17*	—	.10*
R	.17	.22	.21	.25	.31	.36	.24	.30
(N)	(1227)	(1262)	(1758)		(977)		(1365)	(1316)

*p. <01
[a]Table entries are unstandardized coefficients.
[b]This item was unavailable in 1980 and 1982.
[c]The 1988 measures refer to George Bush, all other years refer to Reagan.

tributed significantly to distrust in the 1986–1988 period (see Table 1.4). Unfortunately, the NES survey did not include the caring item in 1980 or 1982, thus making comparisons across all the years impossible.

In summary, over the years various aspects of presidential character have influenced the degree of respect the average citizen has toward government. Nixon's dishonesty in attempting to cover-up the Watergate affair undermined confidence in the early seventies. Public perceptions of Carter's incompetence undermined trust at the end of the seventies. Reagan's strong leadership initially helped to restore confidence, but later his apparent lack of sympathy for human needs contributed to renewed discontent. Nevertheless, these evaluations of presidential character provide less than a complete explanation for either the across time trends or the cross-sectional level of trust in the political system. Moreover, without reference to how the government is performing its responsibilities, or to the policies that are being enacted, it is difficult to understand why people evaluate the president as they do. Most recent analyses have therefore, examined perceived economic performance as a possible causal factor influencing trust in government.

Economic Performance

There are good theoretical reasons for believing that citizens' evaluations of economic performance are strongly related to their willingness to trust government. As Weatherford (1987) has pointed

TABLE 1.5
Trust Index by Economic Performance Items[a]

	1980	1982	1984	1986	1988
Personal Situation[b]					
Better	−21	− 2	+17	− 2	− 2
Same	−25	−15	+ 1	−23	−23
Worse	−38	−25	−14	−25	−30
(Pearson's r):	(.11)	(.12)	(.17)	(.13)	(.15)
National Situation[c]					
Better	0	− 4	+19	+10	+ 8
Same	−19	+ 2	+ 1	8	−13
Worse	−32	−22	−15	−36	−34
(Pearson's r):	(.10)	(.14)	(.18)	(.22)	(.19)
Government Policies Have Made Economy[d]					
Better			+27	+19	+15
Same	N.A.	N.A.[e]	− 4	−20	−21
Worse			−16	−43	−30
(Pearson's r):			(.22)	(.27)	(.24)

[a]Source: Data From CPS National Election Studies, 1980-1986. Entries are PDIs (percentage difference index): Percentage of group in most trusting category—Percentage of group in least trusting category.
[b]Question: "We are interested in how people are getting along financially these days. Would you say that you (and your family living here) are better or worse off financially than you were a year ago?"
[c]Question: "[What] How about the economy [in the country as a whole]? Would you say that over the past year the nation's economy has gotten better, stayed about the same, or gotten worse?"
[d]Question: "Would you say that the economic policies of the Federal government have made the nation's economy better, worse, of haven't they made much of a difference either way?"
[e]An item analogous to the '84 and '80 politicized items was available for '82, but since it mentioned Reagan by name we felt that it would not be comparable to the later "Federal government" items.

out, there is much evidence that citizens attribute credit or blame for economic conditions to the government, thus making economic performance evaluations a likely factor influencing trust in the national government.

Table 1.5 reports the bivariate relationships between the Trust Index for 1980–1988, and three measures of economic attitudes: respondent's assessment of their own economic fortunes, evaluations of national economic performance, and the respondent's opinion regarding the effects of government policy on the economy. As one would expect, in those years for which it was available, the politicized evaluation (perceived effects of government policy) was more strongly correlated with the Trust Index than was either of the nonpolitical items. Without exception, however, the personal and national evaluations show a consistent relationship with the Index: in all years, those who thought that their own fortunes or those of their country had worsened in the past year were less likely to trust government than those who reported improvement.

But, can changes in economic evaluations explain shifts in levels of trust, particularly the decline in trust between 1984 and 1986? Personal economic performance does not appear to be a cause of the 1984–1986 shift as there was no corresponding change in respondents' evaluations of their personal economic circumstances. In short, those who claimed to be worse off in 1986 were somewhat less likely to distrust government than their counterparts in 1984, and there was no appreciable increase in the number of those feeling worse off during the interim. It is difficult therefore, to see how personal economic performance could account for the 20 point drop in the PDI for the Trust Index between 1984 and 1986.

National economic evaluations and attitudes concerning the impact of government policy on economic outcomes are more credible explanations. The individual-level correlations with the Trust Index for measures of these attitudes are moderately strong in recent years. In addition, the direction and magnitude of the aggregate 1980–88 shifts in these evaluations are similar to those in the Index. The combination of a declining proportion of economic optimists between 1984 and 1986 (on both the politicized and nonpoliticized national items), and a stronger relationship in 1986 between economic attitudes and trust, makes a convincing case for perceived economic performance as a source of renewed political distrust.

There are important considerations, however, that warn against assigning too much explanatory weight to economic evaluations when examining variations in trust within and across years. For example, while trust did fall between 1984 and 1986 most sharply for economic pessimists, it declined significantly for economic optimists as well. Among those who thought that the national economic situation had improved, the percentage in the most distrusting category of the Trust Index increased from 20% in 1984 to 29% in 1986. Among those who thought that Federal government policy had helped the economy, the percentage in the most cynical category rose from 17% to 24%. Clearly factors over and above economic performance were responsible for this shift, and we join Citron and Green (1986) in being tentative about the impact of economic evaluations.

Policy Discontent

Dissatisfaction arising from a perceived discrepancy between the citizen's policy preferences and the programs pursued by the government, has also been suggested as an explanation for declining confidence (Miller, 1974). If a series of incumbents are incapable of producing effective and equitable solutions to societies major problems, policy related discontent grows, thereby threatening to undermine confidence in government. Alternatively, citizens who agree with the policy orientation of the incumbent national administration should feel confident that the right decisions are being made more generally, thus promoting trust in government.

Two broad areas of policy that have perennially received considerable attention are spending on social programs and defense. By the end of Carter's term in office, both his domestic and foreign policy had come under attack. His social policies were criticized for promoting "welfare cheaters", and his failure to gain release for the American hostages held in Iran brought the charge that the United States military strength had collapsed. In 1980, the crisis of confidence in government was associated with dissatisfaction expressed toward Carter's policies. Those favoring increased military spending and reduced social spending were significantly more cynical than the rest of the population (see Table 1.6).

Ronald Reagan effectively tapped this growing discontent by articulating an anti-government philosophy, pursuing cutbacks in the scope of social programs, reducing taxes and dramatically increasing military spending. If the policy discontent theory of trust is correct, Reagan's actions should have increased policy satisfaction, which in turn restored confidence in government. The data appear to support that hypothesis, at least during Reagan's first term in office. Policy discontent, measured as the proportion of the public most distant from the policies associated with the incumbent national government, declined significantly between 1980 and 1984 (see Table 1.6).[7] However, by 1986 Reagan's policies were apparently becoming less popular as discontent began to grow again, and the correlation with distrust increased in magnitude (see Table 1.6).

At the outset of his presidency Reagan's policies appeared to satisfy the preferences of those favoring his conservative changes, without further alienating those opposed. In fact, during his first two years in office support for Reagan's position of cutting social spending actually increased. Yet, by 1984 public opinion was already drift-

TABLE 1.6
Social and Defense Spending Policy Discontent 1980–1986

	1980	1982	1984	1986	1988
Social Policy Discontent[a]					
Percent Dissatisfied	40.1	33.2	30.0	34.6	35.1
Correlation with Trust	.15	.08	.18	.26	.27
Defense Policy Discontent[b]					
Percent Dissatisfied	40.6	32.1	30.3	35.8	34.6
Correlation with Trust	.12	.09	.14	.22	.19

[a]Based on response to the following question using a 7-point scale: Some people think the government should provide fewer services, even in areas such as health and education in order to reduce spending. Other people feel it is important for the government to provide many more services even if it means an increase in spending. Where would you place yourself on this scale? Where would you place what the federal government is doing at the present time?
Dissatisfaction is indicated by a distance of 3 or more units between where the respondents places themselves and the federal government.
[b]The survey question was: Some people believe we should spend much less money for defense. Suppose these people are at one end of the scale at point number 1. Others feel that defense spending should be greatly increased; they are at point 7. Where would you place yourself? Where would you place what the federal government is doing?
Dissatisfaction is 3 or more units between self and government placement.

ing back toward favoring increased government social spending and decreased defense spending. The trend continued, and within two years a significant fraction of the American public believed that social spending had been curtailed enough, and that further spending on the military would be excessive. Reagan's undaunting calls for yet further cuts in domestic programs to help balance the budget became seen by many as uncaring and inequitably targeted at the disadvantaged.[8] The net result was that by the end of the Reagan years the policies of the Republican administration had alienated the liberals without fully satisfying the conservatives, thus increasing political cynicism on both the left and the right.

A Multivariate Analysis

To this point three broadly defined sources of political trust have been discussed: popular judgments of the president's character, the government's performance in handling the economy, and agreement with the government's policies. Thus far each of these explanations has been treated independently. Yet as the discussion has proceeded, it has been apparent that none of these factors alone provides a complete explanation for either the level of trust or the shifts in confidence over recent years. moreover, the explanations are not mutually exclusive. It would be surprising if the policy actions of an incumbent administration did not influence public assessments of presidential character or economic performance, and vice versa.

Untangling the interrelationships among the different explanations with a multivariate analysis, however, reveals the relative impact that each factor had on confidence while controlling simultaneously for the other explanations and certain demographic variables. Such an analysis demonstrates that each of the factors independently contributes to an overall explanation of trust, although with changing relative importance across time (see Table 1.7). In every year except 1988 the public's judgment of presidential character was a significant political explanation, offers partial confirmation for previous research (Citrin and Green, 1986). In three of the four years, however, the impact of policy agreement and economic performance either equals or surpasses that of presidential character. Likewise, the absence of significant effects for the character trait variables in 1988 certainly suggests the possibility that the impact of presidential character was unique to Ronald Reagan, rather than a general phenomena. Further research on this point is clearly needed.

The fact that policy agreement was significantly related with trust in each of the years, except 1982, also contradicts Citrin's argument that distrust has nothing to do with disagreement over national policies. Without the growing impact of policy and economic performance in the later part of the period, it would be impossible to provide a meaningful empirical explanation for the dramatic 1984–86 decline in confidence. Furthermore, the time-series correlation between policy satisfaction and trust for the 1980–88 period is quite strong, 4=.9.

The multivariate results, taken as a whole, suggest an explanation for the trend in trust over the entire period from 1980–1988. The rise in trust from 1980 to 1984 appears to have resulted largely from the emerging public perception of Reagan as a strong leader. The recovery in trust began in the early period of Reagan's first term when the public was apparently impressed with his ability to effectively promote policies that carried out his campaign promises. These early successes promoted the image of Reagan as a strong leader; remember he was not widely perceived that way when first elected in 1980. By 1982 this positive image of Reagan as a strong leader had

TABLE 1.7
Multivariate Regressions Predicting Trust Index

	1980	1982	1984	1984	1986	1988
Presidential Character						
Moral	.09**	.02	.10**	.08*	.04	.04
Strong Leader	.07	.12**	.02	.01	.08	.05
Compassionate	—	—	—	.10**	.15**	.04
Economic Performance						
Personal	.10*	.05	.02	.02	.01	.04
National	.08*	.05	−.04	−.04	.02	.05
Politicized	—	—	.14**	.13**	.10**	.07*
Policy Dissatisfaction						
Social	.08*	.05	.11**	.11**	.06	.16**
Defense	.04	.01	.01	.01	.11**	.06
Demographic Controls						
Race	.08*	−.04	.01	.00	.01	.03
Income	−.04	−.09**	−.04	−.03	.01	−.11**
Age	−.03	.04	−.08**	−.08**	−.04**	−.02**
Education	−.10**	−.16**	−.08**	−.08**	−.18**	−.14**
Political Controls						
Party Identification	−.08*	.08	.10**	.11**	.02	.04
Presidential Approval	.10*	.10*	.13**	.11**	.03	.06
R^2	.10	.11	.12	.12	.18	.17
(N)	(746)	(760)	(1177)	(1170)	(649)	(1139)

Trust Index was coded: low values=trust.
* p. < .05 ** p. < .01 Entries are standardized coefficients.

been established in the public mind, and was able to support continued improvement in confidence despite a severe economic recession. It is noteworthy that "strong leader" was the only significant nondemographic predictor of trust in 1982, see Table 1.7). The growth in the predictive importance of public concerns about the unsympathetic character of the Reagan administration is demonstrated by the second set of equations for 1984, 1986, and 1988, which include the question about "compassionate" as a description of the President. When the "compassion" item is included in the equation, evaluations of presidential leadership and morality are no longer as significant. The shift in focus from leadership to compassion in part, therefore, helps explain the decline in trust after 1984.

Another major contribution to the decline in trust came from growing policy dissatisfaction after 1984 (recall Table 1.6). Empirically, the growing impact of policy and performance dissatisfaction on trust is evident in Table 1.7 from the larger coefficients for the politicized economic item and the social and defense policy measures as of 1984. In the later years of the Reagan administration a series of mishandled events began to raise public criticisms of administration policies. For example, the bombing of Libya on the grounds of deterring terrorism, which was followed by the disclosure of a "disinformation" plan emanating from the National Security Council, the failed summit meeting at Reykjavik, a continued military buildup and calls for spending billions on SDI despite a growing national deficit, all raised serious doubts and increased controversy regarding the government's foreign policies. Similar problems also developed in relation to domestic policies. The economic recovery was increasingly seen as helping only certain regions of the country, the tax reform act was unpopular among liberals and conservatives, calls for mandatory drug testing were seen by some as lacking concern for the human suffering involved in drug addiction or an invasion of civil liberties while others demanded even more stringent measures. Along with the increasing policy polarization that was occurring liberals began to see the Reagan administration policies as uncaring and inequitable, while conservatives felt that they did not yet go far enough in reducing the scope of government or promoting traditional values. In short, the rise and then decline in trust, during the Reagan era, was the result of how the public responded to both presidential character and administration policies.

Conclusion

The research reported here holds implications for both theoretical explanations of political behavior, and practical, everyday politics. On the theoretical side, it is becoming increasingly evident that public cognitions and evaluative responses to political phenomena involve a focus on three conceptually distinct factors: policy, performance, and the attributes of political leaders. All of these factors were important in understanding the trends in political trust over the recent past. Yet, the relative impact of each on overall evaluations of government varied across time. From this variation we should not conclude, however, that the relative importance of the factors is a random occur-

TABLE 1.8
Political Trust by Preferences on Government Spending for Social Services and Defense

Preference on Spending for:	1980	1982	1984	1986
Social Services[a]				
Reduce: % favoring	34	40	34	26
Trust PDI	−36	−14	+ 9	− 5
In-between: % favoring	20	29	31	29
Trust PDI	−28	−11	+ 8	− 8
Increase: % favoring	46	31	35	45
Trust PDI	−24	−14	− 2	−25
Defense[a]				
Reduce: % favoring	12	35	33	38
Trust PDI	−27	−10	− 4	−29
In-between: % favoring	17	32	32	30
Trust PDI	−32	−18	+ 8	− 9
Increase: % favoring	71	33	35	32
Trust PDI	−34	−11	+14	+ 2

[a]See Table 1.7 for the wording of the survey questions used here. The 7-point issue scales have been collapsed into the three categories indicated above by combining 1–3, 4 above, and 5–7.

rence dictated by uncontrollable forces. Frequently historical events, such as the hostage crisis Carter faced in 1980, are instrumentally and politically motivated. Moreover, for the maintenance of political trust, what is often most important in these events is how the political leader responds to the event, rather than the initial cause of the event.

We have argued that attributes of the president's character are only part of the explanation of political trust. There has been significant change in the specific character traits exhibiting the strongest relationship with trust, with important implications for how we conceptualize "character". This elusive concept has been the focus of considerable media attention and public scrutiny in recent years because of the Watergate, Gary Hart and Irangate scandals, as well as the emphasis on candidate "character" in the 1988 election campaign. Yet, the social sciences have not fully charted the substantive nature of political character nor determined the scope of its relevance for explaining mass political behavior. The fact that perceptions of Reagan's character, as defined by morality, leadership, and compassion, changed over time, and had varying influence on trust, suggests that character is not simply a stable attribute of the politician's personality. What is meant by character in public cognitions depends partly on historical events, and partly on the policies and performance of the political actor. Political "character" is thus actively created in the public mind from a combination of perceived leadership traits, judgments of policy actions, and the citizen's own political predispositions. The above research demonstrates that citizen confidence in government partly arises from public assessments of politically relevant aspects of presidential character, but not the mere popularity of the current incumbent.

The causes of political trust or distrust are more deepseated than the short-run evaluations of political leaders. Despite the profundity of the causes, some might still argue that the target of distrust is the authorities and not the political regime. Were such an argument valid, it would hardly undermine the substantive importance of declining confidence in government. Even discontent that focused on political authorities would be significant in a system of government where considerable emphasis is given to individual politicians, as in the United States. We suggest, however, that low political trust does hold implications for the regime. We should not be misinterpreted here to mean that distrust reflects desires to change the form of government from democracy to socialism, or from a presidential to a parliamentary system. Rather, we mean that declining trust represents a growing discontent with the institutional arrangements that affect the distribution of resources and political power.

When citizens are dissatisfied with the policies and performance of government over a series of incumbents from different parties, their attitudes toward the political system change. Simple disagreement with the particular policy outcomes of government becomes generalized to a concern that goes beyond the particular decision makers to a real questioning of the rules of the game and the fairness in the process by which decisions are made (Gamson, 1968; Tyler, Rasinski, and MacGraw, 1985). An enduring perception of the government as unresponsive calls into question one of the most profound tenets of democracy, the accountability of elected leaders before the law.

It is apparent that restoring an enduring public confidence in government goes well beyond who wins the presidency. To accomplish this task more than presidential style, leadership or personal popularity are necessary. The restoration of trust awaits a government

TABLE 1.9
Multivariate Regressions Predicting Trust Index

	1980	1982	1984	1986	1984	1986
Presidential Character						
Moral	.10*	.04	.08*	.12*	.06	.06
Strong Leader	.12*	.12*	.05	.10*	.04	.07
Compassionate	—	—	—	—	.08*	.15*
Economic Performance						
Personal	.11*	.06	.05	.01	.05	–.01
National	.07	.04	–.02	.05	–.04	.05
Politicized	—	.05	.13*	.08*	.13*	.08*
Policy Distance						
Social	.08*	.06	.10*	.12*	.10*	.10*
Defense	.05	–.02	.01	.09*	–.02	.09*
Demographics						
Race	.07*	–.03	.00	.03	–.01	–.01
Income	–.05	–.14*	–.05*	–.05	–.05	–.04
R	.27	.27	.29	.37	.30	.40
(N)	(751)	(766)	(1220)	(668)	(1206)	(660)

Entries are standardized regression coefficients.

* $p. < .01$

that provides a match between promises and performance, the merging of rhetoric and reality, and the application of effective and equitable policies.

Notes

1. The NES sample is drawn from the population of households in all 50 states, according to a "multi-stage area probability" design (see CPS/NES Codebook for 1986). The survey was administered in person by NES interviewers; the median length of interview was 70 minutes. The total sample size was 2176; the sample size for many individual survey items may be much smaller due to the use of different questionnaire forms.
2. We selected the 25th of November as the point for dividing the respondents so as to not dilute the potential effect of the Iran-arms scandal on trust. By the end of November the seriousness of the scandal had become evident so those interviewed after that date would show the maximum impact of the revelations. To safeguard against having selected a biased cutting point we redid the analysis using two other sampling splits. One entailed dividing the sample into thirds as designated by time of interview. The other used November 19, the date of

Reagan's first televised news conference dealing with the issue. Both of these alternative sample divisions confirm the earlier finding, namely that the level of trust was the same regardless of time of interview.
3. It should be noted that neither one of these sets of respondents taken alone forms a fully representative sample. There were, however, only minor demographic differences between the two parts of the sample. Controlling for these differences had no effect on the distribution of trust for either subset.
4. The drop in Presidential approval found by the NES study was noticeably smaller than that reported by the Times/CBS poll. The difference in the magnitude of the decline for the two surveys probably reflects differences in time when the studies were done, as well as differences that may arise between telephone and personal interviewing methods.
5. From 1982 to 1986 roughly 90% of Republicans and 73% of Independents consistently approved of Reagan's job performance, at the same time their trust in government first rose and then fell significantly. Over this same period, Presidential approval among Democrats increased from 27% in 1982 to 35% in 1984 and 44% in 1986. Yet between 1984 and 1986, as we have already demonstrated, trust plummeted among Democrats back to the level where it was prior to Reagan's initial election.
6. In 1980, when asked about a set of personal traits that might describe Carter "extremely well", 35% of the NES respondents said "moral" but only 6% said "strong leader".
7. Individuals may differ in their perception of what policies the government is actually pursuing. Therefore, policy satisfaction/discontent is measured by not only asking survey respondents about their own policy preference, but also asking them what policy they think the government is currently following. These policy preferences and perceptions are gauged with a 7-point scale that runs from a liberal alternative on one end to a conservative position at the other end. Policy satisfaction is then computed by subtracting the respondent's scale position from that which they assign to the government. The absolute value of the resulting difference ranges from 0–6. We have defined as "discontented" those respondents who are 3 or more units away from the position they associate with the government. In previous research the incumbent President rather than the government has been used as the point of comparison. Such measures, however, have been criticized as being confounded with presidential popularity (Citron and Green, 1986). By using the government as the referent these measurement problems should be minimized.
8. In 1986 the social spending policy discontent measure and the presidential trait item tapping "caring" were significantly related with survey questions asking if inequality was a problem in the United States. These correlations were particularly strong among low income and black respondents.

References

Citrin, Jack, and Donald Green. 1986. Presidential Leadership and Trust in Government. *British Journal of Political Science*, 16:431–453.

Citrin, Jack. 1974. The Political Relevance of Trust in Government. *American Political Science Review* 68:973–988.

Gamson, William A. 1968. *Power and Discontent*. Homewood, Illinois: Dorsey.

Kiewet, D. Roderick. 1983. *Macroeconomics and Micropolitics: The Electoral Effects of Economic Issues.* Chicago: University of Chicago Press.

Kinder, Donald. 1986. Presidential Character Revisited. In Richard Lau and David Sears, eds., *Political Cognition.* Hillsdale, New Jersey: Lawrence Erlbaum Associates.

Miller, Arthur H. 1974. Political Issues and Trust in Government: 1964–1970. *American Political Science Review,* 68:951–972.

Miller, Arthur H. 1983. Is Confidence Rebounding? *Public Opinion,* 6:16–20.

Miller, Arthur H., Martin P. Wattenberg, and Oksana Malanchuk. 1986. Schematic Assessments of Presidential Candidates. *American Political Science Review,* 80:521–540.

Mueller, Edward N., and Thomas O. Jukan. 1977 On the Meaning of Political Support. *American Poliitical Science Review,* 71:1561–1595.

Page, Benjamin I. 1978. *Choices and Echoes in Presidential Elections.* Chicago: University of Chicago Press.

Shabad, Goldie and Kristi Anderson. 1979. Candidate Evaluations by Men and Women. *Public Opinion Quarterly,* 43:19–35.

Tyler, Tom R., Kenneth Rasinski, and Kathleen McGraw. 1985. The Influence of Perceived Injustice Upon Support for the President, Political Authorities, and Government Institutions. *Journal of Applied Social Psychology,* 15:700–725.

Weatherford, M. Stephen. 1987. How Does Government Performance Influence Political Support? *Political Behavior,* 9:5–28.

Chapter 2

Understanding Public Opinion Polls

Kent L. Tedin

Following the 1980 election, the *Detroit Free Press* ran a headline story "Pollsters Kissed Off by Electorate: Have 1,001 Excuses"[1] Two years later Burns Roper, founder of the Roper Poll, wrote an article entitled "The Polls Malfunction in 1982."[2] Four years later, in 1986, similar complaints were heard. An ABC polling analyst was quoted in the *New York Times* as saying, "I don't think it was a great year for pollsters."[3] According to prominent Democratic pollster Peter Hart, "Polling ranged all over the lot." The *Washington Post*-ABC News polled ten close Senate races in late October. Four of the candidates with leading margins were defeated.[4] These "mispredictions" along with others gave reporters yet another opportunity for a journalistic coup on "What went wrong with the polls."

The analysis of public opinion and elections, using modern survey methods, has now been part of the public landscape for over fifty years. Nevertheless, most popular criticism of public opinion polls seems amazingly ill-informed. Polling certainly deserves a critical look. Many surveys are badly-conceived, poorly executed, and incorrectly interpreted. But few, including those who write about the subject for newspapers and magazines, have an appreciation for why candidates who lead in the final pre-election poll do not always win; why two surveys taken at the same time report different results; or even why Truman beat Dewey when the Gallup Poll poll predicted otherwise.

An understanding of what can and cannot be inferred from political polls has a practical importance that lies beyond the academic world. It is now agreed that a candidate's poor showing in pre-election polls makes fundraising difficult and dampens volunteer enthusiasm. More importantly, democratic governments (as well as others) justify their existence by claiming to respond to "the will of the people." Public opinion surveys have become the commonly accepted tool for uncovering the hopes, fears, wishes, preferences, and values of those whom government serves.

Polls, of course, are not the only way of assessing public sentiment. Prior to the 1930s, party officials, politicians, and leaders of voluntary associations such as labor unions or temperance organizations were able to use as political leverage their claim to understand the political opinions of their constituent members. Today elected officials still claim to have insight into the desires of their constituencies; labor leaders continue to assert that they know and speak for the preferences of the rank and file. However, when faced with contradictory findings from "scientific" opinion surveys, these claims are quickly discounted by the popular press as well as by influential decision makers. In the latter part of the twentieth century, "public opinion" has become that quantity discoverable through of use of modern survey research.[5]

In this chapter we shall outline the major procedures used in conducting public opinion surveys and how they can go awry. Equally as important, however, is that technically correct surveys are often misinterpreted, misunderstood, and sometimes deliberately distorted. We will attempt to provide some guidance which will allow the reader to become an intelligent consumer of the survey product.

Sampling

Most public opinion polls are based on samples. When the *Gallup Poll* reports that 50 percent of adult Americans approve of the way that the President is handling his job, it is obvious that the Gallup organization has not gone out and interviewed 180 million American adults. Instead it has taken a sample. The reasons for sampling are fairly straightforward. First, to interview everyone would be prohibitively expensive. The 1980 census cost well over one billion dollars. Second, to interview the entire population would take a very long time. Months might pass between the first and last interview. Public opinion might, in that period, undergo real change.

Sampling provides a practical alternative to interviewing the whole population—be it national, state, or local. Furthermore, correctly done sampling can provide very accurate estimates of the political opinions of a larger population. The theory of sampling is a branch of the mathematics of probability, and the error involved in going from the sample to the population can be known with precision. However, many surveys of public opinion do not meet the demanding requirements of sampling theory. The attendant result, of course, is a loss in accuracy.

Sampling Theory

The *population* is that unit about which we want information. In most political surveys three different populations are frequently polled: (1) those over 18, (2) those who are registered voters, and (3) those who will (or do) vote in the next election. These are three quite different groups. It is very important that the population be clearly specified. When one sees a poll addressing abortion, presidential popularity, or vote intent in an upcoming election, those reporting the poll should make clear the population about which they speak. It has been shown, for example, that Senator Edward Kennedy is more highly rated among all adults than among registered voters.[6] Evaluations of Kennedy are, in part, determined by how one defines the population.

The *sample* is that part of the population selected for analysis. Usually, the sample is considerably smaller than the population. National political surveys conducted by reputable firms employ samples of about 1500 respondents. State and local surveys by reputable firms may employ as few as 500 cases. But as samples get smaller the probability of error increases. Sample size should always be reported along with the results of a survey. If that information is missing, the alleged findings should not be taken seriously.

When samples accurately mirror the population, they are said to be *representative*. The term *randomness* refers to the only method by which a representative sample can be scientifically drawn. In a random sample each unit of the population has exactly the same chance of being drawn as any other unit. If the population were attorneys in the state of Texas, each attorney would be required to have exactly the same probability of being selected for the sample to be random. Attorneys in big cities could not have a greater likelihood of getting into the sample than those from the Rio Grande Valley or the Panhandle. This situation obviously requires a detailed knowledge of the population. In the case of Texas lawyers, one could get a list from the bar association and then sample from that list. But suppose the population was unemployed, male adults. To specify the population in a fashion to be able to draw a random sample would be very difficult.

As a consequence, obtaining a representative sample of the unemployed is not easy.

A probability sample is a variant on the principle of random sampling. Instead of each unit having exactly the same probability of being drawn, some units would be more likely to be drawn than would others. But this would be a *known* probability. For example, if one were sampling voter precincts in a state, it is of consequence that some precincts contain more people than do others. To make the sample of people in those precincts representative, the larger precincts must have a greater likelihood of being selected than smaller ones.

We will use *simple random sampling* (SRS) to illustrate how the principle of probability works in selecting a representative sample. Let us assume our population is a large barrel containing 100,000 marbles, some of which are red and some of which are green. We do not know the percentage of each. Instead of counting them all (a long and tedious job), we will draw a random sample. The question is: How? We could just dip in our hand and take some out, but that would mean that those within our reach would be picked and those close to the bottom would have no chance of being selected. Or we could spin the barrel and take one out after every spin. That would probably work reasonably well, but it still would not be "scientific." Even with a spin those marbles at the bottom might never get close enough to the surface to get picked. If we are insisting on a pure random sample we would have to employ a table of random numbers, and give each marble a numeral between one and 100,000. Random number tables are computer generated digits that are completely unrelated to one another (i.e., random). They can be found in the appendix of virtually any statistics book. Let us assume we sample 600 marbles. Our first random number might be 33,382. We would then find the marble with that number and note if it is red or green. Our next random number might be 13,343. We would again note its color. The process would continue until we drew 600 marbles and recorded the color of each.

Having completed that task, let us say our sample shows 65 percent red marbles. Given the sampling method, we now know some things about the population. Sampling theory (the central limit theorem) tells us that the most likely percentage of red marbles is 65 percent. Of course, it is very unlikely that the real percentage of red marbles is precisely 65 percent. It might be 65.5 or 64.3, for example. The sample will not get the population value exactly correct for the same reason that flipping a coin 100 times will not likely yield exactly 50 heads and 50 tails—although it should be close if the coin is honestly flipped.

We need at this point to introduce the twin concepts of *sampling error* and the *confidence level*. A sample will rarely hit the true population value right on the nose. Sampling error and the confidence level tell us the probability of being off the mark and by how much. The commonly used confidence level is 95 percent. For a sample of 600 the sampling error is four percent. What all this means is that if we took 100 samples from our population, and each of these samples consisted of 600 marbles randomly drawn, then 95 out of 100 times we would be plus or minus four percent of the true population value. Our sample came up 65 percent red. While this figure may not be exactly correct, we at least know that 95 out of 100 times we are going to be within four points—one way or the other—of the true proportion of red marbles in the barrel. This much can be proven mathematically.

Turning to a political example, *The New York Times* reported that during the crisis over the Iranian arms deal President Reagan's popularity plunged from 67 on October 30, 1986 to 46 percent on November 30 of the same year.[7] Since the sample size in the latter survey was 687, we know that if the poll were repeated 100 times, 95 of the 100 repetitions would produce results that are plus or minus four percent of what we would find if we interviewed all adult Americans. Thus Reagan's popularity on November 30, 1986 could have been as high as 50 percent or as low as 41 percent. The "best estimate" (according to the central limit theorem) is 46 percent. Sampling error does decrease slightly as we move away from a 50/50 split, and it increases as the population has more heterogeneous political attitudes. But by far the most important factor is the size of the sample.

This simple truth can be easily demonstrated by flipping a coin. We know an honest coin should come up 50 percent heads. If we were to flip a coin ten times and mark down the percentage heads, then flip it another ten times and mark down the percentage heads, and so on 50 times we would get results that looked like figure A. But if we flipped the coin 100 times instead of simple ten, our 50 repetitions would look like figure B. Clearly there are more "errors" in figure A than in figure B. Error here does not mean mistake; rather it refers to workings of chance. When we talk about mistakes in sampling, we use the term "bias."

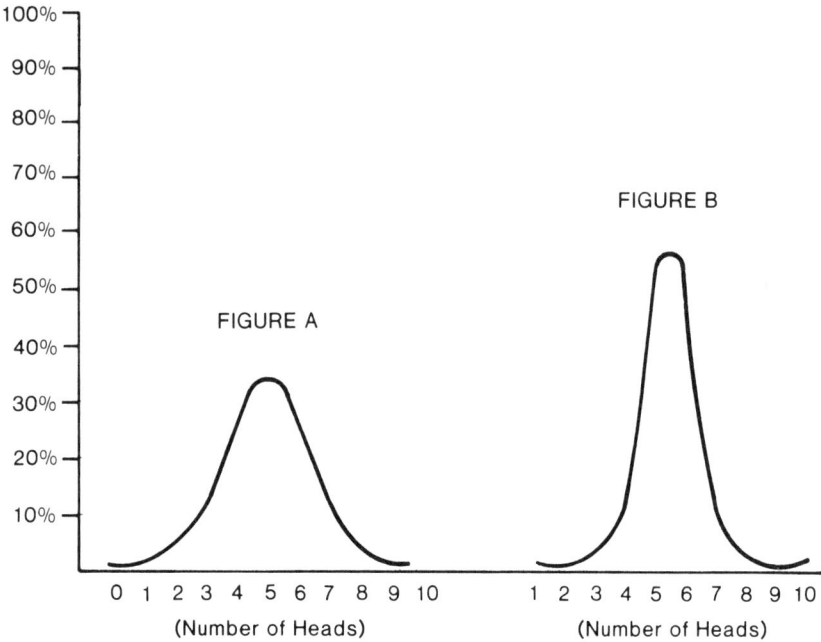

Figure 2.1.

Contrary to what might seem common sense, the size of the population is of little consequence for the accuracy of a survey. That is, it does not make any difference if we are surveying the city of Houston or the entire United States. With a sample size of 600, the sampling error would be identical for both the city and the nation—all other things being equal.[8] Presented in Table 1 are the sampling errors associated with specific samples sizes.

Note that when sample size drops to around 150, sampling error gets very large. While one rarely sees a public opinion survey of 150 people, one often sees survey subgroups (men, college educated, blacks, Republicans, etc.) analyzed where the number of respondents fall below 150. For example, a poll done prior to the 1986 election for governor of Texas showed that among voters over 65 years of age, Mark White led Bill Clements by a margin of 52 percent to 46 percent. However, there were only 91 respondents in that subsample. With a sampling error of 10 percent all we know is that for those over 65 somewhere between 42 and 62 percent favored White, and somewhere between 34 and 54 percent favored Clements. To say that White led Clements among this group in the population is not supported by the data.

TABLE 2.1
Sampling Error and Sample Size Employing
Simple Random Sampling[9]

Sample Size	Sampling Error (plus or minus)
2,400	2.0
1,536	2.5
1,067	3.0
784	3.5
600	4.0
474	4.5
384	5.0
267	6.0
196	7.0
150	8.0
119	9.0
96	10.0
45	15.0

The differences are, in fact, statistically insignificant (i.e., they could have occurred by chance). When reading reports about the politics of those under 30, the gender gap, the politics of the religious right, and similar topics that involve the analysis of subgroups, one should pay special attention to sample size. A difference of five or six percent can be quite *meaningful* in a subsample of 300, and quite *meaningless* in a subsample of 75. If subsamples fall below 100, treat conclusions drawn with great care.

Applied Sampling and Surveys of Public Opinion

Using a large barrel of marbles and a table of random numbers we drew a "perfect" sample. That is, the sampling method fit perfectly with the mathematics of sampling theory. When we sample humans we cannot draw a perfect sample. Although a marble cannot refuse to tell us if it is red or green, a person may refuse to be interviewed. Sampling theory does not allow for refusals. Consequently, surveys of public opinion only approximate the underlying theory of sampling. If these deviations from theory are modest, opinion polls can and do work well. But there are many instances where sampling theory is ignored (or those conducting the polls are ignorant). If the poll simply concerns political opinions (favor/oppose abortion, approve/disapprove of tax reform, keep/abolish the 55 mph speed limit) there is no reality test. The survey may have been done badly and be considerably off the mark, but how would one know?[10] On the other hand, pre-election day surveys have a reality test—election day. In these surveys, sampling mistakes have, in several dramatic cases, cast opinion pollsters in highly unfavorable light.

While we normally think of public opinion polls as being of fairly recent origin, commercial publications were forecasting the outcome of presidential contests as early as 1920. The best known of these publications was the *Literary Digest*. The *Digest* accurately forecast the winner (if not the exact percent) of each presidential election between 1920 and 1932. In 1936, as in previous years, it sent out some 10 million post card ballots "drawn from every telephone book in the United States, from the rosters of clubs and associations, from city directories, lists of registered voters, [and] classified mail order and occupational data. . . ."[11] About 2.2 million returned their postal ballots. The result was 1,293,699 (57%) for Republican Alf Landon and 972,867 (43%) for President Franklin Roosevelt. On election day Roosevelt not only won, but he won by a landslide receiving 62.5 percent of the vote and carrying every state except Maine and Vermont. The *Literary Digest* was not only wrong; it was wrong by 19.5 percent. On November 14, 1936 the *Literary Digest* published the following commentary:

WHAT WENT WRONG WITH THE POLLS?
None of Straw Votes Got Exactly the Right Answer—Why?

In 1920, 1924, 1928 and 1932, the *Literary Digest* Polls were right. Not only right in the sense they showed the winner, they forecast the actual popular vote with such a small percentage of error (less than 1 percent in 1932) that newspapers and individuals everywhere heaped such phrases as "uncannily accurate" and "amazingly right" upon us. . . . Well this year we used precisely the same method that had scored four bull's eyes in four previous tries. And we were far from correct. Why? We ask that question in all sincerity, because *we want to know*.

Why did the poll fare so badly? One reason that can be discounted is sample size. The *Digest* claims to have polled 10 million people. Thus a large sample is no guarantee for accuracy. Rather, their sampling procedure had four fundamental defects. First the sample was drawn in a *biased* fashion. The *Digest* clearly did not use random selection or anything approaching it. Even though questionnaires were sent out to ten million people, a large part of the sample was drawn from telephone directories and lists of automobile owners, during the Depression a decidedly upper-middle class group and one which was predominantly Republican in its political sentiments. In other words, the *Digest* did not correctly specify the population. A second factor contributing to the *Digest's* mistake was time. The questionnaires were sent out in early September, making impossible the detection of any late trend favoring one candidate or the other. Third, 1936 was the year that marked the emergence of the "New Deal Coalition." The *Digest* had picked the winner correctly since 1920 using the same methods as in 1936, but in 1936 voting became polarized along class lines. The working class and the poor voted overwhelmingly Democratic while the more affluent classes voted predominantly Republican. Since the *Literary Digest's* sample was heavily biased in the direction of the more affluent, it is not surprising that their sample tended to favor Landon. Finally, there was the problem of self-selection. The *Digest* sent out its questionnaires by mail. Of the ten million they mailed, only a little over two million responded—about 22 percent. Those people who self-select to respond to mail surveys are often quite different in their political outlooks from those who do not respond. They tend to be better educated, to have higher incomes, and to feel more strongly about the topics dealt with in the questionnaire.[12] So even if the sample of ten million had been drawn in an unbiased fashion, the poll probably still would have been in error due to the self-selection factor. One very fundamental principle of survey sampling is that one *cannot allow the respondents to select themselves into the sample.*

Despite the failure of the *Literary Digest,* several public opinion analysts did pick Franklin Roosevelt as the winner. Among them was George Gallup, Jr. who built his reputation on a correct forecast in 1936. In terms of percentage, Gallup did not get particularly close. He missed by almost seven percent. But he got the winner right, and that is what most people remember. He was, in fact, closer in 1948 (off by five percent) when he made his infamous prediction that Dewey would beat Truman—that too is well remembered.

The technique used by Gallup in 1936 and up until the Dewey-Truman disaster is called *quota sampling.* This technique employs the census to determine the percentage of certain relevant groups in the population. For example, what percentage is male, Catholic, white, and college educated? Within these groups interviewers are then assigned quotas. They must interview a certain percent women, a certain percent with less than high school education, a certain percent black, etc. Once the interviews are completed, the sample is weighted so that it will be representative of the population on those variables. If 15 percent of the population is male, high school educated, and making over $25,000 a year, the sample will be weighted to reflect those proportions. The principle problem with quota sampling is a variation on the problem of self selection. The interviewer has too much opportunity to determine who is selected for the sample. An interviewer who must get a certain number of "female blacks," may avoid certain areas of town or may get the entire quota from a single block. There is a natural tendency to avoid shabby residences, long flights of stairs, and homes where there are dogs. Experience with quota samples demonstrates that they systematically tend to underrepresent the poor, the less educated and racial minorities. Members of those groups who are interviewed tend not to be "typical," The minorities and poor that found their way into Gallup's quota sample were atypical of those groups. They turned out in larger numbers than anticipated and voted overwhelmingly for Truman. A second factor contributing to Gallup's mistake was that he quit polling two weeks before the election. When significant movement takes place it often occurs just before the election. For example, in 1980 Jimmy Carter and Ronald Reagan were virtually even the weekend before the vote. A strong move toward Reagan over the weekend allowed him to pile up a substantial victory. To capture these changes, Gallup and other survey organizations now poll right up to the day of the election.

Contemporary Sampling Methods

We used simple random sampling (SRS) to illustrate the principles involved in drawing a scientific sample. However, SRS is seldom used in actual public opinion surveys. There is no master list of all Americans that could be sampled. Even if there were, the persons selected would be widely scattered throughout the country making in-person interviews prohibitively expensive. For example, an interviewer might have to travel all the way to Kerrville, Texas, just to talk to one respondent. Rather, polls where respondents are personally interviewed use *multistage cluster samples*.

Modern probability sampling is done by household, not by individual. As an example we shall look at the method used by the Gallup Poll.[13] The first step is to use the census and divide the country into four geographic regions. Within each region, the following population centers of similar size are grouped together:

- Cities of one million or more
- Cities between 250,000 and one million
- Cities between 50,000 and 250,000
- Suburbs of 50,000 or more
- Towns between 2,500 and 50,000
- Villages of less than 2,500

The second step is to draw from these groupings a simple random sample of cities, suburbs, towns, and villages. Each population center is then divided into regions of about equal population size. These are sampled using probability methods (the bigger regions have a greater probability of being drawn). Within these regions, smaller geographical units are selected by probability sampling. These smaller units are called *primary sampling units* (PSUs). About 20 persons are interviewed in each PSU. Once selected, PSUs are often used several years before they are replaced.

The primary sampling units are divided into city blocks or areas of equivalent population in rural areas. These areas are then randomly sampled. Once again the compact geographic area saves time and money. Most survey organizations then abandon probability methods at the block level and rely on some type of quota. The problem is that specific individuals are hard to locate. Interviewers working for the Gallup Poll are given a randomly drawn starting point and then instructed to stop at every nth household. The interviewer asks to speak to the youngest man over 18. If he is not home, the interviewer asks to speak with the youngest woman. If neither of these is home, or refuses to be interviewed the interviewer goes to the next adjacent dwelling and tries again until successful. Each interviewer has a male/female quota and an age quota, but this is not a *quota sample* because the interviewer cannot choose who gets into the sample.

Multistage cluster samples work well and are an efficient compromise given the expense involved in a simple random sample approach. The drawback is that cluster samples have a greater sampling error than SRS, as would be expected since the respondents are "clustered" into 75 to 100 small geographic areas. A simple random sample of 1000 has three percent sampling error. A typical cluster sample of 1000 would have a four percent sampling error. Gallup reports that its national samples (cluster samples) of 1500 have a three percent error.

In recent years in-person surveys have increasingly been replaced by telephone surveys. The principal advantage of the telephone is its low cost. It also frees one from having to use clusters, as the physical location of a respondent is irrelevant in a phone survey. However, there are disadvantages as well. Nationwide, it is estimated that 20 percent of all phone numbers are unlisted. In some areas, like San Francisco, it is as high as 40 percent.[14] The solution to this problem is to use a random digit dialing scheme. A ten digit phone number is composed of an area code (the first three numbers), an exchange (the next three), a cluster (the next two), and the two final digits. If one knows the geographic assignment of area codes, exchanges and clusters by the phone company (they will usually provide it for a fee), a population can be defined and sampled. In Houston there are approximately 10,000 of these seven digit codes (if we limit ourselves to Houston we can ignore the area code). An example appears below:

(713) 496-78 ____ ____

The first five digits would be randomly sampled from the population of 10,000. Then the last two digits would be chosen from a table of random numbers or with a computer program that generates random digits. These methods allow persons with unlisted numbers to get into the sample. On the negative side we make calls to a large number of nonworking numbers. But the sample is quite representative.

Another problem with telephone surveys, although it applies to in-person surveys as well, is refusal. The telephone, however, particularly lends itself to abuse as persons selling aluminum siding, upholstery, or West Texas real estate will sometimes attempt to gain a respondent's confidence by posing as a pollster. The sales pitch comes later. A study by the Roper organization showed that 27 percent of a national sample had experienced these sales tactics.[15] People, especially in large cities, are becoming wary of those claiming to be taking polls. It is currently estimated that the refusal rate for telephone surveys is 30 percent. However, the refusal rate is only slightly lower for in-person surveys.[16] Refusals are of consequence only if those who decline the interview are systematically different on the *questions of interest* from those who consent to the interview.

Finally, the exact percentage of households with phones is a question open to debate. It is certainly high, but how high? The 1986 census reports that 92 percent of all households have phone service, although in five states the percentage falls below ninety. On the other hand, a study by the U.S. Public Interest Research Group reports that 27 percent of those with incomes under $15,000 do not have telephone service. The principal reason cited was that service costs too much.[17] Those without phones are found among the least affluent segments of society. This "lumpenproletariat" is one population subgroup that rarely finds its way into any survey, regardless of methodology.

Most reputable polls will report their sampling method in a square box embedded with the news story on the poll results. News stories taken from polls often run for several days, but "how poll was done" is often printed only once. Still at some point the news organization has an obligation to inform the reader of the methods used. A good example of this sort of reporting is taken from the *New York Times*-CBS poll.[18]

HOW THE POLL WAS CONDUCTED

The latest *New York Times*-CBS News poll is based on telephone interviews conducted Sunday and Monday with 1,036 adults around the United States, excluding Alaska and Hawaii. The sample of telephone exchanges called was selected by a computer from a complete list of exchanges in the county. The exchanges were chosen so as to insure that each region of the country was represented in proportion to its population. For each exchange, the telephone numbers were formed by random digits, thus permitting access to both listed and unlisted residential numbers.

The results have been weighted to take account of household size and number of residential telephones and to adjust for variations in the sample relating to region, race, sex, age and education.

In theory, in 19 cases out of 20 the results based on such samples will differ by no more than 3 percentage points in either direction from what would have been obtained by interviewing all adult Americans. The error for smaller subgroups is larger. For example, the potential error for liberals is plus or minus 7 percentage points; for moderates and conservatives it is 5 percentage points.

> In addition to sampling error, the practical difficulties of conducting and survey of public opinion may introduce other sources of error into the poll.

This statement is extremely informative. It tells the reader the dates of interviewing, the sample size, the method of sample selection, the weighting procedure, and the sampling error for the survey as a whole and for subgroups; and it alerts the reader that this survey, like others involving humans, will not be perfect.

The Misuse of Surveys

The *Literary Digest* poll belongs to a general class of surveys called "straw polls" or the "straw vote." They are nonscientific attempts to measure public opinion, like throwing straw in the air to see which way the wind is blowing. Their principal defect is a biased sample, usually the result of respondents being able to "select themselves" to be counted in the poll. Importantly, there is no way of assessing the sampling error, as the factors by which a person gets into the sample are unknown. One might think that with the advent of modern survey methodology straw polls would have disappeared. Not so. They are in fact alive and well—and most are as unreliable now as they were in the 1930s.

Modern Straw Polls

A natural poll that receives a fair amount of media play consists of letters to the president (the media also sometimes pick up on letters to congressmen). When a national crisis occurs which is generally perceived as presenting the president in a poor light, the White House will frequently report that "the mail" is running 10 to 1, 5 to 1, etc. in favor of the president. When Special Prosecutor Archibald Cox was fired during the Watergate scandal, the Nixon White House reported that the mail was running 5 to 1 in favor of the president's actions. Many senators and congressmen, on the other hand, reported that their mail was running 25 to 1 in opposition to the president's action. More recently the White House claimed that the mail was running 10 to 1 in favor of the president when it was revealed that arms were shipped to Iran in return for aid in hostage releases. However, *New York Times*/CBS news poll showed that the public disapproved of this policy by a 3–1 margin.[19] These letters are basically meaningless as an indication of public sentiment. We know that those who "self-select" to write to public officials overwhelmingly tend to write to those whom they feel are sympathetic. If people like the president and support him in the controversy, they will write the White House. If they are hostile, they will write somewhere else or not at all.

Another common straw poll involves surveys sent out by public officials or various partisan organizations. These are often published by the media in bold headlines as if they constituted a reasonable assessment of public opinion. For example, a story in the *Houston Chronicle* carried the following headlines: "Survey Here Shows Opposition to President's Energy Program." The "survey" turned out to be responses to 200,000 questionnaires mailed out by west side Houston Congressman Bill Archer. There were a total of 43,010 responses to this mailout, or about 22 percent (about the same response to the *Literary Digest* poll). The poll also reported that respondents favored production of the B-1 Bomber and retention of "right to work laws."[20] Suffice it to say a survey of this sort measures absolutely nothing. It is severely contaminated by self-selection. There is no way to compute sampling error, given the bias in the way respondents got into the sample. While the information might be valuable to Congressman Archer as an indication of what his attentive constituents think, it has no value as a measure of public opinion.

In addition to reporting the straw polls of others, newspapers have gotten into the business of conducting their own. These are often found on the editorial page labeled "Tuesday Poll," "Voice of the Reader," and "Readers Poll." There is usually a cut-out ballot which is mailed to the newspaper. The results are reported a few days later. The Ft. Lauderdale (Florida) *Sun-Sentinel* "Tuesday Poll" asked readers "Should the state conduct an experiment to ban trucks from the passing or median strip lane of I-95?" The Wisconsin *Capital Times* "Readers Poll" recently inquired into one of the pivotal questions facing state citizens: "Are you satisfied with the job Elroy 'Crazylegs' Hirsch is doing as the University of Wisconsin's athletic director?"[21] As a general rule, those with intense negative feelings are the most likely to "self-select" into these surveys.

A variety of political organizations also attempt to assess public opinion using mail surveys, often combined with highly biased questions. For example, a questionnaire in 1980 from the Republican National Committee with a return deadline of September 29, 1980, included the following items:[22]

1. Recently the Soviet armed forces openly invaded the independent country of Afghanistan. Do you think the U.S. should supply military equipment to the rebel freedom fighters?
2. The Soviets now have a combat brigade in Cuba training Marxist revolutionaries for use in South America and Africa. Do you approve of Mr. Carter's decision to do nothing in response to this direct Soviet/Cuban challenge?
3. Do you believe the U.S. should launch a new program to modernize and increase our Navy in view of the Soviet's massive naval buildup worldwide?

Given the highly loaded questions it should come as no surprise that critics of Mr. Carter would be more likely to complete this questionnaire and return it than those who are undecided or supporters. This survey has many of the same defects as mail surveys that are periodically conducted by *Playboy* and *Penthouse* about sexual habitats. There is a great likelihood that those willing to divulge information about their sex lives differ in important regards from those who are unwilling. Mail surveys are not always meaningless, but they must be conducted with great care by those with specialized training. Most that are done correctly are published in academic journals and rarely show up in the popular media. When one does encounter a popular account, it should be treated with considerable skepticism.

Recently television, including highly regarded network news programs, has been getting into the straw poll business. On October 20, 1980, ABC news asked its viewers to evaluate the Reagan-Carter presidential debate by calling in one telephone number if they thought Reagan won and another if they thought Carter won. This system, called "Dial It" by AT&T, cost each caller 50 cents. Of course, there was no limit on how many times any one person can call—as long as one did not mind paying 50 cents for each call. About 727,000 people called at a profit of $363,500 to the phone company), with Reagan being perceived the winner by a 2 to 1 margin. Other television straw polls involve Warner-Amex's CUBE system which allows for two way communication for cable TV subscribers. The results of these poll have found their way to NBC News and the Cable News Network.[23]

With regard to the findings on the Carter-Reagan debate many of Carter's supporters were rightly outraged. Carter pollster Patrick Caddell argued that since the poll was conducted in the late evening it oversampled callers from the Western time zone (an area of strong

Reagan support) while many of Mr. Carter's supporters in the southeast had already gone to bed. Also callers from urban areas (where Carter would be strong) had a more difficult time getting through than callers from nonurban areas because the dense population led to a clogging of the telephone exchanges. One might also speculate that the poor would be less willing to spend a frivolous 50 cents than would the middle class. However, not all "Dial It" polls are frivolous. They have sometimes been used to decide questions of life and death. NBC's Saturday Night Live posed a question to its viewers as to whether "Larry the Lobster" should be boiled alive at the end of a restaurant skit. Over 466,000 viewers called. Larry was spared by a scant 12,000 votes.[24]

The Dial It procedure has been used several times on the ABC late night news program "Nightline," where attitudes on current topics are assessed. Ted Kopple usually introduces these polls with a disclaimer that "we don't pretend the results are scientific, but here's what we found." Viewers should treat that statement as the equivalent of "certain bored people with strong feelings on some subjects are willing to pay 50 cents to register their views in a poll that means nothing. Here are the results."

Interpreting Scientific Surveys

Polls correctly executed do not always "predict" the actual election day winner. Polls taken at the same time will on occasion show conflicting numbers. Sometimes the numbers will swing wildly over a short period of time. These characteristics do not necessarily mean the polls are defective, but they do require explanation.

Pre-Election Surveys

The media tend to attribute more accuracy to pre-election polls as "predictors" of the election day outcome than even the best designed polls can possibly deliver. First an obvious point. Pre-election polls refer to sentiment at the time they are conducted, not on election day. The "horse race" analogy commonly used to discuss elections is, in this case, appropriate. The horse that is ahead going into the stretch is not always the horse (or the candidate) that wins. With the exception of exit polls (election day polls where respondents are interviewed as they leave the voting booth) no one conducts surveys on the day of the election. At least five percent of the electorate (sometimes more) is normally undecided the weekend before the vote. As one approaches the election, there is often a momentum which favors one of the candidates—the undecideds do not split 50/50. This flow of the undecideds was one reason Truman beat Dewey (the last Gallup poll showed that 19 percent of the electorate was undecided). It is also the reason that Richard Nixon squeaked out a win of less than one percent over Hubert Humphrey in 1968 when the polls had shown Nixon with a substantial lead throughout the campaign. And it is the reason Ronald Reagan soundly defeated Jimmy Carter in 1980 when polls showed the contest to be very close.

But there is a more fundamental problem with pre-election polls as election day predictors. It is impossible to properly define the population. Recall that a random sample must be drawn from a finite population. But it is impossible to define the election day population. Less than 55 percent of adult Americans vote in presidential elections. No one has yet determined a method which with any degree of accuracy predicts who will vote, yet it is those election day voters who constitute the population, not adult Americans or even registered voters. In the final 1986 pre-election survey for the *Houston Chronicle* a sample of registered voters were asked if they were "certain to vote" on election day, would "probably vote," or "would not vote." The results:

Certain to Vote	83%
Probably will Vote	14
Will not Vote	03
	100% N = 666

Actual turnout in Texas was 39 percent.

The problem in accurately assessing turnout is linked to social desirability. People want to be good citizens, and so they say they will vote. Even after the election, respondents will tell interviewers they have voted when in fact they have not. In 1972 the Survey Research Center at the University of Michigan did a "vote validation" study in which they checked poll records to see if those who said they voted did in fact vote. Seventy-two percent of their sample claimed to have voted, but the official record showed that only 55 percent had actually cast their ballot.[25] Clearly, then, pollsters must employ "educated guesswork" in place of science to define the population. Turnout patterns are fairly constant from one election to another but they do change, and that change can often spell the difference between victory and defeat.

Without an agreed-on population, pollsters use a cornucopia of methods for estimating likely voters. Most pollsters ask a series of screening questions designed to identify likely voters (such as past voting behavior, strength of candidate preference, etc.), although the Gallup Poll does no screening and reports the preferences for all registered voters. Those polls that do screen employ a distinctive methodology. Generally speaking, no two polls use the same screening questions, and consequently no two polls look at exactly the same population.

Screens are of consequence for poll results. The tougher the screen in terms of weeding out potential nonvoters and those with weak candidate preferences, the greater the support for Republican candidates. For example, both the NBC poll and the Gallup poll did surveys between August 15 and August 17, 1980. Gallup used all registered voters (an easy screen); NBC interviewed only registered voters who had made up their minds (a tough screen). Gallup showed Reagan with 39 percent; NBC showed him with 48 percent.[26] It is, by the way, the use of screens to define likely voters that allows a pollster working for Democratic candidate Smith to say his client is ahead while the pollster working for Republican candidate Jones says his client is ahead. Neither have "faked" the numbers; rather they disagree on the probable composition of election day voters. The Republican pollster sees a big turnout among affluent whites; the Democratic pollster sees an atypically high minority turnout.

There are also reasons polls may not agree that simply go beyond sampling considerations. Some pollsters ask the undecideds if they "lean" to one candidate or the other. These leaners are then counted as having candidate preferences while other polls may not ask the question and count them as undecideds. In a survey following the 1980 Democratic convention the Gallup, Harris, and Roper polls using the "leaning" question reported only 10 percent undecided when asked to chose between Carter and Reagan. The NBC poll which did not use the "leaner" question reported that 50 percent were undecided.[27]

By far the best strategy in watching pre-election surveys (particularly those conducted early-on) is not to look at the numbers from one specific poll, but at the overall trend. Is one candidate consistently improving or is there no movement? It is the trend that can give insight into progress (or lack thereof) in the campaign.

Volatility in Candidate Choices and Issues Preferences

Example 1: Prior to the 1980 Iowa Caucuses a *New York Times*/CBS poll showed Ronald Reagan ahead of George Bush by a margin of 45 percent to six percent. Two days after the caucuses Reagan led by a margin of only 33—27 percent. Bush had picked up 21 points and Reagan had lost 12 within the span of about a dozen days. Example 2: In the past ten years there has been considerable debate over the Strategic Arms Limitation Treaty (SALT). There have been many attempts to use opinion surveys to determine if Americans favor or oppose it. In early 1979 three surveys taken at the same time showed quite different results. An NBC/AP poll showed 81 percent of the public favored Salt; a CBS/*New York Times* poll showed 63 percent favored it, and a survey by the Roper Organization showed just 40 percent favored SALT.[28]

Both these phenomena are a function of the fact that the mass public has surprisingly little knowledge or interest in politics. Most opinions are not deeply held. In the case of Iowa, Bush was almost completely unknown, and despite his previous run for the presidency Ronald Reagan was in 1980 a fairly dim fixture on the political landscape. George Bush won the Iowa Caucuses, and the media attention he garnered allowed him to make up considerable ground on Reagan in the early going. The same phenomena occurred in 1984 when Gary Hart unexpectedly won the New Hampshire primary. He moved from virtual obscurity in the polls to draw even with Vice-President Mondale. This sort of movement, however, usually takes place only very early in a presidential campaign. Once the electorate becomes better informed about the personalities, these sharp fluctuations are less and less frequent.

Social desirability also contributes to voter volatility. People believe that good citizens have opinions. Consequently, when polled they will volunteer one even if they have given absolutely no thought whatsoever to the subject. In one relevant study respondents were presented with a fictitious issue (the "Public Affairs Act") and asked: "Some people say that the Public Affairs Act should be repealed. Do you agree or disagree with this idea." Fully one-third of the sample expressed an opinion (16 percent agreed, 18 percent disagreed and 66 percent claimed no opinion).[29]

The explanation for disagreement among the polls over the SALT treaty follows very much the same logic. Most Americans have little information about a highly technical subject like the Strategic Arms Limitation Treaty. In fact only 23 percent could accurately identify the two nations who were negotiating the treaty.[30] As topics recede from a people's immediate day-to-day concerns, the wording of the question can make considerable difference in the response. While the questions were essentially the same, the Roper item noted that Salt was "controversial" which probably cued people to give a less positive response. As topics become more salient, minor variations in questions wording have less effect. The abortion issue and attitudes toward the Ayatollah Khomeini would be more likely to generate stable responses than are inquiries about the Salt treaty or the Strategic Defense Initiative (known popularly as "star wars").

The wording of questions can clearly affect the response pattern. One only need page back to those questions used in the survey by the Republican National Committee for an example of items likely to yield distorted results. There are several general principals that are worth noting when looking at questions asked in surveys. Some words are loaded. When the Nicaraguan opponents of the Sandinistas are referred to as "freedom fighters," responses are more positive than when they are called "rebels" or "contras." Clearly, freedom fighter contains a positive cue. People are more likely to agree with statements than disagree with them, favor them than oppose them. Support for continuance of the 55 MPH speed limit will be greater if one is asked to agree or disagree with question A as rather than question B.

Form A: The 55 MPH speed limit should be retained.
Form B: The 55 MPH speed limit should be abolished.

An experiment by the author revealed that with form A 64 percent favored the current speed limit, while with form B only 53 percent were in favor. Sometimes only one option is presented to the respondent: "Do you favor the 55 MPH speed limit?" Note the alternative "oppose" is never mentioned. When looking at questions ask yourself: How could the wording of this item affect the responses? Or given what this question asks, are the results reasonable? A query about freedom fighters in Afghanistan should yield a positive response, and the results must be interpreted in that context.

Conclusion

During the 1930s, 40s and 50s public opinion polls received little attention from the mass media. Reporters saw pollsters as potential competitors—given the technical nature of their subject they might want a byline of their own. Those fears have now subsided. Polls are ubiquitous and commentary on public opinion is fair game for all. There is much to be learned about American democracy from an intelligent examination of polls. Attempts to deliberately mislead occur, but they are not frequent. Rather, the key to understanding polls is a realization that the numbers do not speak for themselves. They require interpretation. While the average American cannot be expected to master the intricacies of modern survey research, an appreciation of the principles laid out in this chapter should allow the reader to do more than simply take at face value the assertions by others about the measurement and meaning of public opinion.

Notes

1. Everett C. Ladd and G. Donald Gerree, "Were the Pollsters Really Wrong?" *Public Opinion* (December/January, 1981). p. 13.
2. Burns Roper, "The Polls Malfunction in 1982," *Public Opinion* (December/January, 1982). pp. 41–45.
3. Martin Tolchin, "The Pollsters Look Back," *The New York Times,* November 8, 1986, p. 17.
4. *Ibid.*
5. For elaboration on this point see Benjamin Ginsberg, *The Captive Public.* (Basic Books, Inc., 1986), chapter 3.
6. Burns Roper, "Reading the Signals in Today's Political Polls," *Public Opinion* (February/March, 1980), p. 48.
7. Reported in *The Houston Chronicle,* December 2, 1986, page 2.
8. National samples are usually larger than state or local samples because one other factor that effects sampling error is variation, and there is likely to be more variation in the attribute measured nationally, as opposed to those in a geographically smaller area. Also, those conducting national samples are often interested in looking at subgroups (like blacks or women). The larger the sample, the lower the sampling error when one is looking at subgroups.
9. Gerald M. Goldhaber, "A Pollster's Sampler," *Public Opinion* (June/July, 1986), p. 48.
10. One's suspicions are aroused, however, if polls on the same topic at similar times show quite different results.
11. *Literary Digest,* 122 (August 22, 1936), p. 3.
12. Don A. Dillman, *Mail and Telephone Surveys* (New York: Wiley, 1978).
13. The method described here is that used by Gallup Poll. See Paul Perry, "Election Survey Procedures of the Gallup Poll," *Public Opinion Quarterly* 20 (Fall, 1960), pp. 531–541.

14. Robert Groves and Robert Kahn, *Surveys by Telephone* (New York: Academic Press, Inc., 1979), p. 20.
15. Charles Turner and Elizabeth Martin, *Surveying Subjective Phenomena* (New York: Russell Sage, 1984), p. 73.
16. Groves and Kahn, p. 64; Seymour Marti Lipset, "Different Polls, Different Results in 1980 Politics," *Public Opinion* (August/September, 1980), p. 20.
17. Based on a survey of 816 respondents with incomes under $15,000. Reported in "One in Five Low-Income Homes lacks Telephone, Survey Finds," *Houston Chronicle* (Sunday, February 1st, 1987), Section 1, page 3.
18. *The New York Times*, December 10, 1986, p. 9.
19. *Ibid.*
20. The *Houston Chronicle*, Saturday, October 8, 1977, p. 3.
21. Barry Orton, "Phony Polls: The Pollster's Nemesis," *Public Opinion* (June/July, 1982), pp. 56–57.
22. Conducted by Survey Research Center, Republican National Committee, 310 First Street, Washington, D.C., 20003.
23. Orton, pp. 57–58.
24. *Ibid.*, pp. 58–59.
25. Michael Traugoota and John Katosh, "Response Validity in Surveys of Voting Behavior," *Public Opinion Quarterly* (Winter, 1979), 359–377.
26. Lipset, p. 20.
27. Roper, p. 48.
28. Michael Wheeler, "Reining in Horserace Journalism," *Public Opinion* (Feb/March, 1982), p. 42.
29. George Bishop, Robert Oldendick, Alfred Tuchfarbre and Stephen Bennett, "Pseudo-Opinions on Public Affairs," *Public Opinion Quarterly* (Summer, 1980), p. 201.
30. Wheeler, p. 42.

Chapter 3

America's Heartland: Examining the Midwestern Myth

Tami Buhr

Farms and farmers dominate the public image of the nation's heartland. Sometimes the image takes Jeffersonian dimensions. Midwestern farmers emerge as everyday heros, people of honest toil, guardians of the land. In this view, rural lives are characterized by simple virtues, by hard work, and by a natural democratic impulse. Farm life is depicted as having a certain timeless grandeur, as representing generations past and yet to come, as an emblem of continuity in a discontinuous world. This image of the heartland suggests a politics of distinctive prudence and even wisdom.

But in another version, the image of farming—and the Midwest has a more negative aspect, emphasizing lives of toil without grandeur, a society of men and women managing a bare living on America's plains. The American dream of upward mobility is undreamed in this heartland. Instead there are hard times, backbreaking work, farm foreclosures. The culture is one of limited horizons. The politics is that of a peasantry, fearful of change and ultimately hostile to all that is foreign.

Both of these images of the heartland are fictitious. And the largest part of this fiction is that farming and farmers are today still a dominant part of economic and political life in the heartland. More prominent in the corn belt than elsewhere in the United States, farmers nonetheless are not a notable proportion of midwesterners. The fact is that the view of the Midwest as an agricultural society is one held mainly by those who live elsewhere.

We look at the Midwest as a region in this chapter. Turning away from popular images and instead to hard data on political opinions and behavior, we ask what is truly distinctive about the heartland? How does the Midwest compare with the rest of the nation?

The context for this study is time in question the 1988 presidential election. Two public opinion polls, the 1988 Heartland Poll and the 1988 National Election Study (NES), will be utilized, as will the 1988 presidential election results.

This will aid in comparing the Midwest with the rest of the nation and will also aid in examining Midwestern voting behavior relative to the rest of the nation in the 1988 presidential election.

Study Descriptions

The 1988 Heartland Poll was the first of what is now an annual poll conducted by the University of Iowa Social Science Institute. Respondents were sampled in Minnesota, Wisconsin, Illinois, Missouri, Nebraska, and South Dakota. Telephone interviews were conducted of approximately 2100 people between October 4 and November 8. The poll contained a number of questions relating to the 1988 presidential campaign, national and Midwest issues, and life in the Midwest.

A sample of 2,100 people was drawn through a random process out of the universe of 20,685,545 people, the voting age population of Iowa, Minnesota, Wisconsin, Illinois, Missouri, Nebraska, and South Dakota. A sample must be taken because it is not possible to interview all members of the universe. It is important for the respondents to be chosen randomly for the information to be generalized to the entire universe. If some kind of random or probability selection process is not used, the results will only be applicable to the sample and inferences from the sample to the universe will not be possible.

The 1988 edition of the National Election Study (NES), conducted biennially since 1956 by the Center for Political Studies at the University of Michigan, included 2040 respondents in the pre-election survey. The NES also includes a post-election survey of 1775 respondents. To make direct comparisons between the two studies, only the national pre-election survey will be utilized since the Heartland Poll did not have a comparable post-election wave.[1] The NES is performed by using multi-stage area probability sampling in which in-house interviews are performed with the interviewer actually going to the designated households to conduct the interviews.

The studies feature a number of identically worded questions about party identification, ideology, feelings toward the candidates, views on specific policies, and the state of the nation. This facilitates direct comparison between the Midwest and the entire nation. Comparing identically worded questions may make us believe the results are directly comparable, but two cautions need to be kept in mind. First, the Heartland Poll was conducted through telephone surveys while the NES was conducted through household interviews. While the information gathered from the two surveying techniques should not differ widely, two hazards of telephone surveying are that low income people who do not have telephones may be inadvertently excluded, and refusal rates for a telephone survey will be higher because refusing a telephone survey is easier than refusing one in person.

Also, we cannot ignore the importance of sampling error, which is the result of having information on only a sample of the population and using that information to draw conclusions about the entire population. For our comparisons of the two studies, we should not jump to any quick conclusions when the studies differ by only a few percentage points on a particular variable. If second samples were to be taken and second sets of interviews completed, the difference originally observed between those two samples may not occur, or the difference could even be in the opposite direction. Therefore, it is important to be cautious when interpreting survey data to avoid hasty conclusions.

Who Lives in the Midwest?

Before we look at public opinion in the Midwest, we must first learn more about Midwesterners themselves. We will examine responses to some of the demographic questions asked in the Heartland Poll and the NES. We will compare the Midwest and the rest of the nation with regards to employment rates, the most common occupations, income, racial diversity, educational levels, and religion. After examining these demographic characteristics we will have a better idea of who actually lives in the Midwest and if they fit the image held by those outside of the Midwest.

Employment Status

Table 3.1 compares the employment status for the Midwest and the rest of the nation. It shows the Midwest had virtually the same unemployment rate and almost the same number of people in the labor force as the rest of the nation in the fall of 1988, and there were slightly more students and retirees. This corresponds to a traditional view of the Midwest as being inhabited by fewer young people. Note that the cultural traditionalism sometimes thought to characterize the farm belt finds no support here. One indicator of that, the degree to which women remain in the traditional housewife role, shows the Midwest just like the nation. Table 3.1 shows the number of housewives in the Midwest is the same as in the rest of the nation.

TABLE 3.1
Fall 1988 Employment Status for the Midwest and the Rest of the Nation

Employment Status	Midwest	Nation
Employed	61.5%	63.5%
Unemployed	2.7%	4.0%
Laid Off	.2%	1.0%
Retired	18.8%	15.2%
Disabled	.9%	3.1%
Housewife	11.2%	11.3%
Student	4.8%	2.0%

Sources: 1988 Heartland Poll conducted by the Iowa Social Science Institute and 1988 National Election Study conducted by University of Michigan Center of Political Studies.

The percentage of working women is also revealing. Table 3.2, which is similar to Table 3.1 except that it applies specifically to women, shows that the Midwest does not lag behind the rest of the nation in working women. Practically the same percentage of women in the Midwest work as do in the rest of nation. By looking at the number of students we find Midwestern women pursuing higher education in equal if not slightly larger numbers than women in the rest of the nation. Both of these figures are hardly indicative of a region that is considered to be "behind the times".

TABLE 3.2
1988 Employment Status of Women for the Midwest
and the Rest of the Nation

Employment Status	Midwest	Nation
Employed	51.3%	53.3%
Unemployed	3.1%	5.0%
Laid Off	.1%	1.0%
Retired	20.7%	14.7%
Disabled	.9%	3.9%
Housewife	19.2%	19.8%
Student	4.6%	2.4%

Sources: 1988 Heartland Poll conducted by the Iowa Social Science Institute and 1988 National Election Study conducted by University of Michigan Center of Political Studies

Occupations

The most common stereotype of Midwesterners is that they are farmers (or work in farm related occupations). To determine what work people do, interviewers ask respondents what their main occupation is, then either type the respondent's answer into the computer or write it down verbatim. All raw responses are later categorized into a number of general groupings such as managerial occupations, service occupations or farm related occupations.

Farmers or farm related occupations in reality make up only 4.7% of the Midwestern labor force. Nationally, farm occupations account for 2.7% of the labor force. If only about 5% of the work force in the Midwest are farmers, what do the other 95% of the work force do? The occupations 95% of Midwesterners work at are not much different from the rest of the nation.[2] Table 3.3 shows the top seven occupations for both the Midwest and the rest of the nation and the percentage of the work force involved in those occupations. As the table shows, the largest number of people in the Midwest hold professional occupations, followed by administrative support occupations. For the rest of the nation, the top two occupations are switched with administrative support first and professional second. Farm related occupations (including fishing and forestry occupations) are seventh in

TABLE 3.3
Top Seven Occupations for the Midwest and the Rest of the Nation

The Midwest		The Nation	
1. Professional	16.8%	1. Administrative Support	16.5%
2. Administrative Support	13.4%	2. Professional	15.7%
3. Managerial	12.6%	3. Managerial	12.4%
4. Sales Related	9.2%	4. Service, excluding protection, household	11.3%
5. Precision Production	9.1%	5. Precision Production	10.4%
6. Operator, Assembly, Inspector	6.4%	6. Sales Related	9.6%
7. Farm, Fishery, Forestry	4.7%	7. Operator, Assembly, Inspector	7.9%

Sources: 1988 Heartland Poll conducted by the Iowa Social Science Institute and 1988 National Election Study conducted by University of Michigan Center of Political Studies.

the Midwest, whereas nationally they are tenth. Since six of the top seven occupations in the Midwest reflect six top occupations in the nation, the Midwest of Table 3.3 clearly is not a bunch of farmers.

Income

Along with farm image often comes the idea of a poverty stricken Midwest, particularly given the much publicized farm crisis of the 1980s. A comparison of income figures for the Midwest and the rest of the nation again suggests otherwise. The income figures are the income for the respondents. Figure 3.1 shows a comparison of (total yearly family) income for the Midwest and the rest of the nation. The Midwest, it shows, has fewer people in the two lowest income categories, those with family incomes under $20,000 a year. For the nation, the lowest two categories account for 41% of the respondents, while for the Midwest, 30% of the respondents fall in these two categories. The Midwest also has more people in the highest income category, yearly family incomes of $60,000 and above.

Some caution should be exercised when interpreting Figure 3.1. While it appears the Midwest is wealthier than the rest of the nation,

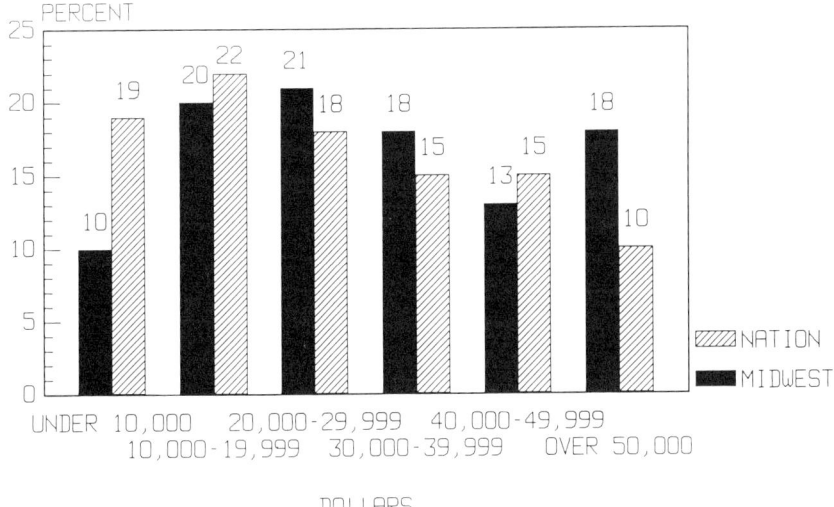

Figure 3.1. 1987 Family Income for the Midwest and the Rest of the Nation

some of the differences between the Midwest and the rest of the nation may be due to the fact that the Heartland Poll was conducted by telephone while the NES was conducted in person. Telephone surveys naturally exclude those lower income people who do not have phone service. The NES is more able to include those people by going to their homes to conduct the interview.

The differences between the Midwest and the rest of the nation are still quite large and not all due to the differing survey techniques. They should not all be discounted. The Midwest has fewer poor people and a larger number of people who can be considered middle-class. Since income and wealth are often related to how one views the world and which political party and candidate one supports, these differences between the Midwest and the rest of the nation should be noted with more than passing interest. After all, the New Deal realignment created a party system split along socioeconomic lines with the traditional Democratic coalition including the working and lower classes, and the more wealthy big business interests tending to be associated with the Republican party. Of course, almost all demographic characteristics of people have an effect on their attitudes and beliefs, but as we will see later, economic factors often influence the vote a great deal.

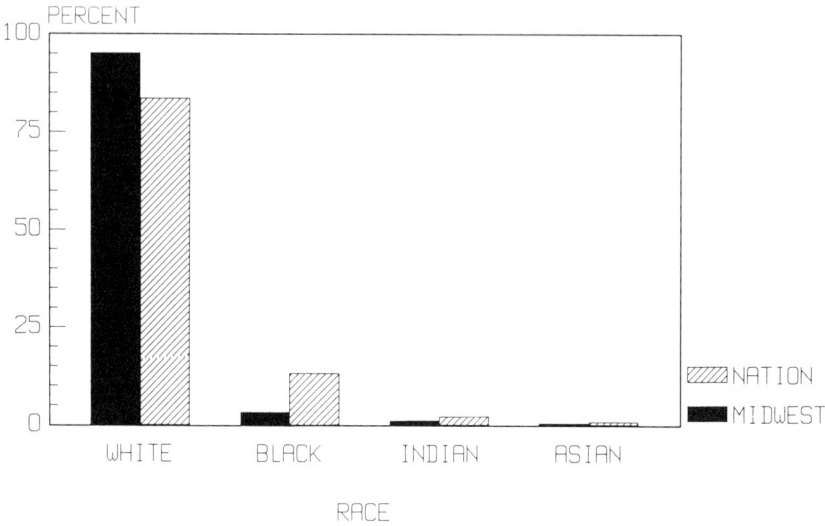

Figure 3.2. Racial Breakdown for the Midwest and the Rest of the Nation

Race

Race successfully predicts the vote, although more so for blacks than whites. Since the New Deal, blacks have also been part of the traditional Democratic coalition and still vote heavily Democratic as a group. In 1988, 90% of the black vote went to Michael Dukakis.

Figure 3.2 compares the racial makeup of the Midwest with the rest of the nation. As expected, the Midwest is not racially diverse, with 95% of the respondents of the Heartland Poll being white and only 3% black. This compares to the NES respondents being 84% white and 13% black. As with income, caution is required when examining these figures. Since people of lower incomes have a greater tendency to be left out of telephone surveys and blacks as a group have lower incomes than whites, the percentage of blacks interviewed for the Heartland Poll may be a little on the low side. But also as with income, the differences between the Midwest and the rest of the nation are too large to be ignored. If blacks tend to be largely Democratic, and the Midwest lacks racial diversity, party identification in the Midwest should be affected.

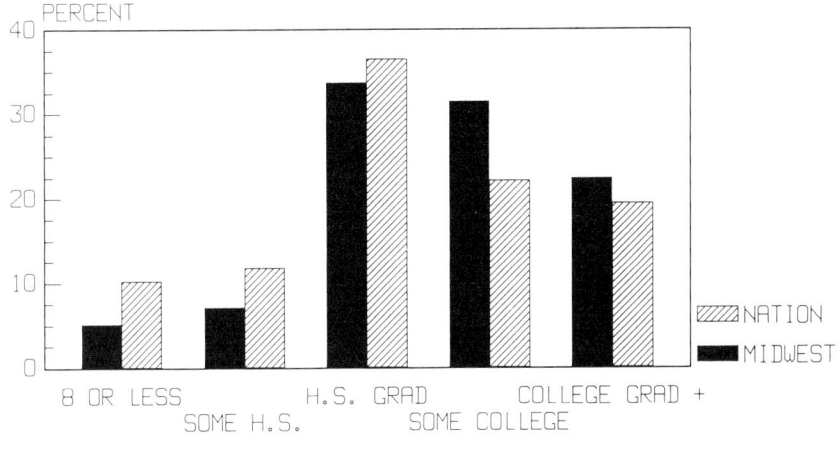

Figure 3.3. Highest Year of School for the Midwest and the Rest of the Nation

Education

The Midwest is often regarded as having a good educational system, an image at odds with its "down on the farm" characterization. A look at the highest year of school the respondents of the two studies completed demonstrates that Midwesterners are not at all less educated but on the contrary are more highly educated than the rest of the nation. Figure 3.3 shows people's highest year of school across five categories. The rest of the nation has more people in every category from the twelfth grade down than the Midwest, but the Midwest has more people in the post-secondary categories. Only 31% of the rest of the nation has had some post-secondary education, for example, compared to 54% of the Midwest.

Education affects how much attention people pay to politics and how well informed they are. Generally, better educated people pay more attention to politics and are thus better politically informed. The more informed a person is, the better able this person is to assess candidates on the basis of issues or performance rather than evaluations based on personality or charisma.

Religion

The Midwest is thought to be more Protestant and less Catholic than the rest of the nation. But figure 3.4 shows this not to be the

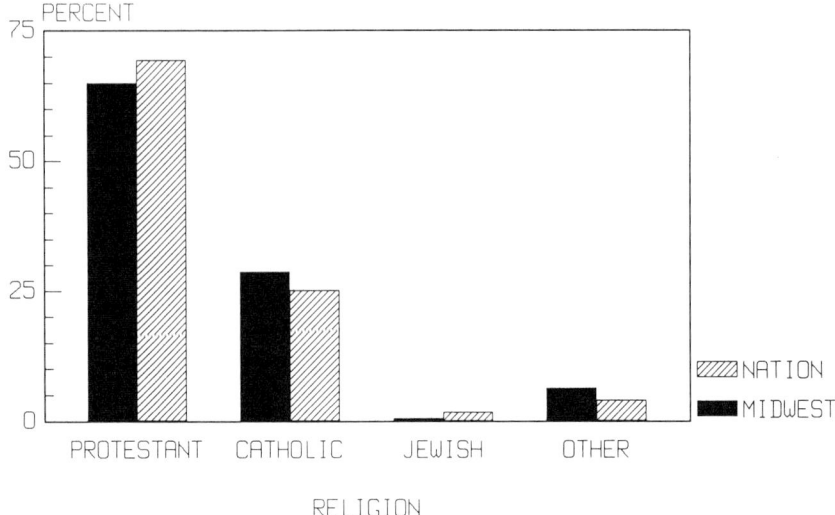

Figure 3.4. Religion for the Midwest and the Rest of the Nation

case. The graph shows the nation to be slightly more Protestant and less Catholic than the Midwest. These differences are so close it is best to consider them sampling error. Once we have taken sampling error into consideration, the differences between the Midwest and the rest of the nation become very slight.[3] The finding here is the lack of difference between the Midwest and the rest of the nation.

Partisanship

The Midwest is usually regarded as a more Republican region, a belief the Heartland data do nothing to disprove. Figure 3.5 is a comparison of party identification, how respondents say they "think of themselves", for the Midwest and the rest of the nation for 1988 during the period in which the surveys were conducted. As the figure shows, the Midwest has more Republicans than the rest of the nation, while the rest of the nation has both more Democrats and independents than the Midwest. Given the demographic information presented above, a larger number of Republicans than Democrats in the Midwest is not a complete surprise. We saw that Midwesterners enjoy a higher level of income than the rest of the nation and that the Midwest has very few blacks relative to the rest of the nation, both of which would tend to produce a more Republican electorate.

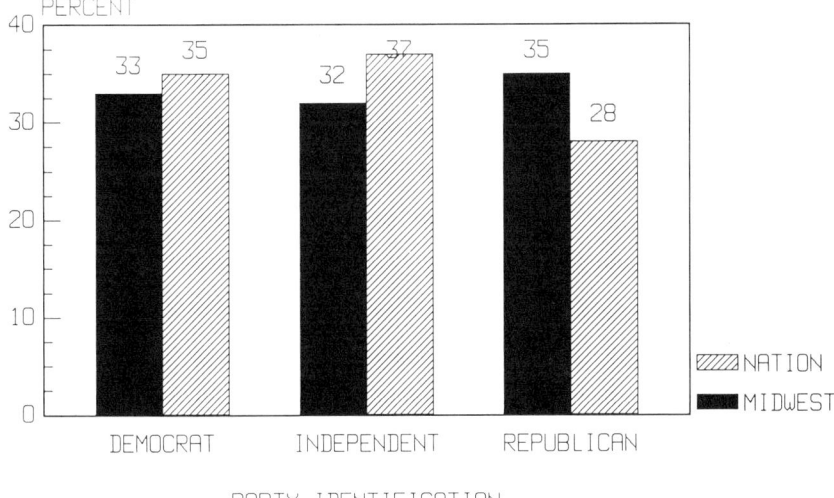

Figure 3.5. 1988 Party Identification for the Midwest and the Nation

Party identification may be measured on a more refined scale. Based upon a series of questions asked of both partisans and independents, a seven point is constructed ranging from "Strong Democrat" through "Weak Democrat" through "Independent leaning Democratic", to pure "Independent" through the three comparable Republican categories. Figure 3.6 is a comparison of the Midwest and the rest of the nation on this seven point scale. The figure shows that the Republican advantage over the Democrats in the Midwest comes more from those who consider themselves weak Republicans rather than from strong Republicans. Generally, weak partisans are more likely to defect from their party and vote for the other party's candidate than are strong partisans. Figure 3.6 suggests that the large Republican advantage in the Midwest shown in Figure 3.5 may not be so large when it comes to party loyalty. As we turn to the 1988 contest, we will see that to be the case.

Partisanship and The 1988 Presidential Vote

In order to further examine this idea of defecting and voting for the other party's candidate, it is helpful to look at which candidate the people in each partisan category are planning to vote for. Because we are working with pre-election surveys that can only tell us who the respondents would vote for if the election were held on the day the

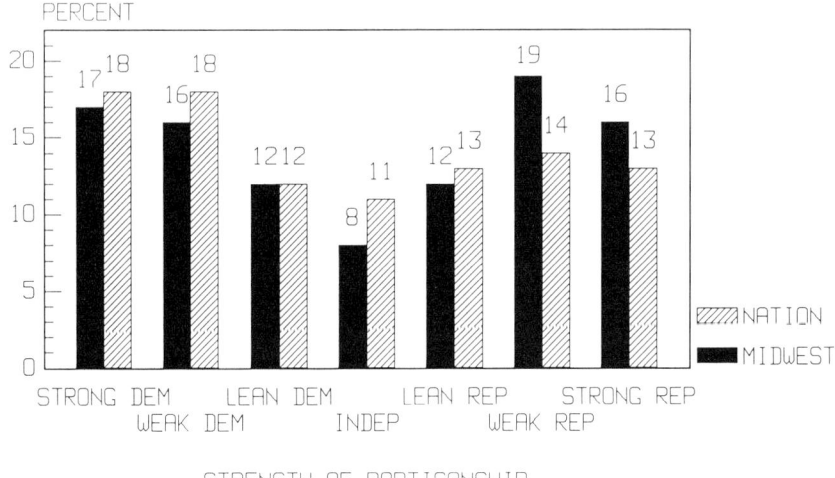

Figure 3.6. Strength of Party Identification for the Midwest and the Nation

interview was conducted, we need to again be cautious when interpreting the findings. After all, 50% of the people who answered the question ended up not voting.

Figures 3.7 and 3.8 show "likely vote" by party identification for the rest of the nation and the Midwest respectively. While for both the Midwest and the rest of the nation, weak Republicans still say they would vote overwhelmingly for George Bush, they are, as expected, less likely to do so than are strong Republicans. Also note that Republicans are less likely to defect to the other party's candidate than are Democrats. An interesting phenomenon in American politics is that people who consider themselves leaning independents tend to vote in a greater percentage for the party they "lean" towards than do the weak partisans of that party. These independents, that is, are less independent than partisans! For the nation, leaning independents say they are more likely to vote for the party they lean towards than weak partisans, although for Republicans this difference is negligible. No similar pattern appears for the Midwest. This is a case where one must be conscious that vote here means likely vote and not actual vote.

A comparison of pure independents shows Midwestern independents less likely to vote for Bush than national independents. As we will see later in our examination of the 1988 presidential election, the traditionally Republican Midwest was the weakest region for Bush. According to the "likely vote" figures, this weakness may

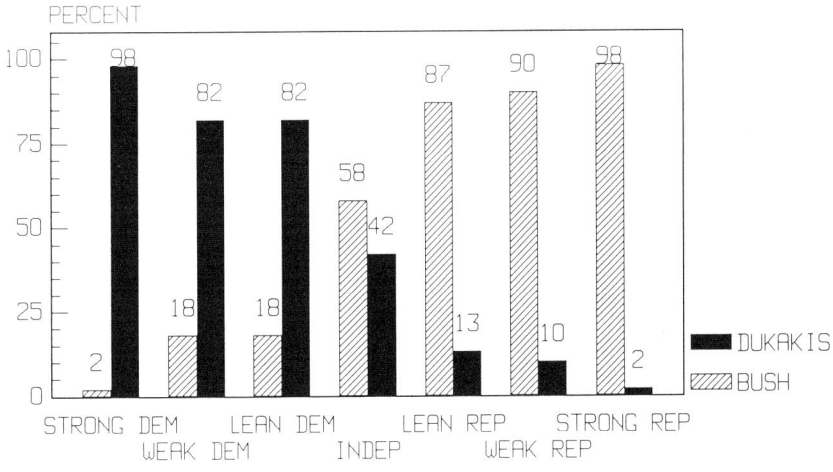

Figure 3.7. 1988 Midwest Vote by Party Identification

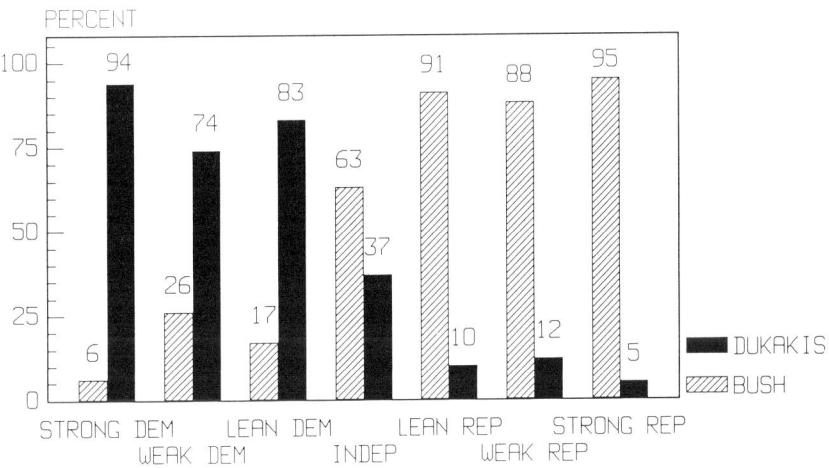

Figure 3.8. 1988 National Vote by Party Identification

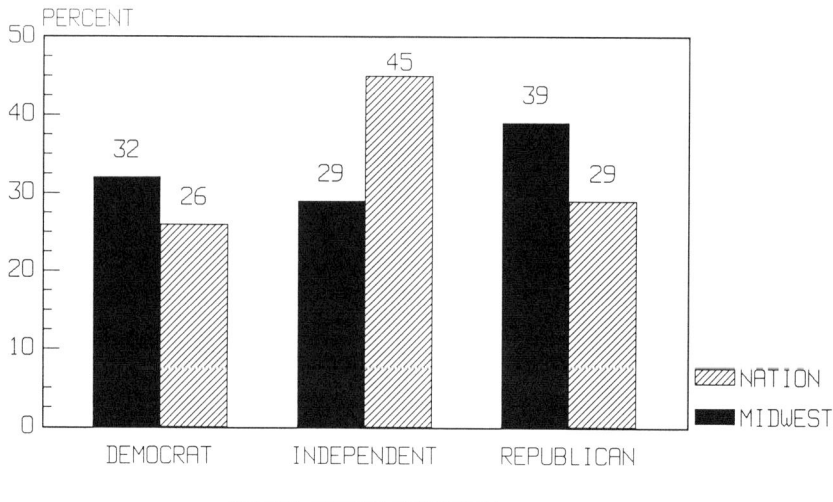

Figure 3.9. Party Identification for 18 to 29 Year Olds

have been in part due to the lesser support Bush received from Midwestern independents. This smaller independent support combined with greater loyalty among Midwestern Democrats for Dukakis would have narrowed the victory margin for Bush in the Midwest if it held in the actual election.

Party Identification Across Age Groups

We have observed that the Midwest has more Republicans than the rest of the nation. What does the future look like for partisanship in the Midwest? If the Republican advantage in the Midwest comes more from younger people than middle and older age groups, the Republican advantage should continue into the future. If the young people of the Midwest are similar to the rest of the nation's young people, we might conclude that the Midwest will look more like the nation with respect to partisanship in the future.

When we break party identification down by age we see that Republicans do not have an equal advantage across the three age groups. Figures 3.9, 3.10, and 3.11 show that as age increases, the difference between the number of Republicans in the Midwest and the rest of the nation decreases. Figure 3.9 shows Midwestern young people to be more partisan than the young people of the rest of the nation, with a sizable Republican advantage. For the middle age

Examining the Midwestern Myth 67

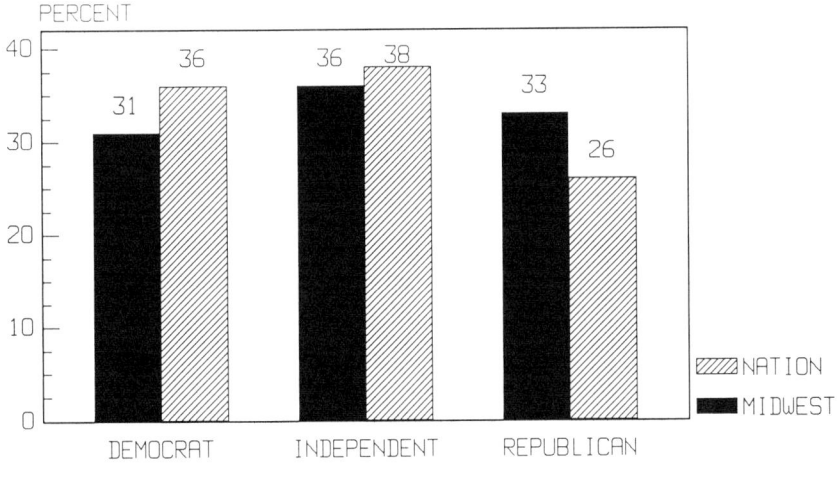

Figure 3.10. Party Identification for 30 to 59 Year Olds

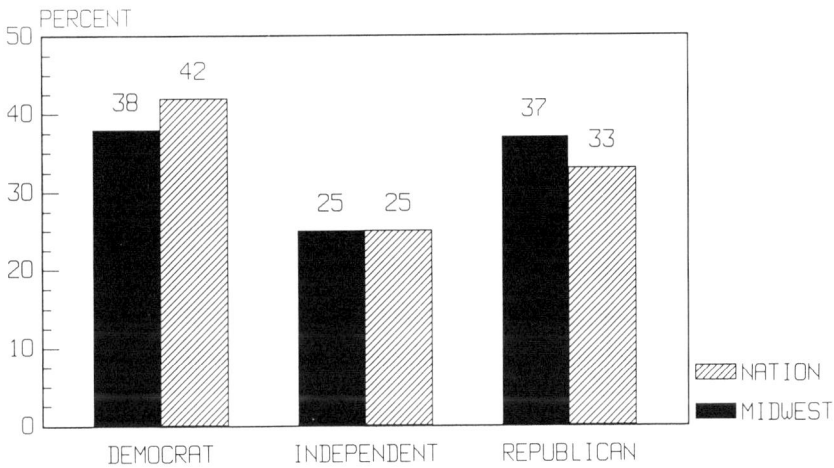

Figure 3.11. Party Identification for Ages 60 and Over

group, the Republicans still have greater numbers in the Midwest, but the contrast between the rest of the nation and the Midwest is shrinking as there are more Midwestern independents. By the time we get to the 60 and over age group, the larger number of Midwestern Republicans relative to the rest of the nation has become slight. But this is due to a larger number of Democrats and not to a larger number of independents as with the 30 to 59 age group. A comparison of the three figures shows the Midwest is more similar to the nation among people over 29 than with regards to its young people. If this were to continue into the future, the Midwest could become an even more Republican region than it already is.

Why are Midwestern young people more partisan than their national counterparts? A theory explaining a generational weakening of partisanship and an increasing number of independents overtime will help to answer this question.

The 60 and over group should have the smallest number of independents. Their partisan attachments were formed during the Great Depression and New Deal with a large amount of commitment and emotion. These people know why they identify with the party they do, and it is likely that this identification has something to do with the events of the Great Depression and Franklin Roosevelt. One would also expect the 60 and over age group to be more Democratic since the Democratic party did become the majority party with the New Deal realignment, and also because partisan attachments become stronger with age.

The middle age group should have more independents than the over 60 age group. Children will often assume the partisanship of their parents at an early age without really considering why they identify with the party they do. As children grow up and begin to question their party identification—and the events of the New Deal that formed the partisanship of their parents recede they will become more unsure of their partisanship and it is likely some will become independents. A particular event or influential politician probably did not form their partisanship. It was just something they inherited from their parents.

For the 18 to 29 year olds the partisanship they inherit is even shakier than their parents' partisanship. The people in this age group know what party they think they should identify with, the party of their parents, but because their commitment to this party is so weak, they are being influenced by events around them. Many of the people in the 18 to 29 age group became more politically aware during the Reagan years and were swayed by this popular president. But for

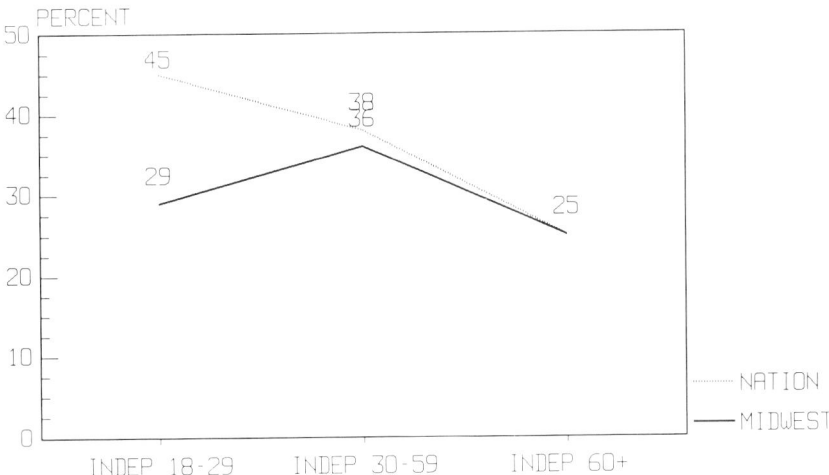

Figure 3.12. Percent Independents by Age for the Midwest and the Rest of the Nation

many, their parents were Democrats and so they faced a dilemma. Their roots tell them they should be Democrats, but their attitudes push them towards the Republicans. Rather than making the big jump between parties, they take an easier way out and fail to identify with either party.

Figure 3.12 shows that for the nation, this theory of a generational weakening of partisanship has some validity. The number of independents increases as age decreases. This theory does not appear to explain partisanship in the Midwest. A reexamination of Figures 3.10 and 3.11 will show that this theory might explain more than Figure 3.12 alone leads us to believe. As we have already observed, Figures 3.10 and 3.11 show the Midwest is more Republican than the rest of the nation. We have seen that the Reagan years might have caused dissonance—and resulted in independence—for young people from Democratic households. If the Midwest had more Republicans than the nation in the parental age groups—as it does—fewer 18 to 28 year olds would have experienced this confusion. More would then easily identify with the Republican party.

Ideology

Along with being viewed as a more Republican region, the Midwest traditionally is thought to be conservative. A look at where respondents place themselves on a seven point liberal-conservative scale shows the Midwest to be ideologically comparable to the rest of the nation. On such a scale, 1 represents extremely liberal, 7 extremely conservative, and 4 moderate. To compare the Midwest with the rest of the nation, the means for both the Heartland Poll and the NES were obtained and compared. The mean value for respondents in the Midwest was 4.40, and for national respondents 4.37. Both the Midwestern and national respondents tended to place themselves slightly more on the conservative side of the scale, but the Midwestern mean value is trivially more conservative than the value for the rest of the nation. When sampling error is considered, a tiny difference becomes no difference. Midwesterners do not think of themselves in more conservative terms than people in the rest of the nation.

Candidate Assessments and Policy Preferences

A comparison of the Midwest with the rest of the nation on the evaluations of political leaders and a few policy areas will give us an indication of how Midwesterners viewed government and politics in the fall of 1988 as compared to the rest of the nation. We will be able to test traditional Midwestern stereotypes, and note any substantial differences that might have affected the presidential vote. First, we will look at how many people approved of the job Ronald Reagan was doing as president in the fall of 1988. About 60% of the respondents in both the Midwest and the rest of the nation expressed approval of Reagan's performance as president. The more Republican Midwest was not more approving of Reagan in the fall of 1988.

Another way of looking at how the respondents felt about Reagan and other political figures is thermometer ratings. Respondents are asked about their feelings toward a person or group on a "thermometer" that ranges from 0 to 100 degrees. Ratings below 50 are cool, ratings above 50 warm, and ratings of 50 are neutral. The results of mean thermometer ratings for Reagan, Bush and Dukakis are summarized in Table 3.4. As the table shows the rest of the nation seemed to feel a little warmer toward Ronald Reagan than the Midwest. The Midwest was quite a bit cooler towards Bush than the rest of the nation. The mean rating for the Midwest was 52 degrees while the rest of the nation's rating was 61 degrees, a difference of nine points. The Midwest was also cooler towards Dukakis but not as

TABLE 3.4
Mean Thermometer Ratings for the Midwest
and the Rest of the Nation

Political Leader	Midwest	Nation
Ronald Reagan	55	61
George Bush	52	61
Michael Dukakis	51	56

Sources: 1988 Heartland Poll conducted by the Iowa Science Institute and 1988 National Election Study conducted by University of Michigan Center of Political Studies.

much so as Bush, with a difference of 5 degrees between the two polls.

On these thermometer ratings overall, the Midwest appears cooler. A number of these questions were asked in the two studies, and almost without fail, the Midwest was cooler than the rest of the nation toward the person or group being rated. One possible explanation is greater levels of dissatisfaction with government (a prominent aspect of which is performance of the national economy) and political leaders in the Midwest than in the rest of the nation. We will examine views toward the economy more in depth later. But as a whole, Midwesterners were more negative on their personal economic state of affairs than the rest of the nation, and this negativity may be showing up in the cooler thermometer ratings and possibly the vote.

The first issue we will look at is spending on social services.[4] The Midwest is often viewed as conservative on government spending except when it comes to spending on farm programs. The question concerning social services in the Heartland Poll asked respondents whether they thought spending on social services should be increased, decreased, or kept about the same. The NES used a seven point scale to measure feelings on social spending where 1 equalled the strongest sentiment toward decreasing spending and 7 the strongest toward increasing spending. A value of 4 is in the middle meaning spending should remain the same. Collapsing the first three categories into a single "decrease spending" category, and doing the same with the upper three categories to get a singular "increase spending" category makes the two questions more comparable. Keeping in mind that the questions were not identical, the Midwest appears less conservative on social spending with 56% saying that we should increase spending on social services while 39% of the nation believed we should increase spending. More telling is the percent who feel we should decrease spending. Only 7% in the Midwest compared to 29% of the rest of the nation. Much of this difference is probably attributable to the differing question formats. But even given this limitation, we have discovered something interesting; the Heartland Poll shows the Midwest to be not as fiscally conservative as traditionally believed.

Similar difficulties are encountered when comparing attitudes towards defense spending. The defense spending questions were asked the same as the social spending questions and will be dealt with in the same manner. The Midwest has conventionally been believed to be less supportive of high defense spending, which the Heartland Poll confirms. Only 9% of the Heartland respondents wanted defense spending to be increased, 59% wanted spending kept at the same level, and 33% wanted spending decreased. The rest of the nation had more support for an increase in spending with 33% of the respondents placing themselves on the "increase" side of the seven point scale, another 33% advocating the current level, and the final 33% wanted spending decreased.

Related to attitudes about defense spending are attitudes about the role the United States should play in the world. Both the Heartland Poll and the NES asked the question, "Do you think the U.S. would have fewer problems if we just stayed at home and did not concern ourselves with problems in other parts of the world?". This question taps at the issue of isolationism, whether the U.S. should be more inward looking and less involved with the rest of the world. Traditionally, the Midwest is viewed as more isolationist than other regions, particularly coastal states that are considered more outward looking. Responses to this particular question show the Midwest not as isolationist as conventionally believed. Only 20% of Midwesterners agreed with the "stay at home" position while 30% of the rest of the nation agreed. This one question does not get at the whole idea of isolationism, but it does contradict a generally agreed upon view of the Midwest.

The 1988 Presidential Election

In 1988 the Midwest was the weakest region for George Bush. This is strange given that the Midwest is more Republican than the rest of the nation. In order to determine what might have been going

TABLE 3.5
Percent Popular Vote for Bush and Dukakis

Geographical Area	Bush	Dukakis
Illinois	51%	49%
Iowa	44%	55%
Minnesota	54%	45%
Missouri	52%	48%
Nebraska	60%	39%
South Dakota	53%	47%
Wisconsin	52%	47%
The Midwest	52%	48%
The Nation	54%	46%

Source: The Almanac of American Politics 1990

on to produce such an outcome, we will need to look at both the pre-election surveys' estimation of the vote for the Midwest and the rest of the nation, and also use the actual election results. First, it will be illustrative to look at the election results. Table 3.5 gives the election results for each state in the Heartland Poll, the Midwest, and the nation as a whole. Table 3.5 shows that within the Midwest support for Bush varied widely from 60% of the vote in Nebraska to only 44% in Iowa. For the Midwest as a whole, Bush received 52% of the popular vote, and nationally he received 54% of the popular vote.

Why was a more Republican region the weakest region for Bush? One possible explanation might rest with economic factors, which have been shown to play a large role in determining the vote. There are two questions asked of the respondents on economic factors that will be helpful, how voters personally are doing financially and how voters perceive the nationally economy to be doing. Both the personal and national factors have been shown to influence presidential voting. The two questions we will be looking at are retrospective judgments, how things have gone over the past year. If things have gone poorly financially for a voter over the past year, theoretically he or she should try to vote the incumbent party out of office, and the same should be the case if the voter perceived the national economy as doing poorly. He or she would vote against the incumbent party

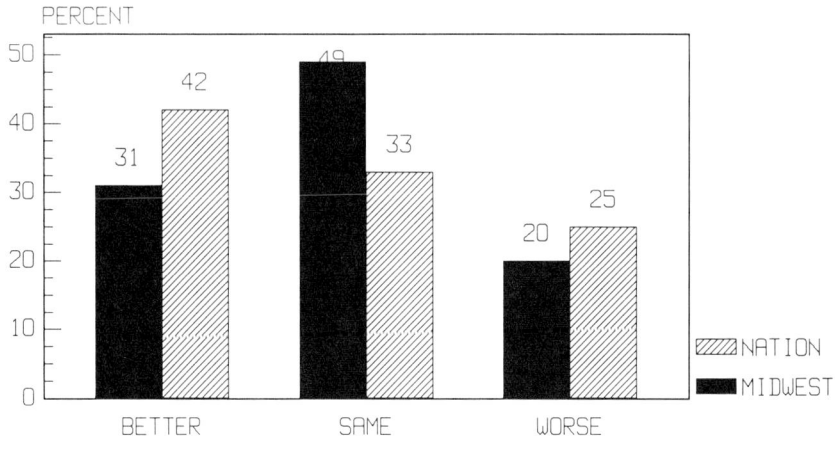

Figure 3.13. Personal Economic Situation Over the Past Year of the Midwest and the Nation

because of poor past performance and the hope the other party would do a better job in the future.

Figure 3.13 shows responses to the question of how things have been financially for the respondents over the past year for both the Midwest and the nation. Midwestern respondents can be seen to be less positive about their personal financial situation than the rest of the nation. Only 31% of the Midwest respondents compared to 42% of the rest of the nation say they are better off financially than they were a year ago. Midwesterners are much more likely to say their financial situation is the same as a year ago than the rest of the nation. Respondents outside the heartland states are slightly more likely to say things have gotten worse than in the Midwest—25% for the rest of the nation compared to 20% for the Midwest.

These numbers are not particularly surprising given the drought that was occurring in the Midwest at the time. It seems natural that many Midwesterners, although not directly engaged in farming themselves, may have been less positive about their financial situation given all the publicity the drought had been receiving during the previous months. The Midwest also did not reap so many benefits from the "Reagan recovery" as some regions of the nation. The fewer positive responses to the question inquiring about the respondent's personal financial situation seem to reflect quite accurately the situation in the Midwest in the fall of 1988.

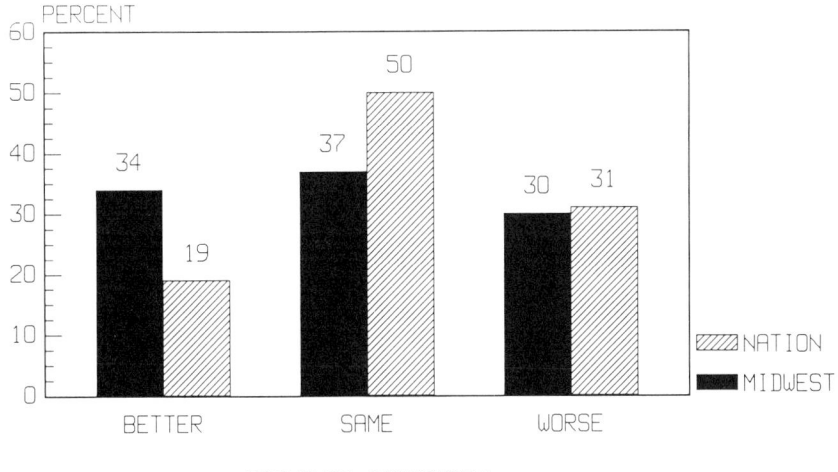

Figure 3.14. National Economic Situation Over the Past Year for the Midwest and the Rest of the Nation

Figure 3.14 compares the responses for the Midwest and the rest of the nation on how the national economy had been doing over the past year. This figure shows something interesting. While the rest of the nation was more positive about personal financial situations, the Midwest was more positive on the national economy than the rest of the nation. According to Figures 3.13 and 3.14, it is possible that the more Republican Midwest voted in smaller numbers for Bush because people saw their personal financial situation remaining the same while the rest of the nation improved. Midwesterners saw themselves left out of the "Reagan recovery" and were less supportive of the incumbent party.

It will also be illustrative to look at how "likely voters" for Bush and Dukakis answered these same economic questions. Figure 3.15 compares Midwestern Bush and Dukakis supporters on their personal financial situations over the past year. As expected, Bush supporters are more positive about their financial situations than Dukakis supporters. If people feel they are doing well financially and attribute some of this good fortune to the Republican's economic management, they would not feel the need to change the political party in control of the White House.

Figure 3.16 is the same graph as Figure 3.15 except that it is for the rest of the nation, and here too Bush supporters are more positive about their personal economic situation than Dukakis supporters. Comparing the Midwestern Dukakis supporters of Figure 3.15 with

76   *The Public: Attitudes, Beliefs and Polls*

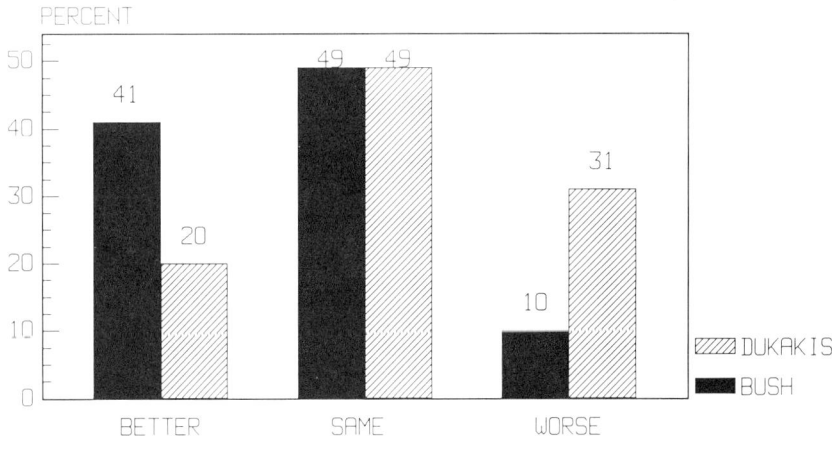

Figure 3.15. Personal Economic Situation of Midwestern Bush and Dukakis Supporters

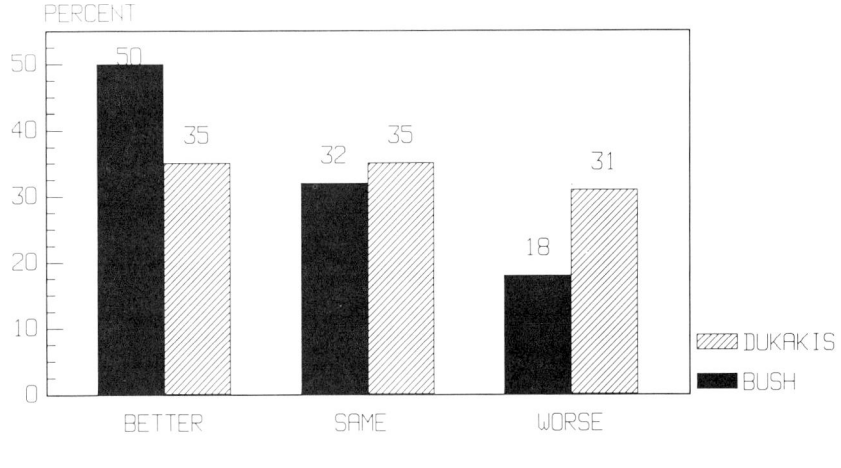

Figure 3.16. Personal Economic Situation of National Bush and Dukakis Supporters

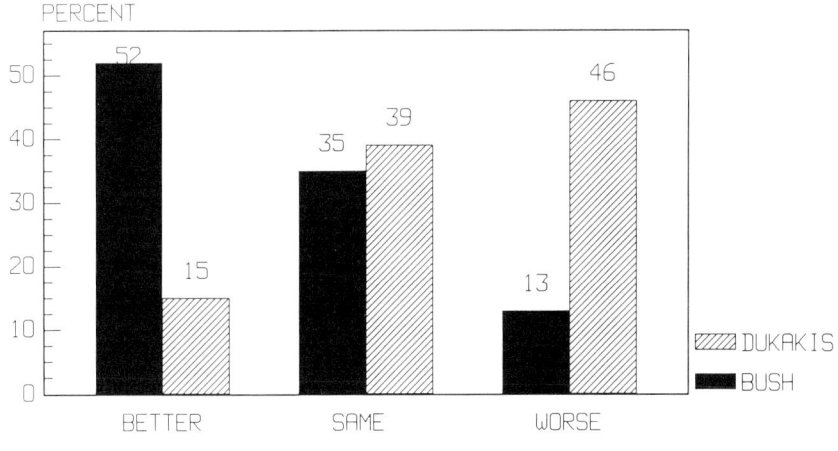

Figure 3.17. National Economic Situation of Midwestern Bush and Dukakis Supporters

the national Dukakis supporters of Figure 3.16 shows the national Dukakis supporters to be more positive than the Midwestern Dukakis supporters. This is consistent with our earlier findings of the Midwest as a whole being less positive on a personal economic level than the rest of the nation. A similar comparison of Midwestern Bush supporters with national Bush supporters is inconsistent with our earlier finding. While a comparison of Figures 3.15 and 3.16 shows 50% of national Bush supporters said they were financially better off than a year ago compared to 41% of Midwestern Bush supporters, 18% of national Bush supporters said they were worse off compared to 10% of Midwestern Bush supporters. The rest of the nation has more people in the most positive category, but also more in the most negative category. National Bush supporters are not substantially more positive than the Midwestern Bush supporters. It appears our earlier differences between the Midwest and the rest of the nation on a personal economic level rests mostly with those likely to vote for Dukakis.

Figures 3.17 and 3.18 are similar to Figures 3.15 and 3.16 except that they concern the condition of the national economy over the past year. Figure 3.17 reflects the Midwest and Figure 3.18 covers the rest of the nation. Once again as expected for both of the Midwest and the rest of the nation, Bush supporters are more positive than Dukakis supporters on the state of the national economy over the past year. Bush supporters may have been planning to vote for Bush be-

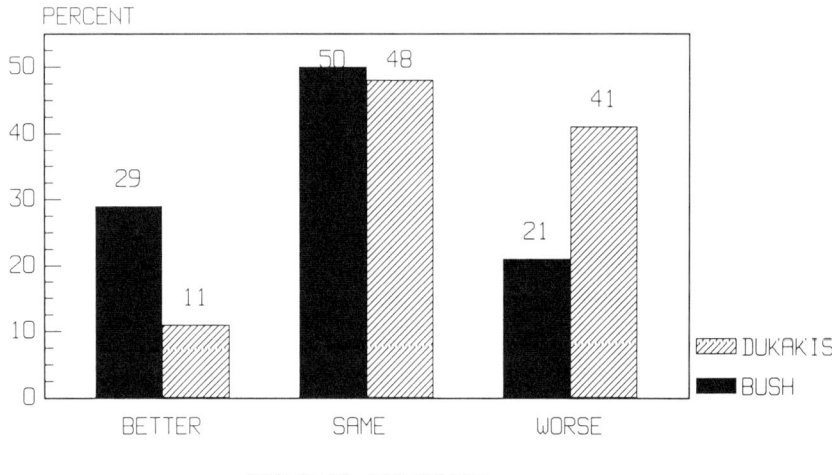

Figure 3.18. National Economic Situation of National Bush and Dukakis Supporters

cause they actually felt the economy had gotten better, or at least not worse. It is also possible that they were planning to vote for Bush for non-economic reasons. Perhaps some were Republicans, people who always vote Republican no matter who the candidate or what the state the nation. They may have just believed the economy was better to keep their attitudes and behaviors consistent. It would seem mildly illogical for Bush supporters to say the economy had not done well over the past year and still vote for Bush. People normally prefer to keep their attitudes and behaviors consistent with one another. A person who is planning to vote for the Republican candidate but feels the Republicans have done a poor job managing the economy is in a state of inconsistency. It is likely that to eliminate this inconsistency, this person will ignore economic evidence to the contrary and will believe that the Republicans have done a good job with the economy, an attitude which is consistent with the support of a Republican candidate.

Such a state of inconsistency does not appear as likely for Midwestern and national Dukakis supporters and national Bush supporters as for Midwestern Bush supporters. Comparing the Bush supporters of Figures 3.17 and 3.18 shows Midwest Bush supporters to be much more positive on the condition of the economy than national Bush supporters. A similar comparison of Dukakis supporters shows smaller differences. Our earlier finding of the Midwest being more positive about the national economy than the nation is attributable to Midwestern Bush supporters and not Midwestern Dukakis supporters.

We are left with a Midwest that is less positive about personal economic factors, which can be attributed to Dukakis supporters, and a Midwest that is more positive about the national economy, which is attributable to Bush supporters. It looks as if both Dukakis and Bush supporters were reacting to a Midwest economy that had not received all the economic benefits of the Reagan recovery. Midwestern Dukakis supporters were more negative on their personal economic situation than national Dukakis supporters reflecting their dissatisfaction with being left out of the recovery. Midwest Bush supporters were viewing their personal situations fairly well and the national economy very well to maintain consistency among their attitudes. Overall, economic factors seemed to play a large role in the Midwest in the 1988 presidential election.

Summary and Conclusions

Our comparison of the Midwest with the rest of the nation supports few of the common stereotypes of the Midwest. An examination of the people of the Midwest showed that farmers account for only 5% of the labor force. While it is true that agriculture does play a role in the Midwestern economy, very few people are actually engaged in farming, and most are employed in occupations typical of the rest of the nation. By comparing Midwestern and national family income, we found the Midwest to be fairly middle-class. We also found Midwesterners pursuing post-secondary education in much greater numbers than the rest of the nation. As expected the Midwest is not racially diverse and has more protestants than any religion, but so does the rest of the nation. Is the image of the farmer an accurate representation of a typical Midwesterner? The answer clearly is no.

As is traditionally thought, the Midwest is a more Republican region but does not always demonstrate it in voting. It is possible the Midwest could become even more Republican if its young people continue to turn away from independence and think of themselves as Republicans in the numbers they did in the fall of 1988. As demonstrated by self placements on a liberal-conservative scale and attitudes toward social spending, the Midwest is not more conservative than the rest of the nation.

Our study of the 1988 presidential election showed economic factors had an influence on Midwesterners' voting decisions. The more Republican Midwest was the least supportive of the Republican candidate than any other region. Dukakis supporters were more dissatisfied with both their personal economic situation and the national economy than their national counterparts. A vote for Dukakis appeared in part to be a vote of dissatisfaction with the economic policies of the past Republican administration. Midwestern voters should be more equipped to vote on the basis of economics given their higher educational levels, which makes this explanation all the more plausible. Other parts of the nation also got left behind in the Reagan recovery, the Southeast and, more notably, the Southwest, and do not show the same apparent economic disaffection as the Heartland. That suggests that a little more than economics is needed to account for Midwestern nonsupport for the Republican ticket.

Our comparison of the Midwest with the rest of the nation has shown us a Midwest that has its differences, as does any region. On the whole, however, the Midwest is both demographically and politically similar to the rest of the nation. Finding few differences between the Midwest and the rest of the country and being able to dismiss traditional Midwestern images is a finding in itself. We have examined the "Midwestern Myth" of a backward, agriculturally dominated region and found it to look much like the nation of which it is a part.

Notes

1. Because some of the respondents from the pre-election wave can not be contacted some months later after the election, the NES sample experiences what is called "sample mortality," the effect of which is that the originally representative sampling becomes a little less so. The people who die, move, become institutionalized, just lose patience with being interviewed, or whatever, can not be assumed to be typical in all regards of the sample. Thus the pre-election wave of NES is the appropriate comparison to the Heartland sample.
2. And the same could probably be said of farm related industries, although this is a more difficult matter to nail down. Some do make their livings manufacturing tractors or packing meat, but the numbers so engaged are not a large proportion of the labor force.
3. For our sample sizes, we can be confident if we were to draw a sample 100 times, that 95 of those times the true population values would lie within plus or minus 2.2 percentage points of the values we obtained in our sample. In other words, for the Heartland Poll, 95 out of 100 times we draw a sample we can be confident the true percentage of Protestants in the population is between 62% and 66%, and for the NES between 67% and 71%.
4. Unlike most of the questions we have been and will be examining, the question concerning social spending used in the Heartland Poll is not identical to the question in the NES. While this is unfortunate and we will need to exercise caution in our interpretations, we can still learn something about differences in attitudes toward social spending.

Chapter 4

The Mood of the American Electorate

James A. Stimson

What Is Public Opinion and Where Is It Going?

What is public opinion and where is it going? These simple questions are at the center of many commentaries on politics. When we ask "what" public opinion is, we usually mean something like "what are the typical preferences of the American electorate?" When we ask "where" it is going, we mean something like "how is it different this year, say, from last?"

Leaders who wish to marshall support for particular proposals—or merely to see themselves returned to power—would do well to know the answers to these questions. Although we lack systematic knowledge on the matter, those who observe political leaders close at hand think that they do know. Elected politicians are seen as most of the time peculiarly sensitive to the shifting winds and changing trends of opinion.

But these sorts of questions, what public opinion is and where it is going, are uncommon concerns of political science. The questions are descriptive of the world of American politics, where our disciplinary emphasis is rather on explanation. And the answers, good ones at least, are more difficult than the questions. We have answers. But since there is little agreement on them, they are evidently not particularly good ones.

How Can We Know What Public Opinion Is and Where It Is Going?

Just because our answers aren't good doesn't stop us from trying them. One way in which we do so is to look at election outcomes to infer the sort of public opinion that might be driving them. If the voters choose conservative candidates over liberals, then they must be in a conservative mood, mustn't they? The surmise is reasonable, but the evidence is much less clear.

If the voters are speaking to us about their preferences through their votes, then they are speaking in riddles. For what they are "saying" over the last twenty years or so is that they like conservative presidents more than liberals and, at the same time, that they prefer liberal Congresses (and often other offices as well) over conservative ones. Which is the true preference? The answer would seem to be both.

If we look at individual contests to make inferences about the mind of the electorate, we encounter similar difficulty. For we see candidates who promise more government involvement and spending doing well, candidates who promise lower taxes, and implicitly less government, doing well, and candidates who promise both doing well. The message of electoral preference over alternatives is confusion. With such disparate results one is tempted to conclude that it matters a great deal *how* candidates deliver their message about public policy, but it matters much less *what* the message itself is.

Elections, in the end, do not speak to our two questions. Perhaps more accurately it should be said that they speak, but we hear a babble of voices. They provide entertaining arguments, but will not answer the questions. For that we need more direct measures of citizen preference.

The Problems of Survey Research "Marginals"

We can of course just go and ask samples of citizens what it is that they want, and how much of it should be provided. A well developed science of survey research tells us that we can do so quite reliably if we just ask the right questions. Suppose, for example, we have the following:

Question: Should abortion be legal as it is now, or legal only in such cases as rape, incest, or to save the life of the mother, or should it not be permitted at all?

Response	
"Legal as now"	49%
"Only to save mother, rape, or incest"	39
"Not permitted at all"	9
"Don't know, no answer"	3
Total	100%

[New York Times survey of April 13–16, 1989]

This does tell us in a sense what public opinion is. But if we were asked to characterize that public opinion, to draw a more general interpretation than the words of the question and the percentage responses, the situation is not promising.

The data tell us several things. (And the *New York Times* is both skilled and reputable in survey research.) But data such as these, even a large collection of them, do not tell us in a very direct sense what public opinion is or where it is going.

The "what" question runs afoul of which questions tap the relevant public opinion. Alas, there are infinite numbers of possibilities and we don't know which should be used. What we know about question wording is that it matters—change the words and you change the responses—but we don't know in any scientific sense what is the "correct" wording.[1] And since the responses must be judged in terms of the words used, to know what public opinion is then, we need to have known what to expect. But we don't. Is 49% advocating "legal as now" a lot, a little, or what?

And a survey question at a single moment in time obviously cannot tell us where public opinion is going, that requires observation of the same question[2] asked repeatedly over time. From such a time series, say the percent who choose the "legal as now" response, we can begin to make statements about where this part of public opinion is going.

Answers to this same question, posed by the *Times* at irregular intervals since 1985, are shown in Figure 4.1. There we see an apparent movement, most notable at the end of the series, toward the "liberal" pro-abortion stance in the four year period. Have we now captured what and why? Well, for this one issue we are close to it. Figure 4.1 gives us a sense of where these public attitudes have been and where they are going. Clearly that is a much better sense than the simple distribution of responses—called "marginal totals" or just "marginals"—to the April, 1989 question.

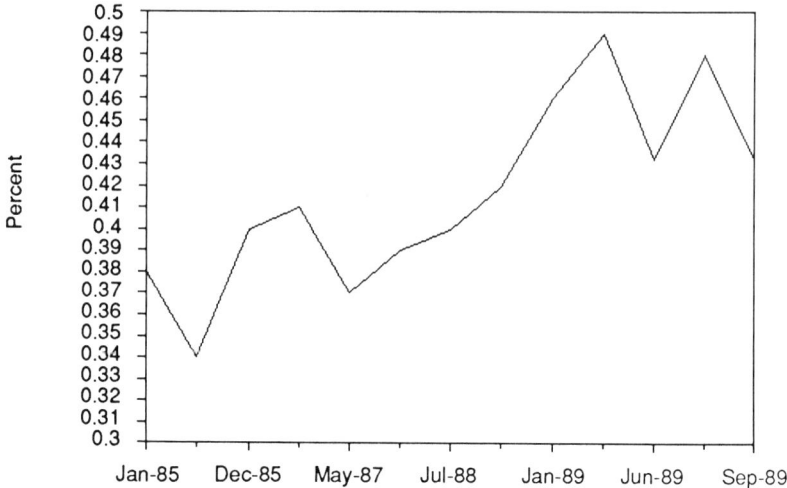

Figure 4.1. Abortion Attitudes, *New York Times:* Percent Saying "Keep Legal as Now"

Informed observers of the abortion issue would probably discount whether the movements of Figure 4.1 could be called a trend. An alternative interpretation is that the big jump in 1989 is a response to the controversial *Webster v. Reproductive Health Services* decision of the Supreme Court.[3] And a one-time movement of opinion following some event carries a good deal less significance than an inexorable trend. But so long as we stick to this one issue, we can't know which it is. If, on the other hand, we knew that other components of public opinion did or did not move at the time of *Webster,* we could make an informed evaluation of the matter. For abortion attitudes might be driven by some underlying movements in national public opinion—to be called "policy mood"—or they might be focused wholly on the specifics of this one controversy. If it is the former, then we have important evidence of a liberal trend in the electorate. If it is the latter, the pattern of abortion attitudes, while still real, would connote much less. It would be something which could be explained by short-term events and by news coverage, something that could go away as fast as it came.

If we wish to speak of "public opinion" generally, not just a specific version of a question about abortion rights, then we need to know if this abortion question is somehow representative or typical. And again we run out of scientific answers. For we have no methodology for determining whether *questions* are a representative sample of some universe of content. We can know whether the people we select to interview are representative by employing random sampling procedures. But there is no comparable sampling methodology for questions because we don't know how to define the universe of possible public opinion questions.

Are individual issues and policies pieces of bundles of views on a wide range of things or each unique, a thing wholly onto itself, to be explained entirely be factors relevant to its specifics? In ordinary commentary we seem to presume bundles. We say all the time things like "the liberal position on . . ." which implies that this word liberal has a general connotation free of issue specifics (and that liberals as a set of people take more or less the liberal position on a wide range of issues). But the policy literature in political science is usually the reverse, stressing the uniqueness of each domain, a thing onto itself only. Which is it? Are issues bundled or separate?

Tackling these issues to derive sensible measures of what public opinion is and where it is going is the focus of this chapter. To do so we will need to look at many more issues and over a much longer time span.

The Lore of Political Eras

Commentaries on American politics all but universally assume that it can be characterized as a succession of eras. The McCarthy years, the Sixties, the Reagan Era—all these connote more than time, much more. They are rich in images of characteristic sets of belief and action. They portray moods of the electorate understood by professional political actors to acquiesce in some kinds of policy direction and sharply to circumscribe the opposites.

Political eras are times of distinctive national ideology, at least in the sense in which we may use that term for whole electorates and their surrounding cultures. Such periods might be characterized as shifts of whole distributions of opinion producing a "center" that moves over time. If the center of the American political spectrum in the McCarthy Era was a rigid conformity, acceptance of the status quo, and hewing to traditional values, that position would have been considerably on the right in the middle 1960s and then back near the center again in the 1980s.

Assertions about political eras are commonplace in the world of political commentary,[4] which is to assert less than that they are true. Skepticism is in order about common beliefs, perhaps especially about universal ones. Skepticism demands rigorous evaluation of national mood; it will not be satisfied by anecdotes or impressions.

Asymmetrical Acquiescence: A Model of Mood

Political lore needs no explicit model. It is what it is without much reflection. But a systematic view of public mood, as it might drive representation, requires more. It requires us to think about what public opinion is, how we come to know it, and how it works its influence. The little model I develop here is a means to give mood a role in the larger picture of democratic politics.

Presume that public opinion, as seen by professionals in the business of government and politics, consists of a tripartite topology, (1) issue positions too far left for public acceptance, (2) those similarly too far right, and (3) a zone of acquiescence between them—not necessarily exactly in the middle.

The zone of acquiescence is a range of incremental policy choices so firmly within established consensus that no public response is to be expected. The public acquiesces because the marginal cost of doing otherwise exceeds its expected benefit. The width of this middling zone is a function of indifference, the degree of which rests on perceived benefits of alternative courses of policy and on the costs of information on those benefits. Where real benefit differentials are modest, or information costs exceed what an inattentive electorate will bear, or both, then this indifferent portion of the policy space might be large. In other cases, abortion comes to mind, the policy space may reduce to unacceptable actions of left or right with no acquiescent zone.

The zone of acquiescence in the general case is asymmetrical, the center need not be equidistant from the bounds. That implies that it might be the case that at any given time the electorate is more willing to tolerate policy innovation and experimentation in the one direction than the other.

The zone of acquiescence notion implies a social (macro) awareness of a left-right continuum, although the process can be so passive, so driven by social communication, that most citizens might act with respect to it without being aware of it. This is not by any means "ideology" in the sense understood in the research on voting behavior. That political psychology orientation toward the structure of ideas requires far, far more than is needed for ideological *influence* to emerge as a macro phenomenon.

If the zone of acquiescence is asymmetrical, it is but a short step to the suspicion that the asymmetry may vary with time. If we allow over time variation of asymmetry, then we would expect to see shifts of public mood. If politicians sense such shifts—and everything we know about the species suggests that such sensitivity is a finely honed attribute—then we have a basis for expecting elite behavior to conform to public mood and for representation. We expect, in other words, the acceptable center of political views to meander over time like a flowing river and for politicians to swim more or less where it goes, not to watch it from the bank.[5]

Zone of acquiescence, combined with common assumptions about cognitive miserliness—the notion that people don't invent difficult and complicated ways of thinking about problems when simple ones seem satisfactory—implies a latent continuum underlying expressed policy preferences, a *common* cause of somewhat diverse opinions which produces observable parallelism in the movements of policy preferences over time. It implies, that is, that it is simpler to see issues in bundles than each on its own terms and that tracks of issue preferences over time should move together, tracing more or less parallel courses. Whether or not issue preferences move together over time is a simple enough matter to observe.

Why Swings in Public Policy Mood?

There are only three possibilities for the development of public mood over time, (1) constancy, (2) unidirectional movement, or (3) cyclical[6] movement. I develop briefly two models of the policy process which suggest, along with intuition and history, that cyclical movements are to be expected. Either is sufficient to produce the result.

Policy Excess

A first explanatory model is an overcompensating negative feedback system. Negative feedback systems, whether engineered, as in missile guidance systems, or natural, as in the auto driver keeping his or her car in the lane by little correction every time it moves too far one or the other way, have the common characteristic of adjusting to inputs of information about how things are going. The adjustments are negative in the sense that what is observed is error, and so correction is always in the other direction.

Assume that policy-makers, both elected and unelected, get satisfaction from the implementation of preferred policies, and a subset of them, elected officials, also seek election and re-election. The electorate benefits from and desires the implementation of a preferred set of policies.

Assume also that the policy preferences of the aggregated mass electorate are not constant, but move over time and further that policy-makers perceive that movement, although imperfectly. Then that subset of policy-makers toward whom the movement occurs sense the possibility of enacting policies closer to their preferred position. The subset of policy-makers who see movement away from their preference sense possible frustration of their policy goals from action at an inopportune time. As a result, even though no policy actor changes preferences, the net policy result shifts in the direction of the movement of mass opinion.

Policy-makers move in policy increments. They move, that is, not to their real preferences (which might be quite extreme relative to current policies and relevant to what the public will accept), but rather step by step in the direction of those preferences. At each time, $t, t + 1, t + 2, \ldots$ they both enact new increments (moving steadily in the direction of mass opinion) and observe the reaction of the public to previous increments. Each observation serves to strengthen and confirm the initial perception of what the public wants. The process continues until some point $t + k$ when the policy-makers sense negative reaction, at which point they correct their imperfect knowledge of public opinion and reverse course. This is negative feedback.

Assume that policy implementation produces a full public response only after several periods $k>1$ because policy implementation is not instant and response has a cumulative character. Response to policy change occurs only after it has been in place long enough for the public to come in contact with it repeatedly. This is a natural result of the fact that the public is inattentive to politics and policy; not paying much attention to policy-making, it comes to be aware of change after it encounters its effects. But numerous encounters with policy change usually will be a matter of some years.

The public also has imperfect information about its own preferences. The sorts of changes it may advocate in hypothetical survey questions may not be supported once the real impacts of change are driven home. It is not adept in anticipating the costs of hypothetical policies and, therefore cannot with certainty be predicted to support policies, once enacted, that is supported previous to enactment. Why this assumption? Because political rhetoric is unbalanced, rational policy advocates will sell policy by presenting it as cost-free sets of benefits. They succeed often in selling policy proposals to the electorate, the *net* effect of which could not have been successfully advocated. Information about costs and other tradeoffs increases after implementation, based upon real experience, leading to apparent flip-flops in public sentiment, caused more by improved understanding than by changed preferences.[7]

Thus the point in which negative public response is sensed is not when policy has gone just beyond what the public wants, but rather k periods later when policy has continued to overshoot public preference for both time and distance, and is now outside the range of acquiescence.

The electorate then reacts to policy excess and, in light of new information about policy effects, shifts preferences in the contrary direction, a shift that gains momentum over the k periods while the excess continues to grow. When policy-makers perceive the shift, the process begins anew in the opposite direction until, eventually, it too overshoots public acquiescence and causes another reversal. The essential requisite for all negative feedback systems to work effectively is that the feedback be timely. If it is not, then small continuous corrections do not produce a smooth path, but rather a sometimes violent jerking back and forth.

Policy Regimes: Performance, and Reaction

Presume that policy-making is characterized by regimes, periods in which policy direction is mainly liberal or mainly conservative. Such regimes might be driven by mass preferences, through elections or otherwise, but they need not be. They could, for example, be the incidental result of throwing out a previous set of rascals on performance grounds. All that is important is that they occur and that they are perceived by the electorate to occur.

Regimes always (are perceived to) fail to perform in the long term. Even if success were possible, perception of failure is likely to cumulate over the duration of the regime. In the worst case even if policy a works brilliantly to solve problem A, the mass electorate will ultimately reject the regime because it fails to perform on some other problem B (which might indeed only become a "problem" because success on A creates a vacuum which needs to be filled by new problems). One can imagine relatively long regimes or relatively brief ones, but it is hard to imagine permanence. Failures must occur and ultimately they must be blamed on the policies in place.

The natural result must be that the longer a regime is in place, the more it will come to be associated with failure, leading to increasing probability of reversing direction. Policy regimes are thus expected to produce policy moods that cycle back and forth over the long term. The process is not so regular or determined that anything like regular periods of alteration can be expected. But it does lead to the reasonable expectation that a mature policy regime is more likely to experience reversal than indefinite continuation.

Schlesinger puts it with more color:

> Disappointment is the universal modern malady.
>
> It is also a basic spring of political change. People can never be fulfilled for long either in the public or in the private sphere. We try one, then the other, and frustration compels a change in course. Moreover, however effective a particular course may be in meeting one set of troubles, it generally falters and fails when new troubles arise. And many troubles are inherently insoluble. As political eras, whether dominated by public purpose or by private interest, run their course, they infallibly generate the desire for something different. It always becomes after a while 'time for a change.' (1986:28)

The Mood Representation Thesis

Here is my thesis: American politics is representative of the forces of American public opinion. That representation emerges over time public policy responds to the changing moods of the electorate.

For simplicity, the thesis is stated as a unidirectional response *of* policy makers *to* mass opinion, but in fact a more complicated interaction is expected. As I have argued elsewhere (Carmines and Stimson, 1989), the issue definition around which representation might proceed cannot reasonably be expected of an inattentive electorate. The pattern more likely to be found is a continuing sequence of cues from policy makers, which mostly fall on deaf ears, but which occasionally stir response to novel definitions of policy debate. The cues thus proceed from professionals in politics and policy, and the response emerges from citizens. The added assertion of the mood representation thesis is that elites respond to that response.[8]

The evidence, if the thesis is true, would be seen in movement between eras of globally different prevailing conceptions of what the American public demands and supports. The relevant changes and differences are to be found not in the district/representative conceptions that so constrain our notion of what "representation" is, or ought to be, but in changes of policy mood over time of an electorate *that is largely a national unit*—and the policy outcome that results.

Two sorts of representation are expected, (1) big bang electoral effects, where the outcome of elections to some degree translates the mood of the moment into choice of candidate, and (2) more subtle movements over time, independent of vote totals. The first is of course the steady preoccupation of political science. It is not our focus here, which turns instead to policy-makers' sensed movement of public sentiment and the relatively small partial adjustments to be expected of those policy-makers. Obviously the two modes are not independent of one another, but the focus is on nonelectoral factors.

Basic policy predisposition—mood—is less than ideology. We know that full blown cognitive structures of an ideological sort are uncommon in mass electorates. Mood instead is a predisposition to acquiesce in policy experimentation in one direction, but not the other, an intellectually passive propensity that nonetheless has real force.

Most would concur, for example, that in the early Reagan era the electorate would have acquiesced in criminal sentencing tougher than previous standards, but not more lenient, in more restrictive approaches to welfare, but not more generous ones, and in reduction of (rates of increase of) Federal spending in variety of domestic areas, but not in expansions. Whether and to what degree any of these remain true in the 1990s is the sort of question that demands measurement of policy mood.

The political eras and representation thesis may be treated as four component assertions. They are (1) that meaningful policy moods exist, (2) that they vary across time in the medium term, (3) that political leaders sense those variations and alter their behavior accordingly, and (4) that public policy therefore comes to represent public mood. We focus in this chapter only on the first two.

Measuring Public Policy Mood: The Marginals as Data

We lack not for measures of public mood. Each individual policy preference comparably measured by survey researchers over time is a candidate measure. Indeed there are many candidates—many preference-marginals time series—no one of which is particularly good. None is available for enough years and, worse yet, given the design motivations of survey researchers, none is available for anything like a representative sample of years. And the validity of each candidate measure—whether, that is, it measures mood or something else—is in question. If we start with the presumption that the longitudinal variation of each consists of (1) *portions common* to all domestic issues (i.e. mood), (2) *portions specific* to the individual issue, and (3) error, then the problem may be restated: When we find evidence of systematic movement over time, we can't know for one issue in isolation whether it is the common or specific portion we are observing. To isolate common variation we must observe issues varying together.

The question is how to uncover a central tendency underlying variation in policy preference over time—i.e., the mood. Were it the case that complete time series of mass preferences over a variety of issue alternatives were available, the answer would be straightforward. This is, except for its longitudinal orientation, a textbook case for principal components analysis;[9] we have n time series from which we wish to extract one or more common elements. But complete time series of preferences over the policies of interest do not and will never exist. To decree that time series must be identically framed questions by a single survey organization rules out the possibility of lengthy series. Often issues are represented by five or six readings over the four decades. In the extreme, a single issue might have but two comparable measures—and yet still have some value.

When account is taken of a data matrix—issues by time—that has far more missing data than measured values, principal components or similar models become swamped beyond believability by the missing data problems. Thus simple though it is in concept, the consequences of missing observations preclude simple estimation of underlying tendency.

Simple methods of creating a summary scale encounter similar difficulties. Linear interpolation, often a reasonable strategy, presents serious difficulties for this problem. On occasions where it would be expected to be reasonably accurate, for example in filling in the missing odd-numbered years in the every two year National Election Studies issue variables, it remains problematic because it induces properties in the resulting time series—year to year similarity in contrast with differences over a longer time scale—that are precisely those in need of empirical test. And often it is clear in the available data that any interpolation would be an act more of creation than estimation. Given that there would be more data values interpolated than measured—perhaps four or five to one—these difficulties are not by any means small.

Adding (or averaging) across issues for a particular year, for example, presumes a common metric, which does not exist. Standardization schemes which could produce common metrics depend critically upon the assumption that the missing values for each issue are representative of all values. That is untenable is the face of the basic thrust of the enterprise, which is the contrary assertion that systematic movement over time is present. Where large portions of decades might be missing, this is no cosmetic issue; missing values not only *can* be atypical, they often *will* be.

The awkwardness of the incomplete data matrix, nonetheless, is just that. It is not the case that insufficient data exist to identify a common underlying tendency. The matrix is information rich. It is only its form that is deficient. One solution to estimating a common thread in policy preferences is to drop the presumption of completely measured time series and its associated mathematics in favor of dealing with pairs or dyads of readings on some policy, not necessarily adjacent. If year t is more conservative than year $t + k$, then we have some simple evidence for the relative conservatism of years t and $t + k$. We don't know from a single dyad the validity of the particular issue as an indicator of mood, nor the degree to which the same dyad of years over a different issue will produce similar evidence. But these matters can be determined empirically. The general approach to the problem, to be called the Recursive Dyadic Dominance method is outlined below.

Recursive Dyadic Dominance[10]

Given an issue time series presenting a subset of readings for the full time series, we have a self-representing indicator of mood for all those years in which measured values are present. If we choose an arbitrary value for the final "base" year of the series, say 100, then the indicator can be scaled for each year t as:

Dominance$_t$ = 100*(Percent Conservative$_t$/Percent Conservative$_b$)

the fundamental piece of information being the ration of measured values in the dyadic comparison. The dominance ratio is then simply the relative conservatism of all available earlier years to the base year, which itself takes on the arbitrary scaling meter value. The ultimate variability of the issue is captured by the dyadic ratios, and although changed in metric, is not standardized by the procedure.

Any other issue which includes a measured value for the base year can be similarly scaled,[11] and then summary values for each year can be obtained as an average of the new metrics for each year in which both issue measures are present. Or, since it is now scaled in a common metric, dominance may be represented by one issue if the other is not available. The process may be generalized across all issues that have a measured value for the chosen base year.

But many issues will not have measured values for the base year. That is where the recursion comes in. Using the preliminary estimates from step one—now in new metric—a second base year, say $t-1$, is selected, and its newly *estimated* value is used as a scaling metric to repeat the procedure for all those issues not available at t (hence already incorporated), but available at $t-1$. The process then is repeated for $t-2$, $t-3$, and so forth until all issue dyads have been incorporated.

Ultimately, every issue available for year t contributes its ratio with all other available years to the summary dominance scale value for t. No missing information enters into the calculation at any point.

[1a] $$\text{sum}_t = \sum_{i=1}^{n} \sum_{j=1}^{t} (\text{Issue}_{ij}/\text{Issue}_{ib}) * \text{Metric}_b$$

[1b] $\text{mood}_t = \text{Sum}_t/n$

where:
Σ (Sigma) is the summation operator
$i=1,n$ is all available issues for year t
$j=1,t$ is all available dyad ratios for issue i
b is the base year for the recursive metric generation
Metric_b is the value of the metric for year b

Given that the issues which contribute their dyadic variation to mood are likely to vary in their association with the latent concept (i.e. their validity) and that it is undesirable to wholly discard numerous issues because their associations are small, the procedure can be modified by including a weighting term u^2, which taps the "communality" of the issue/Mood association, the degree that is that the issue is associated with the underlying concept. The communality may be estimated by correlating the dominance scale with the issue.

The squared bivariate correlations then become workable communality estimates for [2]:

$$[2a] \quad \text{sum}_t = \sum_{i=1}^{n} \sum_{j=1}^{t} u^2 * (\text{Issue}_{ij}/\text{Issue}_{ib}) * \text{Metric}_b$$

$$[2b] \quad \text{Mood}_t = \text{sum}_t / \sum_{j=1}^{n} u^2$$

where the equation is the same as [1] except weighted in both steps by u^2, an estimate of the common variation of Issue_i and Mood.

The result, for a broad range of issue time series, may be seen in Figure 4.2. There, with a little visual smoothing of the pre-1972 data, may be seen a pattern consistent with common interpretations of political eras in American politics. One can easily discern conservatism in the 1950s and the 1980s and a liberal interlude in between. But unlike common interpretations, and of some interest, the series anticipates conventional understandings. The 1960s liberalism is most striking *before* the period we think of with that name had begun. And similarly, the growth of the conservatism of the Reagan period occurs *before* Reagan.[12] If the estimates are to be credited, they suggest that popular awareness lags, that we come to recognize a distinctive political period only after it has been building for some years and then may already be in decline.

The most dramatic mismatch of the estimates with popular perceptions is the end of the series, where the year in which we coined "L-word" to express the unpopularity of liberalism is a near high point of liberal policy preferences. Can this be the case? Two points are relevant. One is that the liberal trend found by the algorithm may easily be seen in the raw data, where widely varying sorts of issue marginals show exactly the same trend. That has not been widely noted, because we don't credit the marginals much; year to year changes of a percent or two *could* be sampling fluctuation. But when they are seen in every issue domain in hundreds of independent samples the evidence is quite decisive that they are not. Second, one needs to explain why no President Dukakis. On that point I note that the policy mood series was used to predict previous presidential outcomes (along with Democratic Macropartisanship and disposable income) and then to forecast the 1988 result. The model made a credible

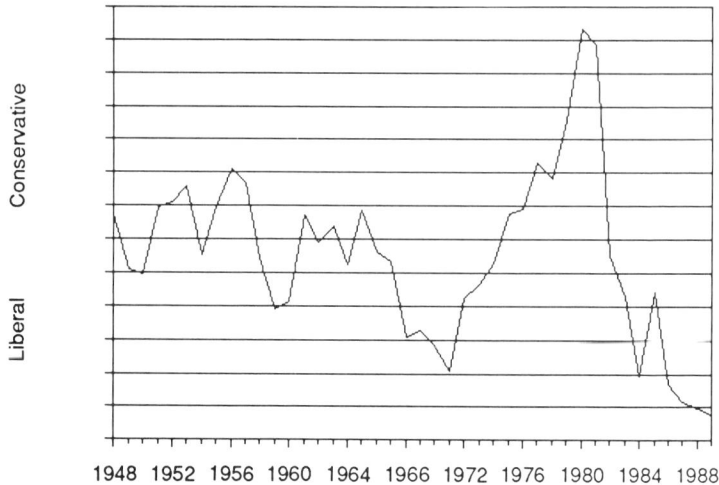

Figure 4.2. Policy Mood, 1948 to 1989: Dyadic Solution from Marginal Data

prediction of a 53.1% GOP share of the popular vote,[13] but more importantly, the contribution of mood was sensible. Both of the other variables were at the extreme pro-Republican end of their range, predicting landslide. The liberal estimated mood moved the forecast 4 points in the democratic direction to a result close to what occurred.

"Mood" or "Moods?"

The conceptual development to this point rests on an assumed single underlying latent dimension of policy attitude. It is presumed that issues which fail to share much of their variation with a single underlying continuum have merely a specific character, rooted in the issue context. Abortion attitudes for example are to be explained as a reaction to *Roe v. Wade* and ensuing public protests against it, not as part of the general back and forth of American political life.

But it could be the case that the reality is "moods," plural, that several issue domains each have their own dynamic. Commentary assuming separate economic and social dimensions to politics is ubiquitous. And other such distinctions are reasonable.

Issues of dimensionality are never easy or straightforward, and that is at least equally the case with a longitudinal perspective. The problems of missing data now exponentially as the data are disaggregated to separate issue domains. What is possible to tap with some reliability with 96 flawed mini time-series is not possible with a hand-

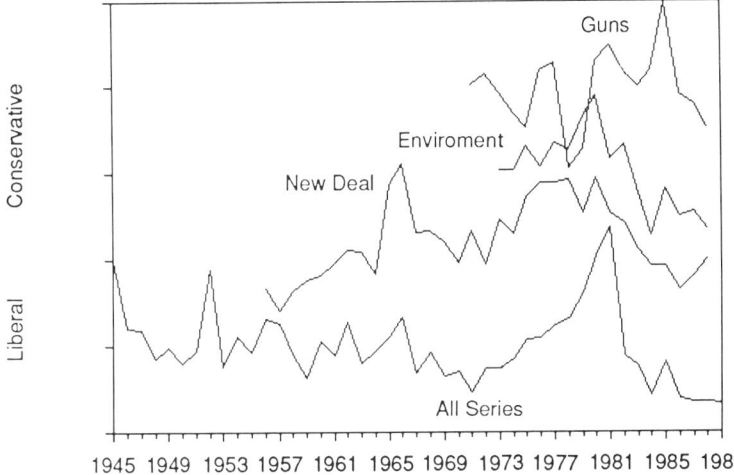

Figure 4.3. Mood and Three Components: New Deal, Environment, and Gun Control

ful; the whole is considerably more reliable than its parts. And issue domain comparisons are even more difficult where their components are central to public debate at different times and the domains become, therefore, associated with both the density and quality of survey research. Race, for example, is arguably separate (at some times) and arguably of central consequences (Carmines and Stimson 1989), but the lack of continuous measures of racial attitudes attenuates the possibility of observing a racial "dimension" which is more than a caricature of the issues as framed. What can be measured is recent responses to a surely atypical set of racial issues, and then only after the period where race was of central importance to American political life.[14] The registration of handguns, in contrast, is an issue for which good measures are abundant, a function of *when* the issue was contested much more than how central it is or was.

But those cautions aside, it is of some use to disaggregate into issue domains. Most importantly, it permits a look at separate sources of variation to see the degree to which they move together. Not anything like a satisfactory test of longitudinal dimensionality, one nonetheless can get some feeling for it by separate measurement and side by side examination of components of the political agenda.

Figure 4.3 portrays the summary mood measure along with three subset measures for which decent estimation of time series is practicable for subperiods.[15] Of these, the "New Deal" measure encom-

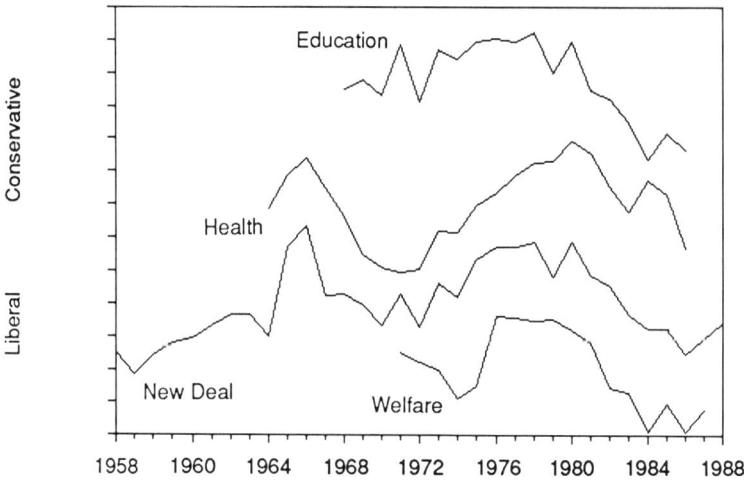

Figure 4.4. The New Deal Disaggregated: Education, Health and Welfare Issues

passes much of the standard content of the various conflicts surrounding expansion of federal activity in health, welfare, and education. It alone is estimated with a number of issue time series that some claim for reliability seems possible (but as with all such scales, reliability is scant in the pre-1972 period where good issue time-series are thin). Measures for environmental protection are available for fewer years and fewer items. The reader in all these cases would be wise to impose smoothing on the raw graphs; year to year zigzags are mainly noise.

What can be seen in Figure 4.3, just barely, is a similar conservative "hump" around 1980.[16] All series but gun control reach conservative peaks for modern times in 1980–81 and move monotonically—more or less—in the liberal direction forward or backward of their peaks. And all reach impressively into the liberal range of their variation by 1988–89. One would see the same by looking at series after series of annual marginals; the evidence there is less striking for the annual movements would be readily written off if it were not the case that so many issue series are simultaneously moving in the same direction.

The New Deal series is substantial enough that it can be further disaggregated into policy components. That is seen in Figure 4.4, where Education, Health, and Welfare series are plotted with the full series. Again applying some (mental) smoothing, these components track the New Deal series closely, rising and falling very largely together. Whether the differences between their time paths are specific variation attributable to issue domain or merely noise, the cross-issue similarity (even with measures where reliability is constrained by small numbers of indicators) is substantial enough to suggest that many analyses of specific policy attitudes over time fail to see that the subcomponents can claim little that is their own. These issues are a package deal.

Ideology and Its Terminology

One of the dependable cliches of American politics is that "liberal" and "conservative" are somehow too gross, too meaningless, too stereotypical to capture much of the meaning of political debate. And then the politicians, journalists, and scholars who utter the cliche will frequently be seen *using* these terms in the next paragraph. The reason that is so is that the terms do in fact capture much of the meaning of political debate, not all but much.

If we accept the premise that the terms are too descriptive not to be employed, then it is natural to ask what exactly they mean. Millions are confused about the issue, and those millions include the politicians, journalists, and scholars who use them on a daily basis. Valuable though they are, they are slippery. Perhaps they are easy enough to define—I could offer several plausible approaches—but we consistently fail to achieve anything like consensus of what they mean. Different people fill them with different content.

Worse yet, it would appear that their meanings shift over time. Over the last half century, "the" core connotation of liberalism might reasonably be argued to be:

1. Advocacy of expanded governmental involvement in the private economy to add stability and enhance opportunities for the lower rungs of the socioeconomic ladder—i.e., "New Deal Liberalism." (In the current politics of the Soviet Union, just to add a bit more confusion, those who wish to *contract* government involvement in the economy are called liberals too.)
2. Advocacy of tolerance of dissent, the key issue of the McCarthy Communist scare period of the early 1950s
3. Advocacy of racial equality in the 1960s
4. Advocacy against the Vietnam War, 1968–1972, during which then Vice-President Hubert Humphrey, an icon of

the earlier liberalism, came to be considered "conservative" solely from his stand on this one issue
5. And some of all of those things in a much more confusing blend in the current era. And after eight years of daily denunciation from that extraordinary public relations machine called the Reagan Administration, probably many millions of Americans don't know what it is, but now know that it is *bad.*

It is not just that alternative themes came and went. More important is that each at the moment was considered virtually the only theme that mattered. And to make things worse, it is not the case that conservatives are simply opposites of liberals (Conover and Feldman, 1981). Rather than something so neat as simple disagreement over basic principles and associated issue, the "two sides" are not really two sides. This is not a tug of war where at least everyone involved can agree that the rope between them is the issue, but often each side is "pulling" on issues the other side does not even see as part of the debate.

Of course all this could lead right back to the cliche: if things are that bad, the terms must be hopeless. But the actors in the political drama we observe use them, and use them in ways that are meaningful to the actor and in the context of the times. And so if we are to see the world of politics as our subjects see it, we too must deal in these messy terms.

How then can we go about getting some handle on the meaning of these terms liberal and conservative? One thing we can do is measure people's self positioning in these terms,[17] and then find out which of their attitudes toward more specific issues are most associated with their self conception on the liberal-conservative continuum. Analyses such as this produced some of the conclusions we have already seen. They show that the core content of the terms varies some between liberals and conservatives and that it varies for everybody over time. We can look at correlations of policy attitudes with ideological self-identification and say which is closest to the core content. But the answer is not constant over time.

Here we set aside individual respondents and ask instead the question "What do liberal and conservative mean?" framed in terms of opinion trends for the whole national electorate. Since both liberalism-conservatism and specific issues move systematically over time, we can learn something by asking which issue movements more or less well map onto net self identification? As we change units of

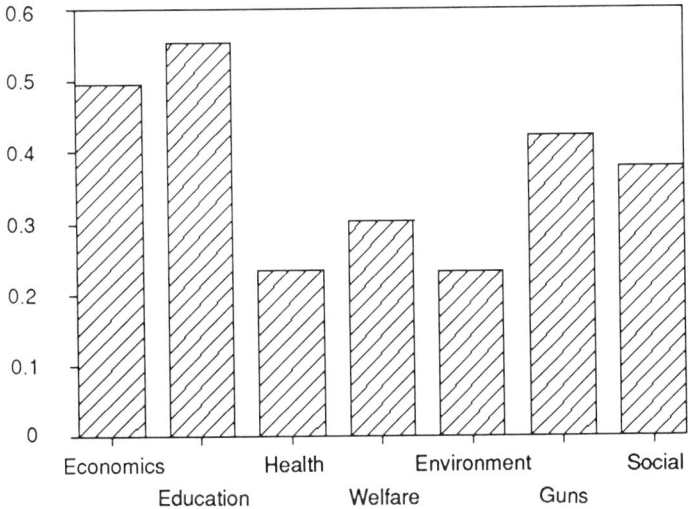

Figure 4.5. Some Components of Ideology: Correlates of Ideological Identification

analysis from individuals to aggregates, it is well known (Robinson, 1950, Erbring, 1989) that the answers to what seem to be similar questions may differ. In fact the questions are not as similar as they seem, and there is little reason to expect similar answers.

What Is It Over Time?

Because of the chameleon-like character of ideological self-identification, any evidence of what it is associated with should be viewed as somewhat tentative. There are considerable limits on what other sorts of issues can be analyzed. Many important candidates such as racial policies simply do not present sufficient time series of survey marginals to undertake the task. And ideological self-identification can be scaled only for the years since 1968.

Figure 4.5 takes up the question of which more specific issue domains move in parallel with self-identification. The bar graph shows correlations of scaled movements in economic policy (interventionism), education, health, welfare, environmental protection, gun control, and a diffuse "social" policy domain, all created as in the figure above by the dyadic scaling solution. Tentative though they are, the results are a disconcerting mismatch with popular conceptions of liberal-conservative. For the highest over-time correlation is with neither of the two normal leading contenders, economic interven-

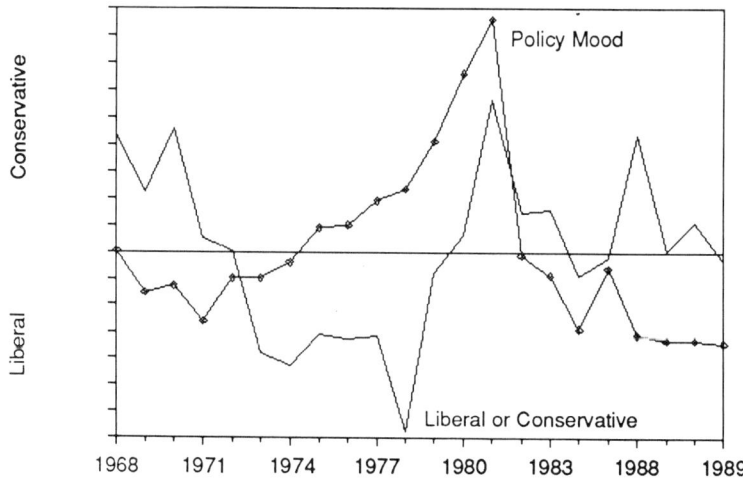

Figure 4.6. Mood and Ideological Self-Identification: One Thing or Two?

tionism or welfare, but instead with education policy, usually not thought to be particularly ideological. The weak associations with the health and environmental protection dimensions are in accord with common assumptions that these matters cut across the standard ideological lines. And the weak association with the social domain, if indeed such a coherent policy domain even exists, suggests that a great deal has been made out of little reality in these matters.

For all its tentative character, Figure 4.5 suggests that the almost universal assumption that ideology consists of two separable dimensions, the economic and social, is creative illusion. Such an interpretation just doesn't fit the facts of the movements of opinion trends over time.[18]

Policy Mood and Ideological Identification

Policy mood is a form of macro electoral ideology, as is the aggregate of scales measuring self-identified liberal or conservative views.[19] Since both are "indicators" of the same ostensible concept, macro ideology, they should be associated, moving together over time. But they are not associated, do not move together over time. Figure 4.6 displays a summary scale of liberal/conservative views together with the mood series. The figure shows some apparent similarity; the conservative jump of 1980 appears in both series. But the statistical evidence says otherwise. The correlation between series (0.007) is effectively zero.

When indicators of the same concept are associated, that is validating evidence for both. When they are not, we are left with skepticism and question marks. We know that both series measure something—and correlational evidence suggests that the "something" is reliably measured in both cases—but we don't know quite what. Policy mood is policy mood; it is the aggregate of policy preference data. What the liberal/conservative indicators and summary scale tap is less certain.

After what is now many years and many analyses, we know that professed liberal or conservative views indicate for some respondents partisanship (Levitin and Miller 1979), for some response to nonpolicy symbols (Conover and Feldman 1981), and for quite a number random error. Conover and Feldman (1981) demonstrate different defining characteristics of liberal and conservative dependent upon self identification. We know, particularly from the Reagan era, that many National Election Study respondents seem proud to call themselves "conservative," all the while expressing predominantly liberal positions on policy choices.

These problems and quandaries become more quirky still when variation over time is considered. Many indicators that are troublesome in a cross-section survey become well behaved from aggregation gain in a time series of the same data. If a few respondents behave systematically and the rest randomly, then the systematic behavior will dominate the aggregate time series. But if there is more than one systematic set of responses, the result of aggregation is a complicated mix of patterns. That very likely is the case with liberal/conservative scales.

We may imagine one set of respondents, informed and thoughtful ideologues, whose responses to direct ideology measures are both systematic and timeless. But it is likely that another set is systematic but with time-bound definitions of ideological concepts. Where campaigns and media bundle issues and ideology somewhat differently from one campaign to the next, the connotation of ideology becomes attached to current circumstance,[20] and probably especially so the less attentive who are likely to be more subject to all sorts of current communications.[21] Thus "conservative" might mean opposition to the New Deal in the 1940s and 1950s, opposition to governmental desegregation in the mid-1960s, support for the war in Vietnam later, support for a massive defense buildup in 1980, and opposition to gun control in 1988. And each of these flavors would be systematic with respect to time, and therefore emerge strongly from the aggregation of individual views. Such a pattern would produce over-time variation in the number of conservatives and liberals that might be quite unrelated to individual or aggregate change of preference. It would reflect instead transitory priming effects.

We are left, after this speculative excursion, with the solid knowledge only that whatever liberal v. conservative scales measure travels a different path through time than does policy mood.

What Then Do We Know about Political Eras?

Political eras exist in the lore of American politics. These analyses suggest that the lore is not wrong, that public opinion is a moving river wandering sometimes left, sometimes right. They don't yet tell us what if any is to be expected from such wandering; answering that very important question is a task now underway.

It is satisfying to develop a concept and measure that seems to produce scientifically what informed observers have thought all along to be the case. It is unsatisfying to find that this measure, ultimately of liberal and conservative views, bears no apparent relationship to professed liberal and conservative views. However, it is not altogether surprising that this is so, for the evidence of contradiction in "ideology" is everywhere to be seen. Whether we deal with what people say or puzzle over what, in aggregate, they do, we have known for some time that there is both a good deal more and a good deal less than strikes the eye from professed ideology.

The terms "liberal" and "conservative" seem so plastic as to lead to much confusion about any constant meaning. Meaningful to the professionals who utter them, they don't seem to mean much to citizens, or mean the same thing to different people or mean the same thing to the same people at different times. "Mood" in contrast is tied to the real policy debates which are its raw materials.

So what is public opinion and where is it going? What it is in the main in the early 1990s is liberal, supporting more government involvement in a variety of areas, education, healthcare, housing for the poor, environmental protection, and so forth. And after a lengthy conservative policy regime, its trend *seems* headed for even more liberal positions in the future. But movements are not trends; there is no inevitability underlying them. They can reverse in the short term. Almost certainly they will reverse in the long term.

But what is intriguing about this 1980s/1990s liberalism is that nobody seems to have noticed it. The almost unbroken commentary about the ubiquity of conservatism in American life is sometimes interrupted by proclamations that change is likely soon. But these data say it is here already. Perhaps observers haven't seen it because it isn't really there. Perhaps they haven't seen it because they didn't know where and how to look.

Notes

1. We can nonetheless avoid obvious errors that bias the response.
2. And what we know about question wording effects tells us that it must be exactly the same question; close isn't good enough.
3. The movement actually occurred slightly before the Webster decision was announced. But because that outcome was anticipated and much in the news before it was announced, it may still deserve credit for the change. The fact that matters here is that it came to be widely believed that abortion rights would be limited by the Court in the early months of 1989, as it never had been before.
4. If we were to inquire why popular commentators see movements that political scientists do not see, the beginning of the answer would be that commentators attend to movements in opinion marginals and political scientists, sharply aware of their methodological limitations, do not. But if, in fact, movements in marginals carry real information—and they do—that suggests the need to develop a methodology for dealing with them, not simply by ignoring their limitations.
5. One can imagine politicians with fixed preferences about policy who nonetheless adjust their tactical views to the currents of the day from the belief that changing the direction of the mainstream requires one to be in touch with it, if not in its center. If we grant the common assumption that professional politicians harbor stronger and more ideological views than the citizens they represent, then such tactical adjustments, adopted consciously or otherwise, must be a well honed skill. This is not a cynical suggestion that politicians adopt views only for expediency—a view I cannot reconcile with first hand experiences with elected politicians—but rather an assertion that the requisite of influence is tactical adaptation to circumstance, an important component of which is the mood of the times.
6. "Cyclical" is used throughout in its weakest connotation, implying back and forth but not regularity of period or amplitude.
7. The process could be ameliorated by analytic treatment of policy proposals in public media, but that tends to be blunted by the conflict between analysis and entertainment, which is the central consideration for commercial media, particularly television. Analysis makes us informed about choices, but isn't entertaining. A profit-driven system of public information, driven by consideration of circulation or ratings, will therefore systematically fail the needs of democracy.
8. Much of the mood conception I develop arises from John Kingdon's (1984) brief, but provocative, treatment of "National Mood." And it is not unlike Fenno's (1966) conception of budgetary moods.
9. Principal components analysis is a technique used to uncover common dimensions which run through multiple variables. One typically wishes to represent a large set of variables by a small number of common dimensions, as few as one.
10. The procedures and formulas which follow are for documentation of what was done. But they are not necessary for understanding the flow of the argument.
11. Note that the methodology presumes that all issues have the same direction, i.e. that higher values always mean the same thing, conservatism in the case at

12. hand. All issues are either naturally represented in the conservative direction or reflected if they cannot be naturally represented.
12. And in the original data, virtually every issue measured in 1980 or 1981 reaches its maximum level of conservatism in that year.
13. Given varying standards of candor in this business, it needs to be said that the forecast was in advance of the event (June/July, 1988), is not a "best" forecast selected after the fact—there is no variation worth noting in the forecasts this stable long-term model could or did produce, employed only indicators that could be known at the time, and contained no fudge factors.
14. The case is worse yet for the presumed central conflict along the lines of labor v. management, which had its day on center stage largely at a time when surveys were much less abundant than now and survey researchers evidently regarded repeating a previously posed item as showing a lack of imagination.
15. The component series are not exhaustive. A bit more than half of the content of the full series winds up in one or another of them. Others which can be discerned are a possible social dimension which, in very preliminary analyses, seems mainly to be noise. National Defense, a topic for another day, behaves systematically, but is highly responsive to short-term debates and events, and seems therefore to have a dynamic at least partly of its own. Racial issues, also not broken out separately, seem mainly common with other aspects of national mood.

    Also included in the data matrix and taken up below is a rich variety of measured self-identified liberal or conservative views.
16. The vertical offsets between series here and in Figure 4 to come are artificial and therefore meaningless. The eye should focus on similar an dissimilar ups and downs over time.
17. The National Election Studies employ the question: "We hear a lot of talk these days about liberals and conservatives. Here is a seven-point scale [respondent shown picture of labeled scale] on which the political views that people might hold are arranged from extremely liberal to extremely conservative. Where would you place yourself on this scale, or haven't you thought much about this?
18. Nor indeed was it ever confirmed in cross-sectional analyses of how individual people see the world. Vastly greater numbers can be shown to have either a single liberal v. conservative structure to all their attitudes or no readily interpretable structure at all.
19. These self-identification scales are based in the main on survey questions that ask respondents to place themselves on the liberal-conservative continuum, most often one labeled from "Extremely Liberal" at one end to "Extremely Conservative" at the other.
20. See Carmines and Stimson (1989: 134–137) for a more complete development of this theory of time bundling.
21. The least attentive, on the other hand, are responding randomly or not at all. See Converse (1982) and Zaller (1989).

References

Carmines, Edward G. and James A. Stimson. 1989. *Issue Evolution: Race and the Transformation of American Politics.* (Princeton: Princeton University Press).

Conover, Pamela Johnston, and Stanley Feldman. 1981. The Origins and Meaning of Liberal/Conservative Self-Identifications. *American Journal of Political Science* 25:617–45.

Converse, Philip E. 1962. Information Flow and the Stability of Partisan Attitudes. *Public Opinion Quarterly,* 26 (Winter).

Erbring, Lutz. 1989. Individuals Writ Large: an Epilogue on the 'Ecological Fallacy' *Political Analysis* 1:235–69.

Fenno, Richard F. 1966. *The Power of the Purse.* (Boston: Little Brown).

Kingdon, John. 1984. *Agendas, Alternatives, and Public Policies.* Boston: Little-Brown.

Levitin, Teresa E., and Warren E. Miller, 1979. Ideological Interpretations of Presidential Elections. *American Political Science review* 73:751–71.

Robinson, W.S. 1950. Ecological Correlations and the Behavior of Individuals. *American Sociological Review* 15:351–357.

Schlesinger, Arthur M., Jr. 1986. *The Cycles of American History.* (Boston: Houghton-Mifflin).

Zaller, John p. 1989. Differential Information Flow in Contested Election Campaigns; Bringing Converse Back In. *Political Analysis* 1:pp-pp.

Part 2

Elections and Their Consequences

Chapter 5

First in the Nation: Iowa and the Presidential Nomination Process[1]

Peverill Squire

Since Iowa's admission to the Union in 1846 the state's political parties have, with one exception (1916), employed a caucus system to select delegates to the national convention. But, what was once a contest of only marginal interest to the presidential candidates and the national media has, in recent years, become a major event in the nomination process. How has a state which in most other regards has become progressively less influential in national politics become so prominent in the single most important nationwide election?

In this chapter I examine the Iowa caucuses. First I discuss how the caucuses went from obscurity to fame, and document their importance by examining media coverage of them. The discussion then shifts to the effect the importance of the caucuses has on the behavior of candidates. The final topic addressed is the role of the caucuses in the nomination process; whether it is a function that should or should not be given to Iowa.

How Iowa Became "First in the Nation"

Iowa's "first in the nation" position did not result from skillful manipulation by its political leaders but as the unanticipated consequence of a series of unrelated decisions by the parties and the state legislature (Winebrenner 1983; 1985; Schier 1980; Mayer 1987, 20-21). A 1969 state law required that both parties hold their caucuses before the second Monday in May, which posed no problem because in previous years the parties had been holding them in March or

April. The decision by the state Democratic party to move its 1972 caucus to late January was prompted by the early July 9 date set by the Democratic National Committee for the start of the national convention. The rules governing the Iowa Democratic party required 30 days between official party meetings—precinct caucuses, county conventions, congressional district conventions, state statutory convention, state presidential convention, and the national convention—therefore January 24 was the last day the precinct caucuses could be held.[2] The 30-day rule had been adopted for practical reasons; party workers needed that time to process paper work in preparation for the next function.

The increased importance enjoyed by the Democratic caucuses which the shift to the beginning of the 1972 campaign calendar—before even the New Hampshire primary—produced came mainly from hindsight. The Democratic state party chairman at the time, Clif Larson, recalls (Lehr 1988, 12), "We didn't realize it at first, but we figured it out. . . . But even then we didn't anticipate the attention we got." The caucuses that year did receive some national media coverage and visits from the candidates which they had not gotten before. But the actual amount of attention was slight; George McGovern, for example, was in the state only a day and a half (Cook 1987, 8) before his "surprise" showing in the caucuses.[3] The network evening news shows had some coverage of the caucuses the day after they were held, but none leading up to them. On January 25, 1972 CBS and NBC spent 4 minutes and ABC 2 minutes discussing the caucus results and the delays in obtaining them, and on the reforms in the Democratic party. The next day CBS gave 30 seconds to reviewing the results, the other networks made no mention of them.

The caucus results seem to have become important only in retrospect, when it became necessary to pinpoint the beginning of the McGovern surge. Witcover (1977, 213), for example, observes,

> In 1972 the rise of George McGovern's barely detected grassroots efforts at the precinct level had been overlooked for a considerable time by the major newspapers and the television networks; their focus was squarely on Muskie. . . . Not even McGovern's show of strength in Iowa shook that perception, and only in retrospect was it realized that something significant had been building for McGovern out in the country.

The same basic point is made by Mayer (1987, 20–21), who notes that politicians in New Hampshire were unaware that Iowa had supplanted their first in the nation status. The caucuses' contribution to McGovern's victory can be exaggerated. Books written following the 1972 campaign (e.g. White 1973; Crouse 1973) make no mention of the Iowa caucuses. The caucuses were the first event of the election year, and therefore worthy of some attention, but they were not deemed important at the time by most observers.

The small amount of national attention that the caucuses had received was, however, noted by the leadership of the state's parties. The Republicans had not benefited because they had held their caucuses in April. The two parties saw cooperation to be in their best interests and they reached an agreement to hold their 1976 caucuses on the same date—January 19. The goal was, of course, to keep the caucuses first on the campaign calendar and receive the substantial amount of attention from the media and candidates warranted by that position. The GOP even changed their procedures, instituting a poll of caucus participants, so that they would have "results" to give the media.[4] The Democratic state party chairman at the time, Tom Whitney, claims that his party actively courted attention (Lehr 1988, 13):

> We convinced the candidates that the most important place to be was in Iowa because that's where the media was going to be. We convinced the media that if you were going to report the story you had to be here because the candidates were.

But, while the state parties positioned the caucuses to be more consequential in the nomination process, it was Jimmy Carter's successful drive to the 1976 Democratic nomination that made them important. The astute plan developed by Hamilton Jordan to exploit the changed rules under which the Democratic nomination was contested gave great weight to the results in Iowa. The Carter campaign was banking on extensive national media coverage, therefore they concentrated many of their limited resources in Iowa. When the results of straw polls in Iowa during the Fall were given coverage in the *New York Times* and other national media the Carter strategy was validated (Witcover 1977, 214-215).

Several other candidates, however, did not anticipate the increased importance of Iowa. Morris Udall, in particular, had to readjust his tactics to give more attention to the caucuses (Arterton 1978a, 15–17). He had initially intended to downplay them in favor of the New Hampshire primary, but by the late fall of 1975 he and his advisors realized the necessity of making an effort to do well in Iowa. His belated attempt fell short, a failure many suggest did great damage to his chances for the nomination.

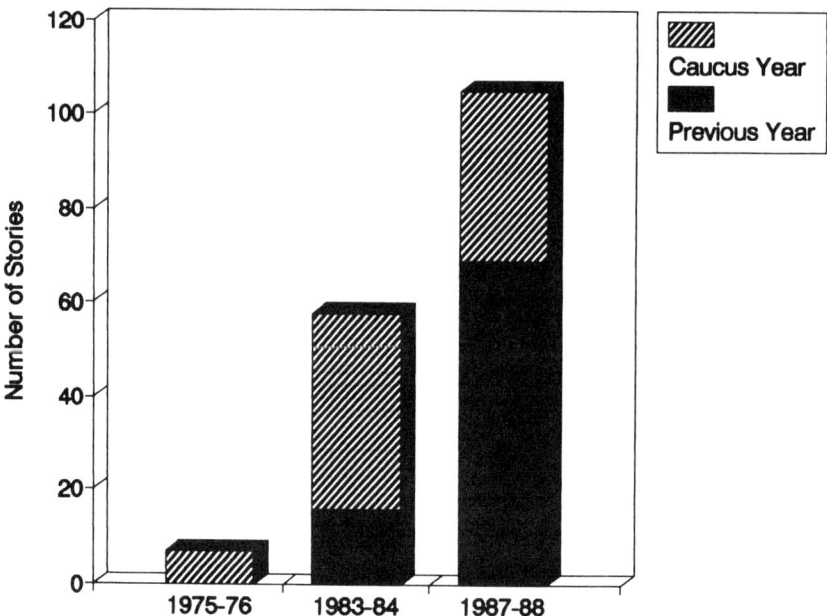

Figure 5.1. News Coverage of the Iowa Caucuses: Number of *New York Times* Stories

Thus it is in 1976 that the Iowa caucuses really achieved national stature in that they were acknowledged by many participants and elite observers as being important before they occurred. The fact that Carter used the caucuses as a springboard to the nomination ensured that candidates in succeeding elections would make great efforts to perform well in them.

The Importance of the Iowa Caucuses: 1976–1988

The Iowa caucuses became significant in 1976, and their importance continues to increase. Accounts of more recent nomination campaigns give great weight to the role of the caucuses (e.g. Witcover 1977; Germond and Witcover 1981; Harwood, 1980; Polsby, 1985). Compare, for example, the amount of coverage given to the caucuses by the *New York Times* and the television network evening news programs during the 1976 and 1984 campaigns. In the months leading up to the January, 1976 caucuses the *Times* carried only 7 stories— none in 1975 and 7 in 1976 (see Figure 5.1). This was a year where both parties had nomination races. The *Times* then published 58 articles on the caucuses in 1983–84 (16 and 42 in the two years), despite the fact only the Democratic nomination was contested. The trend toward increased coverage continues. In 1987–88 the *Times* had 105 caucus stories (69 and 36).

The figures for coverage on the network evening news programs are just as striking. No stories were broadcast in 1975 and just 15 were shown in 1976. The day after the 1976 caucuses the networks spent from 3 minutes (ABC) to 6 minutes (NBC) reporting the results. The 1984 contest received far more attention. Only 1 caucus story was shown in 1983, but 46 were aired in 1984. All three network news programs made Iowa their lead story both the day of the caucuses and the day after them, averaging 10 minutes on the caucuses the first night and 7 minutes the next evening. The obvious conclusion to draw is that the caucuses receive extensive attention from the national media, and that the reporting of events in Iowa has increased over time. Moreover, as several studies (e.g. Robinson and Sheehan 1983; Adams 1984, 1987; Buell 1987a) have documented, the Iowa caucuses get as much attention as the New Hampshire primary and far more coverage than delegate selection contests in most other states.

The result of this intensive coverage is not to make Iowa a "king maker" but rather a "peasant maker." Candidates who finish first are not guaranteed the nomination, as evidenced by George Bush in 1980, or Robert Dole and Richard Gephardt in 1988. But, candidates who do not do well by finishing among the leaders are doomed. Before 1988, no one who had finished below second place in Iowa since 1972 had gotten his party's nomination.[5] In the most recent contest, Dukakis and Bush were able to survive their third place showings for a couple of reasons. First, although two other candidates gained more votes, both Dukakis and Bush received a respectable level of support—each got a higher percentage of the vote than did Gary Hart in his 1984 second place showing. Second, both Bush and Dukakis were well-known, well-organized, and well-funded in New Hampshire, where overwhelming victories eight days after Iowa allowed them to project the image of a winner.

Even in 1988, however, the Iowa caucus results culled the field in each party. Several candidates—Babbit, Hart, du Pont and Kemp—never recovered from their poor performances in Iowa. The dynamics behind this reduction in the number of viable candidate are well established (e.g. Polsby 1983; Bartels 1985; Matthews 1978; Arterton 1978b). Because of the extensive media coverage and the subsequent

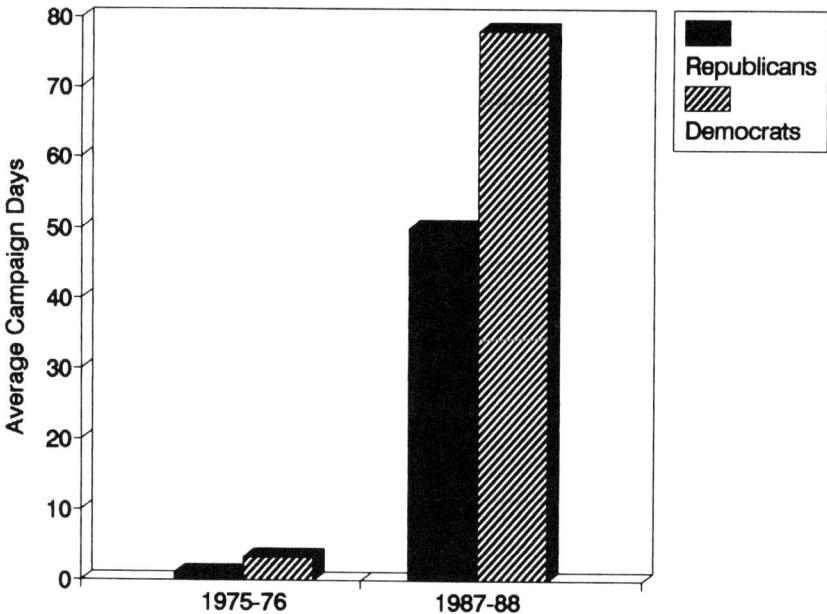

Figure 5.2. The Presidential Candidates Come to Iowa: Average Compaign Days by Party

"winnowing" of the field those seeking their party's nomination must do well in Iowa.[6]

Given the importance attached to the caucus results by the media it is not surprising to find changing candidate behavior. As the media give more attention and meaning to the results in Iowa candidates have found it necessary to spend more time and money campaigning in the state. Table 5.1 presents figures on the number of visits to Iowa made by candidates and the amount of money spent in the state by them in 1976 and in 1988. The figures for days spent are in Figure 5.2 above. The 1976 numbers, compiled by Aldrich (1980, 226–233), show that Udall spent 10 days in Iowa, Carter 7 days, and Henry Jackson just 3 days. On the Republican side Ronald Reagan was in Iowa 2 days and President Gerald Ford did not visit the state as a candidate. While these numbers may not include a number of trips made to Iowa by the candidates well before the caucuses—particularly for Carter—they do give a strong impression of how important the state was thought to be at the time.

These figures contrast sharply with those compiled by the *Des Moines Register* for the 1988 campaign ("Campaign Scorecard" 1988). By the day of the caucuses Democratic candidates had spent a

TABLE 5.1
Number of Days and Amount of Money Spent by Candidates in Iowa: 1976 and 1987–88

1976			1987–88		
			Republicans		
Cand.	Days	Money	Cand.	Days	Money
Ford	0		Bush	16	234,000
Reagan	2		Dole	12	29,000
			du Pont	62	97,000
			Haig	21	18,000
			Kemp	49	149,000
			Robertson	22	201,000
Average	1	66,047		50	155,000
			Democrats		
Cand.	Days	Money	Cand.	Days	Money
Brown	0		Babbitt	80	296,000
Carter	7		Dukakis	46	214,000
Church	0		Gephardt	87	249,000
Jackson	3		Gore	26	114,000
Udall	10		Jackson	30	47,000
Wallace	0		Simon	53	134,000
Average	3.3	49,021		78	176,000

[a] Information collected to October, 1987
Sources: 1976 data from Aldrich (1980, pp. 226, 228, 232, 233); 1987–88 data from "Campaign Scorecard," (1987), and "Campaign Scorecard," (1988).

mean of 78 days in the state; their Republican counterparts had averaged 50 days. Both Richard Gephardt and Bruce Babbitt spent over 100 days campaigning in Iowa and several other candidates came close to that number.

Campaign spending figures demonstrate the same increase in importance attached to Iowa by those contesting the nominations. Aldrich's 1976 data show that declared Democratic candidates spent an average of just over $49,000 in the state, while Ford and Reagan spent around $66,000 each to contest the caucuses. In 1987, with over three months still to go ("Campaign Scorecard," 1987), Democrats had spent an average of $176,000 and Republicans, $155,000.

Contestants for each party's nomination have also taken to trying to win support by directing contributions from their political action committees to campaigns of state politicians. The sums given in 1986 were not trivial: nearly $150,000 was contributed by presidential candidates to those seeking the governorship, statewide offices and state legislative seats. One candidate, Bruce Babbitt, even loaned staff members to a few Democratic campaigns. The idea behind this munificence is, of course, to gain support from state politicians and to use their backing to develop a strong organization.

Thus there is little question about the importance of the Iowa caucuses in the nominations process. National media give the caucuses an enormous amount of coverage, and the candidates lavish the state with attention. The remaining question is whether Iowa, or any state, deserves this role.

The Iowa Caucuses and the Nomination Process

The prominence of the Iowa caucuses has led a number of political observers and a few candidates to suggest that something is wrong with the nomination system—an act referred to in the state as "Iowa bashing" (e.g. Hyde 1987). These detractors support their claims in a number of ways. First, they note that the state is unrepresentative demographically. There is evidence to support this position. The state has a higher percentage of older citizens, and fewer minorities and metropolitan area residents than the national average. It also has lower rates of unemployment, crime, divorce and abortion. A lower percentage of the population is on Public Assistance or AFDC, a higher percentage draw social security. The state exceeds the national mean in the percentage of the population that has graduated from high school and in per capita newspaper circulation.

The rebuttal to this general line of argument is that every state deviates from the national mean on some number of important characteristics. That Iowa does as well is only important if it can be demonstrated that these differences have political consequences. That is, are the candidates chosen by Iowans attending the caucuses different from those who would be chosen by other means?

One way to address this question is to see whether the choices Iowans make on caucus night differ from those held by the nation at that time. Table 5.2 gives the last national Gallup Poll data prior to the caucuses, and the results of the caucuses. In the seven contested races from 1976 to 1988 there are several instances where Iowans deviated significantly—Carter in 1976 and Gephardt in 1988 in the Democratic contests and Bush in the 1980 and Dole in 1988 Republican races. The other three times—Ford in 1976, Carter in 1980 and Mondale in 1984 the votes of Iowans closely reflected national preferences.

Closer examination of Table 5.2 reveals the deviations are not as striking as they might seem. Carter, for instance, had little support nationally before the caucuses, but the first three choices of the Gallup respondents were not active candidates. Thus Carter jumped out of a pack that was, with the exception of Henry Jackson, not nationally known. If it had not been Carter, it might just as well have been another unknown candidate. Moreover, Carter finished behind "uncommitted" suggesting Iowa Democrats, like their national peers, preferred Humphrey, Wallace, McGovern or some other person not in the race. The situation in 1988 was similarly unsettled, with no dominant nationally known contestant in the race, and the added complications of the Jackson and resurrected Hart candidacies. Given the situation the results of that election are not strikingly out of line with national sentiments.

On the Republican side Bush surprised observers with his showing in 1980, but national favorite Reagan finished a very close second and the other Republicans received support roughly equivalent to their Gallup figures. Similarly, in 1988 Bush was shocked by Dole, but the Senator from Kansas received support comparable to national figures.

Another complaint, one registered by Democrats, is that a state which has voted for their party's candidate only twice in the last ten elections—Johnson in 1964 and Dukakis in 1988—should not be given so much influence over who becomes their standard-bearer. There are a number of weaknesses in this argument. First, since 1972, when the nomination rules changes went into effect, only the District of Columbia has voted for the Democratic candidate in all five elections, and only Minnesota—Iowa's northern neighbor—has backed the party's ticket in four elections![7] Iowa has, in fact, been among the states most supportive of Democratic presidential candidates. Iowans have either reflected the national vote, or been more in favor of the Democrat than the national mean. Second, while during this time period the Republicans have controlled the state's governorship, Democrats have held Senate and House seats and, much of the time, have been in the majority in both houses of the state legislature. More Iowans are registered as Democrats than as Republicans (Cook 1987,

TABLE 5.2
National Preferences and Iowa Caucus Results
(in percent)

	Pre-Caucus Gallup Poll	Iowa Caucus
1976		
Democrats		
Humphrey	29[a]	—[b]
Wallace	20	—
McGovern	10	—
H. Jackson	9	1
Muskie	6	—
Bayh	5	13
Shriver	5	3
Other/DK	16	
Carter		28
Harris		10
Udall		6
Uncommitted		37
Republicans		
Ford	53	45
Reagan	42	43
Undecided	5	11
1980		
Democrats		
Carter	51[c]	59[d]
Kennedy	37	31
Undecided	12	10
Republicans		
Reagan	40	29
Ford	18	—
Connally	9	9
Baker	9	16
Bush	7	32
Dole	4	2
Others/DK	12	
Crane		7
Anderson		4
Undecided		2

TABLE 5.2—Continued

	Pre-Caucus Gallup Poll	Iowa Caucus
1984		
Democrats		
Mondale	49[e]	49[f]
Glenn	13	4
J. Jackson	13	2
McGovern	5	10
Askew	3	3
Cranston	3	10
Hart	3	17
Hollings	1	0
None/DK	11	
Uncommitted		10
1988		
Democrats		
Hart	—[g] (30)[h]	0[j]
Jackson	22 (20)	9
Dukakis	14 (15)	22
Simon	8 (8)	27
Gore	7 (5)	0
Gephardt	5 (2)	31
Babbit	1 (2)	6
Uncommitted		5
Republicans		
Bush	47 (44)	19
Dole	22 (35)	37
Robertson	7	25
Kemp	4	11
Haig	4	0
du Pont	1	7

[a] January 2–5, 1976
[b] January 19, 1976
[c] January 4–6, 1980
[d] January 21, 1980
[e] February 10–13, 1984
[f] February 20, 1984
[g] October 23–26, 1987
[h] ABC/Washington Post Poll, December 15–18, 1987
[j] February 8, 1988
Sources: The Gallup Poll; Public Opinion 1984; Public Opinion, (Jan/Feb) 1988.

120; see also Squire, forthcoming): 35 percent Democrats, 31 percent Republicans and 33 other (primarily independents). The state is now competitive between the two parties with the Democrats holding the edge (Squire forthcoming). Finally, in 1976, when Iowans did deviate from national preferences in the Democratic candidate they supported, they started Jimmy Carter on his way to the White House — the only Democrat to win that office since 1964! Evidence does not seem to support the notion that Iowa is too Republican to play a prominent role in Democratic affairs.

Some Democrats also criticize Iowa on the grounds that those who participate in the party's caucuses are too liberal, giving support to candidates who are too far to the left to be successful in the general election. The results of past caucuses belie this notion. Iowa Democrats preferred Muskie to McGovern, Carter to a number of liberals, Carter to Kennedy, and Gephardt to Simon. Only in 1984 did they support a liberal, Walter Mondale, who was also the overwhelming choice of Democrats nationally. If there is a valid complaint that the caucuses back liberal candidates it is in the Republican party, where Reagan lost close races to Ford in 1976 and Bush in 1980.

Finally, the caucuses are assailed on the more general grounds that too few people participate in them to be representative. As can be seen in Table 5.3, no certain turnout figures exist. Rough calculations of participation rates in the 1976, 1980 and 1984 caucuses by registered Democrats and Republicans puts the figures between 14 and 20 percent. These numbers are impressive for caucuses (cf. Ranney 1977, 16) and approach turnout levels in some primaries (cf. Ranney, 1972, p.24, Ranney, 1977, p.20). As a device for allowing mass participation in the democratic process the Iowa caucuses seem to fare almost as well as the less time consuming and less demanding primaries.

Thus many of the charges leveled at the caucuses do not seem well founded. The choices made by Iowans who attend the caucuses are not particularly different from the preferences of their party identifiers nationally. Participation levels are not notably different. If any state is to be given sole possession of the first spot on the election calendar Iowa is as good a choice as any. This can be argued without any reference to less empirical and more metaphysical qualities, like civility, goodness and honesty, that Iowans are purported to possess.

The question then becomes not whether Iowa should be first but whether having any single state first is good for the political process. On the one hand, a nomination system where candidates make multi-

TABLE 5.3
Participation in the Iowa Caucuses, 1972 to 1988

Year	Democrats Estimated Turnout	Republicans Estimated Turnout
1972	20,000[a]	
	60,000[b]	
1976	38,500[abc]	20,000[a]
		22–26,000[c]
1980	100,000[acd]	106,051[ac]
		115,000[d]
1984	75,000[ac]	
	85,000[d]	
1988	120,000[e]	110,000[e]

a figures reported in Cook (1987, p. 11)
b figures reported in Maisel (1987, p. 66)
c figures reported in Winebrenner (1985)
d figures reported in Iowa Official Register, 1985–86
e figures reported in "Iowa's Stars Take a Back Seat in New Hampshire" (1988).

ple trips to a particular state far in advance of the election, as happened in Iowa during recent campaigns, (e.g. Yepsen 1985a, b, c, d) may discourage many attractive candidates from entering the race. Putting presidential hopefuls in the position of spending their "vacations" bicycling across the state (Yepsen 1986), or visiting all 99 of the state's counties may not provide voters much insight into the kind of chief executive particular candidates might make.[8] On the other hand, in a "mixed system" of the sort advocated by Polsby (1983) the caucuses provide information about the appeal of candidates when voters can give them close scrutiny which is unlikely to be produced by other delegate selection procedures.

If we accept the proposition that the current system is flawed, what are the alternatives to it? As I have argued, Iowa is as good a choice as any state to start the process, so substituting another state does not seem to be a satisfying answer. Other proposals suggest a series of regional primaries, or a single national primary, ideas which also have flaws (e.g. Ranney, 1978; Polsby and Wildavsky, 1984, pp.223–241) because, among other problems, they are biased in favor of well-known and well-financed candidates.

The main point to keep in mind is that there is no perfect system which is guaranteed to produce ideal candidates. The current system has problems—too much power is given to Iowa and New Hampshire to narrow the field of candidates. Chances are, however, that little will be done to change the current rules under which both parties contest their nominations. The battles which were fought over which state would come first in 1988 (Buell 1987b) have probably settled the issue for some time to come. Even before the 1988 caucuses the respected Democratic party insider Robert Strauss—an Iowa critic—commented, ". . . if we have another reform commission I might take the gas pipe." Others are resigned to Iowa's leadership role. For example, Don Fowler, who headed the last Democratic reform commission, has commented (Hyde 1987), "The truth is we've tried to soften the impact of Iowa and New Hampshire and it's never worked. Let me put it this way: As long as Iowa and New Hampshire insist on having their events early, and as long as the candidates continue to go there, there's not much the Democratic Party can do about it." A preconvention suggestion by Jesse Jackson to diminish the importance of the caucuses was dropped as part of an agreement with Dukakis regarding the rules governing the 1992 campaign (Hyde 1988). Even if California moves its primary just behind Iowa and New Hampshire, the Hawkeye state's "first in the nation" status will keep its voters among the most influential in the nomination process.

Notes

1. Much of this chapter is drawn from my article in Peverill Squire, ed., *The Iowa Caucuses and the Presidential Nominating Process*, Westview Press, 1989.
2. The Iowa caucuses are a four-tiered process. The initial event is the precinct caucuses which are widely covered by the media. The precinct caucuses elect delegates to the 99 county conventions, which then select delegates to the six congressional district conventions, which in turn elect representatives to the state convention. A somewhat different version of the events leading to the movement of the Democratic caucuses to the beginning of the election calender is given in Lehr (1988).
3. Winebrenner (1985, 107) reports McGovern was in the state for three days. McGovern's surprise finish was behind Muskie and uncommitted. See Table 5.2 for the actual results.
4. The Republicans employ a voting procedure at the precinct level which does not translate well into either overall voter preferences or candidate delegate totals. Using a preference poll provides the party information of interest to the media. In 1976 these data were generated by a survey of 62 precincts. In 1980 all precincts were polled.
5. The examples are numerous. Among them are Udall and Henry Jackson in 1976, John Connally and Robert Dole in 1980, and John Glenn in 1984. Note,

however, what is being discussed is rank order among the candidates—in 1976, for example, uncommitted votes outnumbered those for Carter, but little attention was given to that result.
6. In his discussion of the New Hampshire primary, Mayer (1987, 23) observers, "The 'winnowing' function . . . is now performed almost entirely by the Iowa caucuses."
7. The Republicans have won at least the last five presidential contests in a number of states, including New Hampshire, Connecticut, New Jersey, Michigan, Illinois, Colorado, and California. Mondale was on the ballot three times his native Minnesota voted for the Democratic ticket.
8. Candidates do visit almost every city of any size in the state with one exception: West Branch. The site of Herbert Hoover's birthplace and presidential library is bypassed by Republicans and Democrats alike (Carlson 1987).

References

Adams, William C. 1984. Media Coverage of Campaign '84. *Public Opinion*, 7:9–13.

Adams, William C. 1987. As New Hampshire Goes . . . In Gary R. Orren and Nelson W. Polsby, eds., *Media and Momentum.* Chatham, NJ: Chatham House Publishers, Inc.

Aldrich, John H. 1980. *Before the Convention.* Chicago: University of Chicago Press.

Arterton, F. Christopher. 1978a. Campaign Organizations Confront the Media—Political Environment. In James David Barber. ed., *Race for the Presidency.* Englewood Cliffs, NJ: Prentice-Hall, Inc.

Arterton, F. Christopher. 1978b. The Media Politics of Presidential Campaigns: A Study of the Carter Nomination Drive. In James David Barber, ed., *Race for the Presidency.* Englewood Cliffs, N.J.: Prentice-Hall, Inc.

Bartels, Larry M. 1985. Expectations and Preferences in Presidential Nominating Campaigns. *American Political Science Review,* 79: 804–815.

Buell, Emmett H. 1987a. Locals and Cosmopolitans: National Regional and State Newspaper Coverage of the New Hampshire Primary. In Gary R. Orren and Nelson W. Polsby, eds., *Media and Momentum.* Chatham, N.J.: Chatham House Publishers, Inc.

Buell, Emmett H. 1987b. First-in-the-Nation: Disputes Over the Timing of Early Democratic Presidential Primaries and Caucuses in 1984 and 1988. *The Journal of Law & Politics,* 4: 311–342.

Campaign Scorecard. November 1, 1987. *Des Moines Register.*

Campaign Scorecard. February 7, 1988. *Des Moines Register.*

Carlson, John. December 20, 1987. Ghost of the Depression Spooks Candidates. *Des Moines Register.*

Cook, Rhodes. 1987. *Race for the Presidency.* Washington D.C.: Congressional Quarterly, Inc.

Crouse. Timothy. 1973. *The Boys on the Bus.* New York: Random House.

Germond, Jack W., and Jules Witcover. 1981. *Blue Smoke and Mirrors.* New York: Viking Press.
Harwood, Richard, ed., 1980. *The Pursuit of the Presidency 1980.* New York: Berkley Publishing Co.
Hyde, John. December 6, 1987. Rising Chorus of Complaint on Caucuses. *Des Moines Register.*
Hyde, John. June 26, 1988. Jackson Drops Call to Change Iowa Caucuses. *Des Moines Register.*
Iowa's Stars Take a Back Seat in New Hampshire. 1988. *Congressional Quarterly Weekly Report,* 46:287–290.
Lehr, Jeff. 1988. Iowa's Primary Caucus. *The Iowa Alumni Review,* 41: 12–13.
Maisel, L. Sandy. 1987. *Parties and Elections in America.* New York: Random House.
Matthews, Donald R. 1978. Winnowing: The News Media and the 1976 Presidential Nominations. In James David Barber. ed., *Race for the Presidency.* Englewood Cliffs, N.J.: Prentice-Hall, Inc.
Mayer, William G. 1987. The New Hampshire Primary: A Historical Overview. In Gary R. Orren and Nelson W. Polsby, eds., *Media and Momentum.* Chatham, NJ: Chatham House Publishers, Inc.
Norman, Jane. November 23, 1986. Caucuses a Windfall for State Politicians. *Des Moines Register.*
Polsby, Nelson W. 1983. *Consequences of Party Reform.* New York: Oxford University Press.
Polsby, Nelson W. 1985. The Democratic Nomination and the Evolution of the Party System. In Austin Ranney, cd., *The American Elections of 1984.* Durham, N.C.: Duke University Press.
Polsby, Nelson W., and Aaron Wildavsky. 1984. *Presidential Elections,* 6th ed. New York: Charles Scribner's Sons.
Ranney, Austin. 1972. Turnout and Representation in Presidential Primary Elections. *American Political Science Review,* 66: 21–37.
Ranney, Austin. 1977. *Participation in American Presidential Nominations 1976.* Washington D.C.: AEI.
Ranney, Austin. 1978. *The Federalization of Presidential Primaries.* Washington D.C.: AEI.
Robinson, Michael J. and Margaret Sheehan. 1983. *Over the Wire and on TV.* New York: Russell Sage Foundation.
Schier, Steven E. 1980. *The Rules of the Game: Democratic National Convention Delegate Selection in Iowa and Wisconsin.* Washington D.C.: University Press of America.
Squire, Peverill. Forthcoming. Iowa and the Drift to the Democrats. In Maureen Moakley, ed., *Party Realignment in the American States.* Columbus, OH: Ohio State University Press.
White, Theodore H. 1973. *The Making of the President 1972.* New York: Atheneum.
Winebrenner, Hugh. 1983. The Evolution of the Iowa Precinct Caucuses. *The Annals of Iowa,* 46: 618–35.
Winebrenner, Hugh. 1985. The Iowa Precinct Caucuses: The Making of a Media Event. *Southeastern Political Review,* 13:99–132.

Witcover, Jules. 1977. *Marathon.* New York: Signet.
Yepsen, David. 1985a. Trade Barriers no Solution, GOP Hopeful Kemp says. *Des Moines Register,* September 14.
Yepsen, David. 1985b. Deficit attacked by Democratic Hopeful in D.M. *Des Moines Register,* September 30.
Yepsen, David. 1985c. Kemp cites Need for Judges Against Abortion. *Des Moines Register,* October 6.
Yepsen, David. 1985d. Delaware Senator Opens fire on Presidential Race. *Des Moines Register,* November 3.
Yepsen, David. July 20, 1986. Babbitt Hopes Bike Ride gets his Campaign in Gear. *Des Moines Register.*

Chapter 6

Localism in Presidential Elections: The Home State Advantage

Michael S. Lewis-Beck
Tom W. Rice

In American political folklore, it is axiomatic that the "hometown boy" has a natural electoral advantage over his out-of-town rival. And the forces of localism are believed to operate in presidential races, as well as in lesser ones. Indeed, every national contest brings forth numerous claims of home state advantages for presidential candidates. These claims have prompted the suggestion that presidential candidates are generally from large two-party swing states precisely because the home state advantage can mean a home state victory. Some argue that presidential candidates "must" come from such states.

The importance of carrying large states lies in our winner-take-all electoral college presidential process, which emphasizes winning the popular vote within states rather than across the nation as a whole. Consequently, a home state victory in a large state is substantially more important than a win in a small state; it could even prove the difference between winning and losing the entire presidential race. Evidence suggests the major parties recognize this. Since 1884, 58 percent of the presidential candidates have come from the six most populous states.

While the hypothesis of a home state advantage in presidential races is attractive, it is yet to be tested. The purpose of this brief study was to assess the magnitude of the home state advantage in presidential elections. Second, we wanted to establish whether there had been any trend over time, such as a declining home state advantage, in response to the nationalization of political forces. Third, we wanted to discover factors that help predict a presidential contender's potential home state advantage.

Is There a Home State Advantage?

At first glance, the evidence from presidential contests between major party candidates over the past century suggests that the notion of a home state advantage is mythical. Grover Cleveland failed to carry New York in 1888, and William Jennings Bryan lost Nebraska in 1900. Woodrow Wilson could not achieve a majority in New Jersey, despite two attempts. George McGovern did not win South Dakota in 1972. Moreover, these examples of the failure to gain a home state majority are hardly atypical. Out of 42 major party presidential candidates since 1884, only 23 polled 50 percent or better in their home states.

Does this mean that, contrary to the popular view, the home state does not favor its native son in a White House race? No, it simply means that this criterion of home state advantage (i.e., winning a majority) is inappropriate. To determine a presidential candidate's home state advantage, we should assess how many votes he got beyond what was expected. For example, a Democratic candidate from a traditionally Republican state may cut significantly into the Republican vote majority in his home state but still not manage to carry it. In other words, he showed the presence of the home state advantage by reducing the normal Republican vote—even though it was not enough to attain victory.

Such is the actual scenario for McGovern. Republicans usually win the majority of the popular presidential vote in South Dakota. In the five presidential contests previous to the McGovern-Nixon race, Democratic candidates had averaged only 42.3 percent of the popular vote. We see that McGovern, however, in gathering 45.8 percent, bettered this past figure by an additional 3.5 percentage points. Therefore, it appears that because he hailed from the state, he was able to improve upon the usual Democratic performance in South Dakota.

But this slim gain (3.5 points) understates the extent of McGovern's home state advantage. Recall that the 1972 presidential contest was a national debacle for the Democrats, who polled only 37.5 percent of the total popular vote, a share much below historic proportions for the party. In fact, over the prior five presidential elections, Democratic candidates had averaged 48 percent of the vote countrywide. Viewed in the context of his general lack of popularity, then, McGovern's gain in South Dakota appears rather impressive. Whereas in a randomly chosen state his expected vote share would be 10.5 percentage points less than the average of the five earlier

Democratic candidates, in his home state of South Dakota he actually achieved 3.5 percentage points more. In other words, once his national level of popularity is taken into account, his total home state advantage comes to 14 percentage points.

In general, the home state advantage (H) of a presidential candidate can be conceived of as the deviation of his actual vote share in his home state (A) from his expected vote share in that state (E), adjusted for his national popularity. This calculation begins with the actual vote share (A) as a percentage of the popular vote in the home state. Subtracted from that is the expected vote share (E), which is the average popular vote percentage for the candidate's party in the previous five presidential elections. This tells us how much above or below the normal state average this candidate's state vote falls.

The adjustment for national popularity involves subtracting another number, this one indicating how much above or below the national expectation the candidate's national vote falls. (National expectation (NE) is the average percentage the candidate's party received in the previous five elections.) To judge the candidate's national performance we simply subtract the expected national vote share (NE) from the actual national vote share (NA).

The entire calculation of home state advantage can be represented by the following formula:

$$H = (A-E) - (NA-NE)$$

Illustrating the formula with the McGovern case yields:

$$H = (45.8-42.3) - (37.5-48.0),$$

which when worked out gives an advantage of 14.0.

We calculated this measure for major party presidential candidates from 1884 to 1980, drawing the data from various issues of the Statistical Abstract of the United States. The party realignments of the Civil War years prevented an extension any further back in time. (And because of the Civil War years, the expected votes for the 1884 and 1888 races had to be calculated with only three and four previous elections, respectively). Also, the races of 1904, 1920, 1940, and 1944 had to be excluded, because both candidates were from the same state. Note that in our work, "home state" is defined as the state where the candidate established his political career. (Eisenhower, whose political career began after his military experience, was assigned to Kansas, the state he claimed as his home).

These procedures yielded 42 observations and revealed a clear home state advantage for presidential candidates. In some instances, this advantage is large. Among contemporary candidates, the largest has gone to Jimmy Carter in 1976, who scored a Georgia advantage of 18.4 percentage points. But this is a dramatic case. In general, the vote margins for candidates in their home states do not achieve the magnitude of the Carter triumph. For the total sample, the average home state advantage is 4.0 percentage points.

While this is not a huge margin, it should be underscored that by such margins many election races are decided. And, as mentioned earlier, winning a close race is especially important for the candidate when the state is large. California, for example, may have gone to Nixon in 1968 because he was a native son. Over the previous five presidential elections, Californians had given fewer than half their votes to Republican candidates. However, Nixon registered a home state advantage of 3.6 percentage points and carried the state's electoral votes. Without this state in the Nixon camp, no candidate would have received half of all the electoral votes and the election would have been thrown into the House of Representatives. Since the majority of state delegations in the House were controlled by Democrats, it is quite possible that Humphrey would have been chosen the next president!

Of course, such momentous consequences cannot typically be traced to the simple presence or absence of a modest home state advantage. Still, it remains clear that political strategists in presidential nomination campaigns are acting rationally when they seek a candidate who is from a large two-party swing state. Without doubt, there is a home state advantage worth capitalizing on.

Has the Home State Advantage Declined over Time?

A number of scholars and pundits have argued that the United States has experienced a "nationalization of politics." In other words, these observers believe that local factors and idiosyncratic state or regional concerns have gradually diminished as determinants of election outcomes. National concerns, they find, have become progressively more important. With this in mind, one might wonder whether votes in presidential races are less likely to favor native sons now than in the past. Put another way, has the home state advantage declined over time? To test this possibility, we did statistical analysis of the data, looking for any indication of linear or nonlinear decline. We found none. The home state advantage just has not changed its strength over time. Whatever forces of nationalization that may be operating elsewhere, they have left undiminished that purely local support for a presidential candidate.

What Explains the Home State Advantage

It is difficult to give a full account of the persistent strength of local bonds. Nevertheless, certain ideas merit special consideration. Of all public offices, the presidency is by far the most visible. Each of us learns the home states of presidential candidates, and we are particularly aware of the fact if the state is ours. This piece of candidate information is repeatedly reinforced through the radio and television network that now embraces our nation. It gives us a chance to show "pride in our own" by voting for a native son. Such local loyalty is not wholly unreasonable. We are offered the psychological satisfaction of identification with a president who is more like our "friends and neighbors." Further, we might hope that as president he would remember "the folks back home" when distributing federal largess.

How sure can a presidential candidate be of his home state advantage? What strengthens or weakens it? We hypothesize three factors that should go far in predicting the magnitude of a particular candidate's home state advantage. The most important of these is state population, whose dominant influence would seem obvious. All of the aforementioned conditions for strong local bonds are maximized in small states. The citizens of these states are more likely to know the candidate's home town, his friends, even the candidate himself. As studies of name recognition and congressional voting suggest, such candidate knowledge is a strong incentive to candidate support. Moreover, in addition to extensive knowledge, locals are more affectively tied to the candidate, in part because he is one of their "group." Beyond these cognitive and affective links, self-interested voting has plausibility, since the president can more easily reward all the folks back home when they are few in number.

Besides state population, we expect two other variables to determine, albeit to a lesser extent, a candidate's home state advantage—namely, political party and incumbency. Let us consider them in turn, beginning with political party. Democratic candidates should receive a larger home state advantage than Republican candidates, because Democratic voters turn out at lower rates than Republican voters. Therefore, Democratic candidates have the opportunity to mobilize relatively more votes from traditionally nonvoting partisans, who may be especially responsive to such "nonissues" as the candidate's home state. In other words, Democratic candidates have more nonvoting Democrats to work on with their home state appeal.

With regard to incumbency, we hypothesized that incumbency would dampen the home state advantage somewhat because of "ceiling effects." For example, presidential incumbents usually are not only returned but as well are awarded a larger vote the second time. Given this increased vote in a reelection bid, it becomes more difficult for home state gains to keep ahead of national gains. We may imagine that some who were originally home state voters now vote for the candidate because of his incumbency status.

We tested the impact of these three factors in a statistical analysis and found that as hypothesized, presidential candidates from smaller states have a greater home state advantage, along with those who are Democrats or incumbents. These three variables are statistically significant predictors and together have substantial impact. Among these predictors, state population is clearly the most important. Our figures indicate that a candidate from a small state could expect a much greater home state advantage than could one from a large state.

For the political party strategist, the central role of state size in shaping home state advantage poses a paradox. Benefits are maximized, of course, by winning the electoral votes of a large state. However, the home state advantage, which brings this win closer, is greatest in a small state. Looking at past presidential nomination contests, party leaders often appear willing to risk the narrower home state advantage of the larger states in order to gain their greater benefits.

Summary and Conclusions

Like many truisms of American politics, the notion that presidential candidates have an advantage in their home states has never been tested. When the evidence is carefully examined we find that, indeed, this home state advantage exists. On average, a presidential candidate can count on an increase of about four percentage points in his home state vote share beyond what he would otherwise expect. Although this is not a great advantage, it can obviously make the difference in a close race. Interestingly, the strength of this local support has remained undiluted since the turn of the century, despite the forces of nationalization that seem to be overtaking other aspects of the electoral process. Among the several explanatory variables that seem important, state population size stands out. The smaller the home state, the larger the margin of the candidate's advantage. But paradoxically, party strategists aiming to maximize the electoral college vote must often seek this advantage in states where it is thinnest.

Chapter 7

The Paradox of Ignorant Voters but Competent Electorate[1]

James A. Stimson

After four decades of carefully studying the American voter political scientists continue to be faced with a central paradox—individual Americans seem to pay relatively little attention to politics and consequently appear quite ignorant on the topic, yet taken as a whole the American electorate appears to have accurate perceptions concerning the positions of candidates and parties and thus seems to be well informed. How is it possible that voters could be ignorant as individuals yet collectively informed? That is the question motivating this chapter.

We shall survey some evidence of what the electorate does and does not know, ponder some proposed explanations for the conflicting evidence of ignorance versus knowledge among voters, and suggest a resolution for the apparent paradox based upon the intermediary role of citizen political activists. The model used as the basis for the resolution is derived from communication theory. In the two-step theory of mass communication, a relatively small percentage of the public is tuned into public affairs and is the primary conduit of information to the majority who are not so attuned. In the political sphere this means that those who are more interested in politics convey information about candidates and political parties, and those not attentive to political matters evaluate candidates and party positions on the basis of how they evaluate those among the activists who are conveying such information to them.

Thus, for example, a political "activist" may somehow convey the information that one candidate is in favor of a freeze on the production of nuclear weapons, and express approval for the candidate. Those to whom the information is conveyed will then project onto the candidate the views of the activist, and evaluate the candidate in terms of how they evaluate the activist. If, for some reason, the member of the inattentive public is inclined to evaluate the activist conveying the information in a positive fashion, the inattentive citizen will project onto the candidate a positive response, as well as a positive response with respect to the issue. If the inattentive citizen has reason to evaluate the activist conveying the information in a negative light, this negativism will be projected onto the candidate and issue.

This process of political information being conveyed by, and filtered through a cadre of political activists is described by the model of "mediated cognitions." The political knowledge of most citizens is seen as being mediated by political activists. As it turns out, the model of mediated cognitions can be used to account for the apparent paradox of the United States having ignorant voters but an informed electorate.

A Paradox and a Model

Voters repeatedly tell those studying American voting behavior that they don't follow public affairs, have little interest in politics or governmental policies, view government as relatively remote from their lives, and have little concern over which group of public officials is in charge. Yet, taken together as an aggregate, these same voters seem surprisingly well informed about the choices they make. This contradictory set of facts has produced one of the longest running conflicts among political scientists, and the length and bitterness of the conflict seems to indicate there is no easy way out of the paradox. We can deny one or the other set of facts, but after decades of arguments between the "voters don't pay attention" and "voters are not fools" schools of thought, the evidence marshalled on both sides is impressive.

For example, the area of economic policy-making provides a stark contrast between ignorant citizens and informed electorate. Citizen ignorance of the basic facts of economics and government economic policies has been long noted. Even matters as simple as the relationships between government expenditures, revenues, and deficits seem to elude most citizens. But research also demonstrates that electoral support for government economic policy is based upon a relatively sophisticated level of information so that the electorate as a whole will consistently support neither full employment policies nor anti-inflationary policies, but rather support the right policy at the right time given national economic circumstances.

In a similar vein, public officials such as members of the United States Congress repeatedly tell researchers that the public seems wholly unaware of how their representatives behave and what policies they support despite the best efforts of the representatives to inform their respective constituents. At the same time, these members of Congress worry a great deal about the consequences of their actions for reelection. Are members of Congress irrationally fearful and ignorant of the true level of public information, or is there some way in which the general public does not know about a single act by a congressman, such as a vote on a particular bill, yet somehow comes to understand the congressman's general pattern of behavior?

Furthermore, there are many examples in electoral history where voter perceptions on important matters are contrary to the facts, at least as can best be objectively determined, yet the general electorate manages to choose the party or candidate that in fact is closest to voter preferences. For example, in 1972 McGovern was widely, and incorrectly, perceived to be in favor of "acid, amnesty, and abortion," a rather radical agenda, when McGovern in fact had a mixed, and largely private view of the abortion issue, and certainly did not favor the legalization of LSD or illegal drug use in general. However, as inaccurate as those perceptions were, the electorate ended up seeing McGovern accurately as the more congenial of the two major candidates to the counterculture to which these issues were tied.

Even more striking was the widespread belief in 1980, a belief of considerable consequence to the election's outcome, that Jimmy Carter was opposed to increased spending on defense. In fact, Carter instigated perhaps the most impressive peacetime increases since the beginning of the Cold War in the late 1940's. But applied to the choice between Carter and Ronald Reagan, the public's misperception of Carter was the basis of an accurate relative assessment of which candidate would be more likely to spend even more on defense in the future.

Most debates over public policy are very technical, and even the basic alternatives are usually very difficult to communicate for mass consumption. Such debates usually revolve around specific and complicated facts and assumptions. Competing values are also usually involved, but the role of values in public policy debate is often so subtle that only experts following the day-to-day process can sort out their impact. Still, despite the complexities and subtleties, voters frequently make choices in deciding whom to support which accurately reflect their underlying preferences.

If we are to resolve these apparent contradictions and paradoxes, we must begin by abandoning the image of individual citizens as isolated fact-collectors and decision makers. If instead we view the collection of factual information as a social process, including a two-step flow of communication, we can come to understand how millions of inattentive citizens acquire reasonably accurate information about policy positions and policy choices.

We have long known that inattentive citizens are likely to obtain information from the more politically attentive people with whom they have contact, but for some reason political scientists tend to forget this fact when analyzing general voting behavior. Perhaps this fact is often forgotten because democratic theory tends to idealize the citizen as an individualistic, self-contained decision maker. Also, the study of voting behavior in political science is dominated by survey research, which constantly directs our focus to the individual as the unit of analysis, producing a tendency to revert to the psychology of individuals. Whatever the reason, our inclination is usually to view decisions by voters as if they occurred in a social vacuum—the lonely vigil of the individual citizen in front of his or her television set trying to figure things out alone.

Consider the problems of gathering facts about policy choices. The citizen who would express his preference between candidates and parties must know what the choices are, who stands for which choice, how each policy choice is likely to affect himself and others, and so forth. Two major barriers stand in the way of gathering such information. First, the activity is extremely expensive in time and energy. It requires a level of attentiveness to government and politics well beyond what most citizens seem willing to attain. Second, a citizen who pays the high price of attentiveness to public affairs could still end up being wrong—that is, taking a position contrary to what he would support if he had more expert knowledge on the matter. Put another way, even a highly attentive citizen may often not have enough information to make a rational decision.

On the other hand, a citizen might prefer to be inattentive to politics, thereby avoiding the costs of attentiveness, and instead look to someone in his personal environment, someone whose views he knows (often, perhaps, without wishing to). The following pattern of inference is simple, yet accurate enough on average to make it a reasonable guide: Joe Blow supports candidate X, therefore X probably stands for the same things as Joe Blow does. If one fills in television's "Archie Bunker" for Joe Blow, and Richard Nixon for candidate X, one inference that follows, for example, is that Nixon is not warmly disposed toward black Americans.

This sort of inferential reasoning is probably very common. It provides a simple and at times impressively accurate means for making sense out of complicated political alternatives without having to pay the costs of high attentiveness. Indeed, one of the more interesting aspects of this type of political reasoning is that it can proceed without ever having to listen to the candidate at all.

Who would be those of known views in the individual's environment? Citizen political activists, those relatively ordinary people who take the opportunities for political participation that most shun, would seem to be prime candidates. They are the citizens who pay attention to politics when others do not. Their views are public, on display through lawn signs, campaign buttons, and bumper stickers. Sometimes their views have been conveyed directly to those around them, in which case they convey considerable information about the party and candidates they support. Sometimes their views are not known directly, but are advertised along with candidate support. A peace symbol and a McGovern sticker on the same bumper told a story in 1972. Sometimes the association of political support with a subculture of life-style is the basis of inferences of an aging Volkswagen van, the symbolic association of the candidate with a cluster of liberal political views might be inferred.

The process of inferring candidate and party issue positions from the views of activist supporters would be most direct and powerful for members of primary groups like families. An activist member of the family would provide information on issue positions as a result of direct conversation over a long period of time. That might be supplemented, in some cases replaced, by figures who are highly visible but not personally known, such as movie stars. A Jane Fonda endorsement in the 1970's and 1980's could tell us a good deal about a politician's set of views. And then, of course, there are the entirely anonymous and impersonal mechanisms such as the bumper sticker. By combining the "cues" we receive from these various sources, it may be possible to develop a reasonably sophisticated picture of what different candidates and parties stand for.

We assume for this analysis that one of the things which distinguishes activists from non-activists is the public expression of political views. Indeed, "talking about politics" is one of the activities used to define activism. If we assume, furthermore, that the visibility of a citizen's views is in rough proportion to his or her activity, a matter of degree rather than of kind, then a method of examining visible party positions suggests itself. Thus, the citizen who reports no activity beyond voting is altogether removed from this public opinion analysis, while the more active are weighted by degree of activism.[2]

Party and Candidate Policy Positions: How Much Does the Electorate Know?

We begin the analysis with evidence of what the public knows using the National Election Series (NES) national surveys. Since 1972 similar information has been obtained in each election about candidate positions. Looking at Table 7.1, we can see that there is a close fit between how voters perceived a party and the party's actual issue positions.

Not only do voters uniformly perceive the Democrats to be more liberal on most issues in most elections, but these perceptions appear sensitive to variations in party positions from election to election. For example, in cases where a new party position is defined—race in the 1960's and women's rights around 1980—citizen perceptions follow closely. One important feature is that while perceptions follow actual party positions, they tend to exaggerate the differences between parties.

After hearing all the appalling stories about how little citizens know about politics, it should come as some surprise that such essential information about policy choices is perceived with commendable accuracy by the American electorate. Table 7.1 suggests strongly that American citizens see little confusion or randomness in the political world.

The perceptions of candidate positions shown in Table 7.2 tell a similar story. Since candidates have much less time than a political party to establish what they stand for, and since there is apt to be considerable variation from candidate to candidate, the ability of the American electorate to sort them out as well as it does is quite impressive. What can be said about both tables is that there is little evidence of a confused or ignorant electorate. Although we find ignorance, confusion, and serious misperception among individual voters, there is none to be seen in the electorate as a whole.

TABLE 7.1
The Positions of Party Activists and Perceptions of Party Positions

Issue	Party Activist Positions			Perceived Party Positions		
	Democrats	Republicans	Difference	Democrats Liberal	Republicans Liberal	Difference
Women's Role						
1972	52.86	49.86	3.00	30.4	9.6	20.8
1976	52.01	49.22	2.79	34.2	8.2	26.0
1980	52.89	56.04	2.85	60.4	8.6	51.8
1984	53.11	46.58	6.53	59.3	13.2	46.1
Minority Aid[a]						
1956	49.72	49.83	−.11	20.1	22.1	−2.0
1960	51.52	50.28	1.24	22.7	21.4	1.3
1964	52.69	45.10	7.59	60.4	7.3	53.1
1968	53.64	48.29	5.35	51.0	10.8	40.2
1972	53.95	47.97	5.98	53.3	11.3	40.0
1976	51.63	49.24	2.39	53.3	14.5	38.8
1980	52.41	47.63	4.78	76.2	9.4	66.8
1984	52.31	46.52	5.79	63.1	17.7	45.4
Jobs and Standard of Living						
1956	51.32	46.83	4.49	34.8	15.9	18.9
1960	50.38	45.82	4.56	51.2	12.5	38.7
1964	50.93	44.95	5.98	60.8	8.1	52.7
1968	54.06	48.12	3.94	53.0	13.1	39.9
1972	52.92	45.48	7.44	69.6	11.7	57.9
1976	52.84	45.91	6.93	62.8	12.5	50.3
1980	45.43	38.08	7.35	72.5	9.3	63.2
1984	53.09	44.53	8.56	65.8	10.6	55.2
Education Aid						
1956	51.70	48.13	3.57	29.7	14.9	14.8
1960	51.85	44.81	7.04	41.0	13.1	28.8
1964	52.41	43.75	8.66	52.9	11.7	41.2
1968	52.97	45.38	6.59	43.3	15.8	27.5
School Desegregation						
1956	49.61	50.80	−1.19	22.8	25.0	−2.2
1960	50.71	49.88	.93	15.7	20.4	−4.7
1964	52.03	47.70	4.33	56.4	6.9	49.5
1968	52.59	49.44	3.15	51.7	8.7	43.0

[a]The item used for 1956 through 1968 refers to "fair treatment in jobs and housing" for minorities.

TABLE 7.2
The Positions of Candidate[a] Activists and Perceptions of Candidate Positions

Issue	Candidate Activist Positions			Perceived Candidate Positions		
	Democrats	Republicans	Difference	Democrat More Lib.	Republican More Lib.	Difference
Liberal/Conservative						
1972	60.62	44.20	16.42	84.0	9.2	74.8
1976	56.92	42.55	14.37	74.7	13.1	61.6
1980	57.32	40.85	16.47	71.1	22.2	48.9
1984	56.65	42.12	14.53	68.9	20.5	48.4
Women's Role						
1972	55.48	51.05	4.43	36.4	12.7	23.7
1976	50.72	49.51	1.21	25.6	16.6	9.0
1980	58.76	54.15	4.61	65.0	10.3	54.7
1984	55.24	46.00	9.24	65.5	14.8	50.7
Defense Spending						
1972	50.18	38.82	11.36			
1976	51.17	46.81	4.36			
1980	47.61	42.48	4.93	77.8	13.6	64.3
1984	56.29	44.80	11.49	82.2	8.5	73.7
Minority Aid						
1972	58.02	47.90	10.12	65.2	11.5	53.7
1976	51.77	46.81	4.96	46.0	16.5	29.5
1980	47.61	42.68	4.93	76.4	12.0	64.4
1984	53.60	46.37	7.23	63.6	17.9	45.7
Jobs and Standard of Living						
1972	55.89	45.55	10.44	79.6	10.8	68.8
1976	54.76	44.59	10.17	58.5	16.5	42.0
1980	47.81	38.08	9.73	71.1	12.9	58.2
1984	54.81	44.26	10.55	69.3	10.0	59.3

[a] "Candidate Activists" are party identifiers who report voting for their party's presidential candidate.

To recapitulate, research tends to portray individual voters as disinterested, uninvolved, ignorant, unsophisticated, and nonideological; while at the same time portraying the general electorate as aware, knowledgeable, sophisticated, and reasonably ideological. The precise manner in which the paradox can be resolved is yet to be explained, but an important conclusion for democratic theory can already be derived. If the key for developing an informed, effective electorate is to create an aggregation rather than a mass of individual voters, then the importance of elections becomes obvious since elections are our primary means for creating that aggregated whole. There is thus added empirical support for the utility of representation, and the elections that representation requires, in creating the kind of citizenry that democratic theory assumes. The critical link in all of this is something here termed the "citizen activist." We need to take a closer look at this crucial link.

Citizen Activists: Who, What, and Why?

Citizen activists are in many respects very normal people, but they have the one atypical attribute of being intensely involved with politics. While they are clearly not a cross-section of the electorate, they also have very little in common with professionals in the world of politics. The citizen activists do not hold or seek office, and their involvement in politics, counted in hours or days, is intense only relative to most members of the electorate who do little or nothing.

The literature in political science has little to tell us about the attributes, behavior, or institutional role of citizen activists. The citizen activist falls between the well-studied mass electorate on the one hand and the professional politician on the other.

Public activism is occasional in American politics. Wearing political buttons or ringing doorbells on behalf of candidates are intermittent activities because elections occur only periodically. Furthermore, different citizens become active in different campaigns. Each campaign faces anew the problem of recruiting "foot soldiers." Political campaigns need citizens with the personal attributes of good salesmen in order to sell the party or candidates. At the same time, political activism is costly in terms of time, energy, and emotional involvement, with little in the way of compensation other than the sense of being a good citizen, advancing one's personal views, or perhaps the social rewards that come from working with others. Given the high costs and low compensation of activism, it is not surprising that the failure to recruit adequate numbers of workers is a normal attribute of political campaigns. Sometimes a presidential campaign will succeed in inducing widespread political activity, but the normal campaign, whatever the level of politics, usually involves relatively small numbers of people rather than the "armies of volunteers" usually described by media hype.

Activism is occasional in a second sense. The pool of potential activists is much larger than the number of actual activists in any given year. All activists are occasional activists; they are active only periodically. But quite a number participate in some elections but not others. They are occasional in the sense of being active only during elections, and also in the sense of being active only in some elections. Generalizations about activists and activism must therefore be based upon information gathered over many elections if we are to draw a reasonably accurate picture of the "normal" activist.

At the same time we want to examine the variation in activist attributes from election to election. Although activists may have many similar attributes from election to election, different candidates and different issues will bring out activists of a different "coloration, and this tendency of elections to activate people of varying values, ideologies, and commitments is part of what we want to study. In a sense, it is the tendency of a given election to recruit selectively from the vast pool of potential activists that allows the citizen activist to respond so quickly to changes in the political context, and makes the citizen activist the most variable set of actors in the political system. This tendency for selective recruitment also suggests an important role for the citizen activist in any explanation for the dynamics of political change.

Data and Method

The remaining discussion is based upon an analysis of all presidential elections between 1956 and 1984 using data from the National Election Series. The eight elections allow us to identify a pool of over fifteen thousand citizens interviewed in the studies. Although activists comprise a small percentage of the general electorate, from this very large pool the method used here allows the identification of almost one thousand citizen activists over the eight elections, more than enough for a systematic analysis.

Two overlapping sets of activists can be isolated from the election study samples. The first, and most important for our analysis, are "campaign activists." These are identified by their reports of having engaged in more than one of the following activities: (1) voting; (2) attending political rallies or meetings; (3) wearing a campaign button or displaying a bumper sticker; (4) working for a party or candidate through the formal organization; (5) attempting to influence the opinions of others through conversation; and (6) donating money (not including the one dollar federal income tax checkoff). Anyone who engaged in four or more of these activities was classified as a "citizen activist, which placed them in the most active five or six percent of the electorate.[3]

"Informational activists," the second set of citizen activists, were identified by their reports of having paid attention to the campaign through various media (newspapers, magazines, radio, and television). Not activist at all in a behavioral sense, informational activism measures passive involvement in the world of politics. There was only modest overlap between the two types of citizen activist, and thus we will have little need to pursue analysis of informational activism in this study except for a crucial test at the end. Our ability to clearly distinguish the two types of activism shows that those who actually do something are quite different from those whose involvement is only psychological or intellectual.

Citizen activists, particularly those active in campaigns, have been identified and described. We are now able to pursue the fundamental thesis that mass perceptions of party and candidate issue positions are "driven" by these activists, and that through their efforts ignorant individual citizens are aggregated into a knowledgeable total electorate.[4]

Examining Mediated Perceptions in Two Policy Areas

The model of "mediated perceptions" outlined earlier held that most voters use information provided by citizen activists as the basis for their perceptions of parties and candidates. If an activist attributes a policy position to a party or candidate, those exposed to the activist will likewise attribute that policy position to the party or candidate. A positive assessment of those activists encountered leads to the projection of a positive assessment onto the party, candidate, and policy the activists supported, a negative assessment leads to a negative projection. In this way the perceptions of the general electorate are mediated by that portion of the electorate we have identified as the citizen activist.

If the mass electorate projects party and candidate positions on the basis of information provided by citizen activists, then we should expect to find a correlation between activist positions and the perceptions of the general electorate. As activist positions change from election to election, we should expect mass perceptions to "track" or follow the activists. To test our model we will focus upon two issue areas—policies related to the encouragement of full employment, and policies related to the promotion of minority rights.

These issue areas were chosen for a number of reasons. First of all, they were issues in all eight elections. Second, the election studies asked questions about voter perceptions on these issues so that data are available for our analysis. Third, there turns out to be no substantial regional variation on these issues (even on matters of race). This lack of variation permits us to exclude any possible effects due to geography or regional subculture. Fourth, every issue shows significant variation over time, from election to election, so that we can see whether or not there is indeed "tracking." If there were no variation, we would have no basis for seeing if changes in voter perceptions follow changes in citizen activist positions.

Our first issue area has to do with creating full employment. The degree to which government should intervene in the private economy to secure full employment was one of the central issues of the New Deal. Since 1932 the two major parties can be easily differentiated by their respective stances on this issue. From Figure 7.1 we can see that during the period 1956–1984 the Democrats were perceived as the party more likely to pursue an active federal role. Figure 7.1 also shows that perceptions on this old and stable issue have fluctuated considerably over time. The high points of party differentiation in 1964, 1972, and 1980 correspond with the candidacies of strong ideologues—Barry Goldwater, George McGovern, and Ronald Reagan. In each of these three elections the issue of governmental intervention in the economy was unsettled by the taking of new positions, and the electorate's perception of these changes.

Figure 7.1 also shows graphically the strong relationship between the party activist positions and the perceptions of the general electorate. The relationship is clearly evident in every campaign except that of 1984. The electorate seems to know where the parties stand on the issue of full employment, and this is no trivial matter,

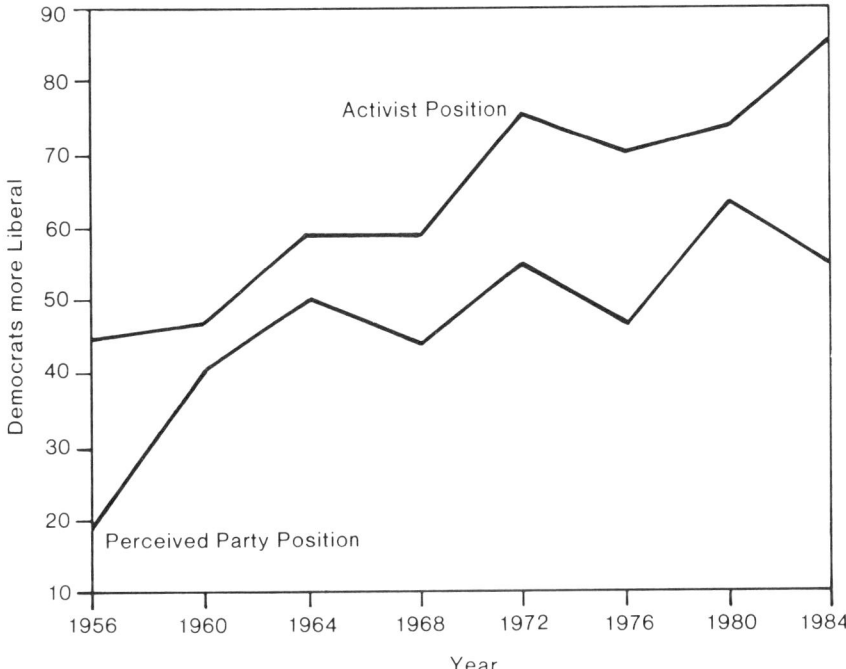

Figure 7.1. Jobs and Standard of Living: Party Images and Activist Positions

but these results by themselves are not as convincing as they might be because Democrats and Republicans have maintained such consistent positions for so long. For half a century the Democrats have been more liberal, activist, and interventionist than the Republicans, and the electorate does not need to have very current information in order to correctly reflect the party positions.

A more demanding, and thus more convincing, kind of evidence would be data which show the electorate accurately perceiving change from election to election. Such knowledge would imply that the electorate is in fact responding to current political debate despite their apparent indifference, and thus significantly strengthen the utility of the mediated cognitions model. It would also imply that the outcome of elections represents more of a mandate to the winning side than is usually credited in the voting behavior literature.

The other policy area we have chosen to examine illustrates the sensitivity of the electorate's perceptions to changes in the activists' positions, which makes mass perceptions of party positions on matters of race more interesting than our first issue area. During the 1950's the Republican Party was on balance slightly more liberal on matters

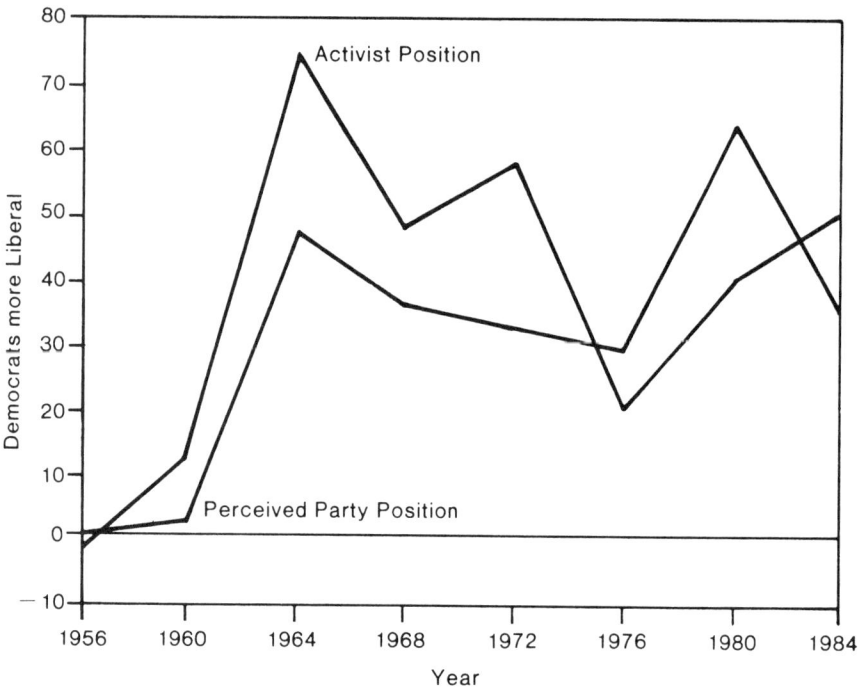

Figure 7.2. Treatment of Minorities: Party Images and Activist Positions

of race than the Democratic Party. Since 1964 there has been a dramatic shift to the left among Democrats so that the Democrats are now much more liberal on race than the Republicans. Although this does not mean Republicans have become less supportive of racial equality than they once were, they have not kept up with the Democratic change, and thus the parties have reversed position on the issue in terms which is more strongly supportive.

Because racial issues present more changes in party positions, and because these changes occur with some rapidity, they present a greater challenge to the mediated cognitions model. Figure 7.2 shows that the model works very well on these issues as well, thus strengthening our confidence in its utility. The prediction of mass perceptions from citizen activist positions is even better than with the issue of full employment. Looking at changes from election to election, the evidence supports the thesis very nicely. When American political parties change their customary policy positions, American voters know it, and supposedly indifferent and ignorant voters appear to learn of these changes from citizen activists. Put another way, mass perceptions track activist positions.

There is always the danger that these results are spurious. That is, the electorate might be tracking the party positions directly through their own efforts rather than by learning from activists. In this case activist positions being close to party positions is irrelevant since the electorate would perceive parties as they do without ever noticing a citizen activist.

We can test for this by using the other kind of activist, the informational activist, as a kind of control group. Informational activists are those who report paying close attention to the campaigns through the media of radio, television, newspapers, and magazines, and therefore should possess a high level of information on their own. They constitute the very part of the electorate that does not rely upon campaign activists for their perceptions. If the mediated cognitions thesis has substance, the informational activists' positions should be as good at predicting the perceptions of the mass electorate as the positions of the citizen activists. As it turns out, the positions of the informational activists, whose positions remain essentially private, do not predict the perceptions of the mass electorate as well as the positions of the citizen activist positions is not spurious. The connection appears to be a causal one otherwise the mass electorate would do no better, and probably worse, than the informational activists in matching actual party positions.

The Implications of Mediated Cognitions

What matters most about the thesis of mediated cognitions is that it accounts for the paradox of inattentive voters versus well informed electorates. It means that the presence of many inattentive and ignorant voters does not prevent the American electorate from being well informed and making rational choices among parties and candidates. It suggests that the many studies demonstrating the ignorance of individual votes has less to tell us about how the political system works than it does about how not to go about testing the health of democratic processes. It suggests that electoral mandates are real, not fictions of the overactive imaginations of successful candidates for public office.

The thesis of mediated cognitions also redirects our attention to some basic aspects of democratic theory. Elections, with the opportunity they provide for producing aggregate results, are an effective and efficient way of maintaining popular control of government. Also, it emphasizes once again the importance of political participation for democratic government, although it suggests that not every voter needs to have a high level of participation. In the long run it may be highly rational for most voters to rely on cues from those who are activist as a means of both conserving their time and energy, and as a means of electing the kind of government that they most desire.

Notes

1. The author would like to acknowledge the assistance of Carolyn Lewis in undertaking the massive data manipulations that are a necessary part of analyzing data from the National Election Study series, and of Mark Hartray who also aided in the task. The chapter has benefited from the critical wisdom of Chris Achen, Lee Epstein, John Ferejohn, James Kuklinski, Carolyn Lewis, Bob Luskin, Paul Sniderman, and Aaron Wildavsky. None will have to bear the consequences, however, of any errors by the author. The data used in this chapter were made available by the Inter-University Consortium for Political and Social Research. The data were collected under a grant from the National Science Foundation.
2. This weighting by visibility technique is borrowed from the work of Converse, Clausen, and Miller.
3. Necessarily excluded by the design of the election studies are the sizable numbers of young people who became activists before attaining the right to vote. This exclusion is no doubt more serious in the years before 1972 when the national eligibility age was lowered to eighteen.
4. For full details on the design, method, and analysis used here see James A. Stimson, "The Process of Perception of Party Issue Position: A Longitudinal and Regional Perspective," a paper presented at the annual meeting of the Midwest Political Science Association in Chicago, 1985.

References

Paul Allen Beck and M. Kent Jennings, "Political Periods and Political Participation," *American Political Science Review,* 73 (1979), pp. 737–750.

Henry E. Brady and Paul M. Sniderman, "Attitudes Attribution: A Group Basis for Political Reasoning," *American Political Science Review,* 79 (1985), pp. 1061–1078.

Edward G. Carmines and James A. Stimson, "The Structure and Sequence of Issue Evolution," *American Political Science Review,* forthcoming.

Henry W. Chappell and William R. Keech, "A New View of Political Accountability for Economic Performance," *American Political Science Review,* 79 (1985), pp. 10–27.

Philip E. Converse, Aage R. Clausen, and Warren E. Miller, "Electoral Myth and Reality: The 1964 Election," *American Political Science Review,* 59 (1965), pp. 321–34.

David Nexon, "Asymmetry in the Political System: Occasional Activists in the Republican and Democratic Parties," *American Political Science Review,* (1971), pp. 716–730.

Sidney Verba and Norman H. Nie, *Participation in America* (New York: Harper and Row, 1972).

Part 3

The Actors in Washington: Congress, Presidents, Courts, and Bureaucrats

Chapter 8

Strategies for Building Coalitions in Congress: Majority Versus Minority Party Presidents

Cary R. Covington

During his first year in office, Dwight Eisenhower was asked by a supporter why he was not more partisan in his dealings with Congress. The President responded by noting that "Every measure we deem essential to the progress and welfare of America normally requires Democratic support in varying degrees" (quoted in Greenstein, 1982, p.232). Even when his own party controlled both houses of Congress, Eisenhower was sensitive to the need to appeal for support across party lines on behalf of his legislative agenda. How much more must the need for bipartisan support have weighed on his mind when Republicans lost control of the Congress in the 1954 elections?

This paper compares the coalition-building strategies of Eisenhower, a minority party president, with those of two majority party presidents, John Kennedy and Lyndon Johnson. I will identify several coalition building techniques and discuss how a president's status as a member of the majority or minority party in Congress affects his use of those techniques. On the basis of those considerations, I will generate a set of hypotheses about coalition building strategies by minority party presidents relative to majority party presidents. Then, I analyze the differences between Eisenhower on the one hand and Kennedy and Johnson on the other. Finally, I discuss conclusions about the effects of minority party status on presidential legislative strategies.

Presidential Strategies for Congressional Coalition Building

General Coalitional Considerations: A president with a partisan majority in Congress is likely to be more aggressive and partisan in both his legislative agenda and in strategies for gaining its passage (Jones, 1983). The reason is the built-in advantages that a majority party president enjoys over a minority party president.

First, most members of Congress are, on the basis of shared partisanship, predisposed to support the president. This basic sympathy is, of course, evanescent, and can quickly evaporate when exposed to the heat of ideological or constituency-based policy differences. Nonetheless, at a minimum, a shared partisanship opens doors, creates a willingness to listen, and provides a nonpolicy basis for persuading a majority of members which, if adroitly employed, can give a president an important 'leg up' on his legislative agenda (Edwards, 1980, pp. 58–66).

Second, a majority party president has the advantage of being able to work closely with the institutional apparatus that runs the Congress. Members of his party hold the party and committee leadership positions that set the agenda for the Congress. These members, particularly the party leaders, usually feel a strong responsibility to aid the president with his program (Sinclair, 1983, pp.114–115). This creates a level of cooperation and access to the institutional apparatus that is not available to a minority party president.

The final (and most ethereal) consideration is that majority party status engenders an expectation of presidential leadership and initiative, particularly when the president is succeeding a minority party president. The trend over the last half-century is for greater presidential leadership in government. On top of that trend, however, rests a cycle in which newly elected majority party presidents are expected to usher in a new era of presidential-legislative cooperation producing new policy initiatives. Franklin Roosevelt, John Kennedy, and even Jimmy Carter were expected to provide new life to a deadlocked legislative process.

Thus majority party presidents are likely to be more aggressive and partisan in both their agendas and in how they pursue them. An extended review of Stephen Wayne's contrast of Eisenhower's attitudes toward Congress with those of Kennedy and Johnson is instructive. On the one hand,

> the approach of Persons and Harlow [Eisenhower's key congressional aides] was low-key and generally bipartisan . . . [avoiding]

'noisy strong-arm tactics.' . . . Eisenhower and his staff tried to avoid alienating Congress (1978, pp.142, 144, 145). On the other hand, Kennedy's and Johnson's staffs were more active and more assertive . . . [with] a clear sense of both general and specific goals. Kennedy wanted a well-organized, well-run, aggressive operation, one that would vigorously push his program . . . Johnson, too, desired a high-powered and well-oiled operation (1978, p.146).

The differences in approach extended even into staff hiring practices. Where Harlow avoided partisanship in hiring his staff, Larry O'Brien "chose a staff with solid Democratic credentials" (Wayne, 1978, p.148). As Wayne concludes: "differences in style not function distinguished the operations . . . Kennedy-Johnson liaison was conducted in a *more partisan and forceful manner*" (1978, p.155 [emphasis added]).

Thus, majority party presidents can take issue positions that are more extreme than those of minority party presidents. Strategy pressures minority party presidents to be more moderate. This, in turn, should engender higher levels of partisanship on the part of the members of Congress during majority party presidencies, while patterns of bipartisanship should appear during a minority party presidency. Ultimately, majority party presidents are likely to be *polarizers* who generate high levels of support from their copartisans and low levels of support from the opposing party. Minority party presidents are likely to be *moderators* who fail to inspire the high levels of loyal support from their own party, but attract more 'crossover' support from the opposition party.

Specific Strategic Considerations: We can examine in this context the particular strategies that presidents might employ to create legislative majorities on behalf of their agendas. Three distinct strategies for building majority coalitions on roll call votes in Congress can be identified.[1] These strategies are: a 'mobilization' strategy that is used to ensure the participation of known supporters on key votes; a 'staying private' strategy that is directed toward *cross pressured* supporters of the president in order to maximize their willingness to support the president; and two 'partial support' strategies that are also used to maximize the support the presidents garnered from cross pressured supporters from within his own party in Congress.

The *mobilization strategy* occurs when a president targets his *core supporters* (in whose support he has high confidence) to ensure their participation on key votes (Covington, 1987a). Members of Congress are often subject to time demands that prevent them from voting on the floor of the Congress. To counteract those pressures, members of the White House Office of Congressional Relations (OCR) keep in touch with supporters to let them know when important votes are coming up and what the president's position is, so that they will be sure to attend and vote on the president's behalf. This strategy is employed at all voting stages of the legislative process, although data constraints limited the analysis to roll call votes.

The *staying private* strategy is employed when a president chooses to not publicize his position on a pending vote in order to reap some political advantage (Covington, 1987b). There are four possible reasons why a president might avoid publicizing his position.

First, silence can improve his chances of winning. When the president's position requires support from marginal, cross pressured members of Congress, publicizing his preferences may activate his opposition, who will then bring pressure to bear on those marginal supporters. This would reduce their willingness to support the president. Working for their support 'behind the scenes' may improve the president's chances of winning over those marginal supporters.

Second, silence avoids the appearance of defeat. If a president wants to exert influence, he must appear successful. Therefore, he may have an incentive to avoid taking a public position on a motion he might lose, while nonetheless working on its behalf in private.

Third, silence creates maneuvering room for the president. On close votes, the president may need to be able to alter his position to acquire needed support. Taking a public position could lock the president into a position which would then be difficult to change. Staying private keeps the president's options open.

Finally, silence avoids the appearance of contradictions. Often a president find himself taking positions on particular motions for short-term tactical reasons that seem to contradict his long-standing or more fundamental positions on the broader issues. Some of Johnson's compromises on civil rights legislation and minimum wage laws fall into that category (Covington, 1987b). However, a president wants to avoid the appearance of being indecisive or opportunistic. To avoid those labels, he may forego taking a public position.

The *partial support* strategies consist of two supportive actions that a president can encourage members to take that fall short of actually casting a vote for his position (Covington, 1988). They are directed at *cross pressured* supporters of the president. These supporters are members of the president's party whose constituencies that oppose much of the president's agenda. The common partisan tie between the president and these members predisposes them to want to help him win, but the views of their constituencies pressure them to oppose the president. They are often willing to help the president, but do not want to be publicly seen as siding with him.

The first method of providing partial support consists of an 'abstention' strategy, where members do not vote if they feel they cannot support the president. Abstaining reduces the size of the opposition coalition, which makes it easier for the president to achieve majority status.

Second, members can 'pair for' or 'pair against' the president rather than voting. A member can join with another member from the opposing side of an issue and come to an agreement that neither will vote. This agreement is usually made when one of the participants in the 'pair' cannot be present for a vote, but nonetheless wishes to have his or her position noted. The former strategy enables cross pressured members to express their support in the form of a 'pair for' the president's position. It is a preferred method of supporting the president because it is less visible to constituents than a vote. The latter strategy permits cross pressured supporters to express the opposition demanded by their constituencies in a form that minimizes the damage to the president's cause because the member's opposition is automatically counterbalanced by a nonvoting supporter. Each strategy helps the president achieve a majority while reducing the members' risks of retaliation by constituents.

Historical accounts of the presidency make it clear that all these strategies are used. There is no way, unfortunately, to directly observe their use. Since we cannot test directly for the use of these strategies, an alternative, indirect approach must be developed. That approach consists of making inferences about how members of Congress should vote in response to the use of those strategies, and then comparing the inferences against the actual votes. I now will assess how the use of these strategies might be affected, according to whether the president is from the Congress' majority or minority party.

The Strategic Impact of Minority Party Status

Presidents with a congressional majority are likely to be more aggressive and more partisan in their approach, and so may be predisposed toward certain of the strategies described above. Presidents from the minority party are likely to take a more passive, bipartisan, approach, and so prefer other strategies.

To assess the impact of party status on a president's strategic choices, I will describe why a majority party president would use each strategy, and then assess how the constraints of being from the minority party might alter those preferences. In this section I explore what testable implications—hypotheses—flow from the strategic impact of minority party status. Later the hypotheses will be subjected to tests.

General Patterns of Presidential Support: Majority party presidents have an incentive to act as polarizers, while minority party presidents have an incentive to act as moderators. Thus,:

$H1_A$: Majority party presidents should promote legislative agendas that are more extreme (liberal or conservative) than minority party presidents.

These incentives in turn should affect congressional voting patterns:

$H1_B$: Majority party presidents should generate higher levels of support from their own party and lower levels of support from the opposition party than do minority party presidents.

The Mobilization Strategy: When the president puts the machinery of the White House into action to mobilize his own core supporters, he is also alerting the opposition to his intentions. This, in turn, increases the likelihood that they will 'countermobilize' in an effort to defeat him. If a president's efforts at mobilization are to create a net benefit, he must either have a larger group to mobilize or be assured that his mobilization efforts are significantly more effective than those of the opposition. Given the generally high turnout on roll call votes, a significant difference in effectiveness is unlikely. As a result, the efficacy of this strategy rests more heavily on the presumption that the president is of the majority party. Therefore, minority party presidents should engage in mobilization efforts less frequently than majority party presidents. As a consequence,

H2: The difference in mobilization scores (see below) between a president's core and peripheral supporters should be lower for minority party presidents than for majority party presidents.

The Staying Private Strategy: The logic of this strategy suggests that votes on which the president 'stays private' should have narrower margins of victory, consist of a higher proportion of procedural motions, and solicit support from cross pressured members of Congress to a greater degree than those votes on which the president does not 'stay private.'[2] Whether a president is in the majority or minority does not change those expectations. Therefore, the predictions remain unchanged for minority party presidents.

However, since, on balance, a minority party president is likely to provoke more opposition than support from publicizing his preferences, minority party presidents have an incentive to engage in the staying private strategy more frequently than do majority party presidents. This leads to the following hypothesis:

H3: The proportion of motions on which presidents do not take a public position on should be higher for minority party presidents than for majority party presidents.

The Partial Support Strategies: Presidents employing partial support strategies are seeking limited support from members who do not feel free to provide unqualified support. All other things equal, a president who starts out with a larger base of support faces less need to acquire limited forms of support. In particular, a majority party president should feel less need to seek out partial support than does a minority party president. Therefore, minority party presidents should engage in partial support strategies more frequently than majority party presidents. As a consequence,

$H4_A$: Cross pressured supporters of minority party presidents should exhibit higher rates of abstention than do cross pressured supporters of majority party presidents.

$H4_B$: Cross pressured supporters of minority party presidents should express their support in the form of a 'pair for' the president's position more often than cross pressured supporters of majority party presidents.

$H4_C$: Cross pressured supporters of minority party presidents should express their opposition in the form of a 'pair against' the president's position more often than cross pressured supporters of majority party presidents.

Data And Methods

The Data Base

This analysis is based on archival records obtained from the Eisenhower, Kennedy, and Johnson Presidential Libraries. In each administration, staff members of the White House Office of Congressional Relations (OCR) kept track, on an annual basis, of how members of Congress voted on those motions that they deemed to be of particular importance to the president. These records were used to compute annual presidential support scores. These are analogous to those constructed by *Congressional Quarterly* (CQ), a compilation of member votes on all those roll-call votes where the president took a position pro or con, in the judgement of the CQ editors. The key difference is that CQ includes in its computations every motion on which the president took a clear public position before the vote took place, while the OCR list consists of those votes that the White House itself deemed to be of critical importance, even if the president did not establish a public position on the motion.[3] Thus OCR may include votes not in CQ ("important, but not public") and exclude some which are in CQ ("public, but not important"). The motions are categorized and will be discussed according to whether they appeared on the OCR list (OCR), the CQ list (CQ), only on the OCR list (OCR exclusive), *only* the CQ list (CQ exclusive), and *both* the OCR and CQ lists (CQOCR).

Measurement

Presidential Support Scores: These scores were computed annually for each member on the basis of the motions included on the OCR lists. In keeping with OCR practice, Presidential Support Scores (PSS's) were computed as the number of times a member cast a vote or a 'pair' for the president's position divided by the number of times a member cast a vote or a pair on motions on the OCR list. Absences, in keeping with OCR practice, were excluded from the calculations. On the basis of these scores, each member was categorized as a 'strong supporter' (PSS 90% or more), a 'weak supporter' (PSS between 50% and 90%), a 'weak opponent' (PSS between 10% and 50%) or a 'strong opponent' (PSS less than 10%) of the president.

The only exception in the use of this measure of support occurred in the analysis of the 'pairing for' and 'pairing against' strategies. Inasmuch as the pairs are the focus of study, they were excluded from the calculation. Instead, a member's support was measured as the number of votes cast for the president's position divided by the number of times the member voted on motions on the OCR list.

Cross Pressure Scores: The cross pressuring effects of interest groups, party loyalty, constituency wishes, and personal ideology are not susceptible to direct observation. Therefore, a surrogate measure is employed. Cross pressures were defined as the ideological distance between the member and the president as measured by the absolute value of the difference in the scores assigned to the members by the (liberal) Americans for Democratic Action (ADA) and a similar score calculated for the president using both ADA and the (conservative) Americans for Constitutional Action (ACA). These difference scores were then categorized according to whether the ideological distance between the president and the member was Low (0–33%), or High (34–100%).

These differences are a reasonable substitute measure of cross pressures, because members with low ADA scores are likely to serve conservative constituencies and to hold conservative positions themselves, while those with high ADA scores are likely to be similarly situated regarding liberal interests. Thus a high ideological distance score indicates for a particular member that he or she is at the other end of the scale from the president.

During Republican administrations, cross pressured members consist of Republicans with highly discrepant ideological scores. They are caught between party pressures to conform to the president's position and ideological-constituency pressures to break with the president. Consonantly pressured members consist of Republicans with ideological scores similar to the president's.

By an analogous logic, during Democratic administrations cross pressured members consist of Democrats with highly discrepant ideological scores. Consonantly pressured members consist of Democrats with ideological scores similar to the president's.

Mobilization Scores: Mobilization consists of the decrease in a member's absenteeism rate on votes that are important to the president (OCR motions), compared to the member's absenteeism rate on votes that are not important to the president (CQ exclusive motions).

This difference is then normalized by the sum of the member's absenteeism rates on important and unimportant motions:

$$\text{Mobilization Score} = \frac{\%\text{ Absent on CQ Exclusive Motions} - \%\text{ Absent on OCR Motions}}{\%\text{ Absent on CQ Exclusive Motions} + \%\text{ Absent on OCR Motions}} \quad (1)$$

Abstention Rates: Abstention consists of the number of times a member failed to vote or form a pair on an OCR motion divided by the total number of OCR motions:

$$\text{Abstention Rate} = 1 - \frac{\text{Number Votes} + \text{Number Pairs}}{\text{Number Motions}} \quad (2)$$

It is possible that differences in abstention rates between cross and consonantly pressured members could occur for reasons other than presidential involvement. To control for other possible influences, abstention is also calculated in a normalized form, dividing for each member their Abstention Rate (EQ.2) by their rate of absenteeism on all the motions on which the president took a position (CQOCR Motions) regardless of their importance:

$$\text{Normalized Abstention} = \frac{\%\text{ Absent on OCR Motions}}{\%\text{ Absent on CQOCR Motions}} \quad (3)$$

'Pairing' Scores: Pairing refers to a member's decision of how to register support or opposition, not the decision of whether to support or oppose. Therefore, the numerators of these two measures are the number of times a member paired for (or against) the president on OCR motions, while the denominators are the sum of the votes and pairs actually cast, for and against the president's position, respectively:

$$\text{Pairing For} = \frac{\#\text{Pairs Cast For the President}}{(\#\text{Pairs Cast} + \#\text{Votes Cast}) \text{ For}} \quad (4)$$

$$\text{Pairing Against} = \frac{\text{Pairs Cast Against the President}}{(\text{Pairs Cast} + \text{Votes Cast}) \text{ Against}} \quad (5)$$

Findings

General Patterns of Support

The results generally support the expectations set forth in $H1_A$ and $H1_B$. Table 8.1 presents the mean ideology scores of presidents Eisenhower, Kennedy, and Johnson based on the positions they took on motions used by ADA and ACA to calculate the liberalism and conservatism scores of members of Congress, as well as the mean OCR presidential support score (PSS) by party for Eisenhower versus Kennedy-Johnson. $H1_A$ predicted that Eisenhower would be more moderate in his ideological stance than Kennedy or Johnson. The evidence in Table 8.1 reveals that where Eisenhower's average ADA score is a moderate 52%, Kennedy and Johnson average in the mid-90's. Thus, the evidence supports the hypothesis. This conclusion warrants the immediate caveat that, at this point, we cannot distinguish the effects of the presidents' strategic considerations concerning how liberal or conservative an agenda they could pass through the Congress, from their sincerely held beliefs about what constitutes appropriate public policy, on the liberalness of their scores. In all likelihood the two sets of factors are mutually reinforcing. However, anecdotal evidence reinforces the conclusion that strategic considerations were at work, witness for example, the opening quotation concerning Eisenhower. In a similar fashion, Kennedy (despite his high ADA scores) was known to have watered down his legislative agenda in recognition of the slender nature of his own electoral victory and that of his partisan majority in Congress (O'Brien, 1974). At this point, I would simply point out that the evidence is supportive of the proposition and warrants further investigation.

The expectation concerning patterns of support for the presidents is also confirmed. Kennedy and Johnson, as majority party presidents, engendered much higher levels of support from their core partisan base of northern Democrats than Eisenhower evoked from Republicans (92.1% versus 73.5%).[4] Similarly, support levels for the Democratic presidents from the opposition camp (30.4%) were much lower than Eisenhower's opposition support from northern Democrats (49.2%) and somewhat lower than Eisenhower's support from southern Democrats (35.8%). Thus, the incentive Eisenhower had to moderate his stances and avoid partisanship appear to have resulted in the predicted results of lessened support from his own minority party and increased support from the opposition majority party.

TABLE 8.1
Mean Liberalism and OCR Presidential Support Scores

	Eisenhower	Kennedy	Johnson
Mean ADA Score	52%	98%	94%
Mean PSS Score			
Republicans	73.5%		30.4%*
Southern Democrats	35.8%		60.2%*
Northern Democrats	49.32%		92.1%*

*Since both Kennedy and Johnson were majority party presidents, the scores for members of Congress were analyzed in terms of their means across both administrations.

Mobilization

H_2 predicts that Eisenhower should make less use of the mobilization strategy, and that as a consequence, differences in mobilization scores between core and peripheral supporters should be less for him than for majority party presidents. The evidence in Table 8.2 bear out this conclusion. The differences in mobilization scores between core and peripheral Eisenhower supporters is negligible (28.2% versus 26.1%). By contrast, the corresponding differences for Democrats during the Kennedy-Johnson administrations is much larger (40.3% versus 28.4%). Interestingly, the rate of mobilization for Eisenhower's core supporters is only roughly equivalent to the presumably less mobilized peripheral supporters of Kennedy-Johnson.

Another interesting comparison can be made by evaluating the relative size of the mobilization scores of Eisenhower's core supporters and those of Kennedy-Johnson's core supporters. The Democratic presidents' supporters had mean mobilization scores of 40.3%, while the scores of Eisenhower's supporters were less than three-quarters of that rate (28.2%). Thus, Eisenhower did not significantly mobilize his core supporters compared either to his own peripheral supporters or the core supporters of Kennedy and Johnson.

TABLE 8.2
Mobilization Scores for Strong and Weak Presidential Supporters

	Eisenhower	Kennedy-Johnson*
Republicans		
Strong Supporters	28.2% (105)@	62.5% (1)
Weak Supporters	26.1% (511)	23.8% (194)
Democrats		
Strong Supporters	— (0)	40.3% (987)
Weak Supporters	29.9% (426)	28.4% (578)

*Since both Kennedy and Johnson were majority party presidents, the scores for members of Congress were analyzed in terms of their means across both administrations.
@number in parentheses is the number of members within that category.

'Staying Private'

The third hypothesis holds that minority party presidents should avoid revealing their preferences in public on important motions more often than majority party presidents. Table 8.3 presents the results.

The evidence clearly supports the hypothesis. Where Kennedy-Johnson 'stayed private' on 10.2% of the important OCR motions, Eisenhower did so on 15.8% of them, or more than half again as frequently. Moreover, there is virtually no overlap between the Democratic presidents and Eisenhower in terms of the proportion of times they stayed private. A ranking of the years by proportion of 'staying private' motions places 1957–1959 at the top as the three highest proportions in the ten year series.

The table also provides an additional interesting insight concerning the expansiveness of the presidents' agendas and the aggressiveness of their leadership. Kennedy and Johnson took positions on an average of 51.6 motions per year, compared to Eisenhower's average of only 30 motions per year. This reinforces Stephen Wayne's observation that:

TABLE 8.3
Measures of the Frequency of Engaging in the 'Staying Private' Strategy

	OCR Motions	OCR Exclusive Motions	OCR Excl. Motions / OCR Motions
Eisenhower			
1957	32	6	18.8%
1958	27	5	18.5%
1959	39	6	15.4%
1960	22	2	9.1%
Total	120	19	N/A
Mean	30.0	4.8	15.8%
Kennedy-Johnson*			
1961	43	3	7.0%
1962	57	7	12.3%
1963	44	1	2.3%
1964	35	5	14.3%
1965	81	8	9.9%
1966	51	6	12.0%
1967	50	6	12.0%
Total	361	37	N/A
Mean	51.6	5.3	10.2%

*Since both Kennedy and Johnson were majority party presidents, their scores were analyzed in terms of their means across both administrations.

> Eisenhower and his staff . . . deferred to the Democratic leadership, pushing hardest on the *relatively few* issues that were of genuine presidential concern. As a consequence, their legislative record was viewed by some as the product of the lowest common denominator and by others, as low volume, high quality (1978, pp.145–146 [emphasis added]).

Partial Support

In this section, I examine the results for three subhypotheses concerning how cross pressured supporters of a minority party president should vote in response to his strategies seeking their partial support compared to cross pressured supporters of a majority party president: first, they should abstain more often; second, they should express their support in the form of a 'pair for' the president's position more often; and finally, they should express their opposition in the form of a 'pair against' the president's position more often. The analysis addressing these three subhypotheses is found in Table 8.4.

The *'Abstention' Strategy:* The evidence concerning $H4_A$ appears to disconfirm the hypothesis. Eisenhower's and Kennedy-Johnson's cross-pressured supporters both abstained an average of 9.5% of the time on OCR motions. Thus, in a direct comparison, the Eisenhower voters do not abstain more often than the Kennedy-Johnson voters.

Moreover, a comparison of Eisenhower's cross pressured supporters with his consonantly pressured supporters brings into question whether the former group engaged in the abstention strategy at all. On the one hand, the cross pressured supporters do indeed abstain more often on important votes than do consonantly pressured supporters. However, the virtually equivalent values for the two groups on the Normalized Abstention variable indicates that the cross pressured supporters appear to abstain more often in general, regardless of whether the vote is or is not important to the president. Thus, it is doubtful whether Eisenhower's cross pressured supporters engaged in the abstention strategy, and it is clear that they did not do so more often that Kennedy-Johnson's cross pressured supporters. This subhypothesis is not confirmed.

The *'Pairing For' Strategy:* The support for this subhypothesis is somewhat stronger. Eisenhower's cross pressured supporters expressed their support in the form of a 'pair for' his positions 8.1% of the time, compared to a 4.8% rate for cross pressured Democrats during the Kennedy-Johnson era. Moreover, the rate of increase between cross—and consonantly pressured supporters for Eisenhower's supporters is 55.8% [(8.1%–5.2%)/5.2%], while the comparable rate of increase for Kennedy-Johnson's supporters is only 14.3% [(4.8%–4.2%)/4.2%]. Thus, the 'pairing for' strategy does appear to have been used during the minority party Eisenhower administration, and, as predicted, more often than during the majority party Kennedy-Johnson administrations.

The *'Pairing Against' Strategy:* The support for this subhypothesis is the strongest of the three. Eisenhower's thirteen cross pressured strong supporters expressed their opposition to the President in the form of a 'pair against' rather than a vote a whopping 42.7% of the time. That means almost one-half of their registered opposition

TABLE 8.4
The Use of 'Partial Support Strategies': Abstention, Normal Abstention, Pairing for, and Pairing Against Among Strong Supporters of the Presidents

	Eisenhower	Kennedy-Johnson*
Abstention:		
Cross Pressured Supporters	9.5% (13)@	9.5% (112)@
Consonant Pressured Supporters	4.0% (99)@	4.8% (864)@
Normalized Abstention:		
Cross Pressured Supporters	51.4% (13)	72.1% (112)
Consonant Pressures Supporters	50.4% (99)	47.3% (864)
Pairing For:		
Cross Pressured Supporters	8.1% (99)	4.8% (864)
Consonant Pressured Supporters	5.2% (99)	4.2% (864)
Pairing Against:		
Cross Pressured Supporters	42.7% (13)	7.5% (112)
Consonant Pressured Opponents	17.4% (3)	4.4% (89)

*Since both Kennedy and Johnson were majority party presidents, the scores for members of Congress were analyzed in terms of their means across both administrations.
@number in parentheses is the number of members within that category.

on roll call votes was in the form of a pair rather than a vote. By comparison, Kennedy and Johnson's cross pressured strong supporters expressed their opposition as a pair against only 7.5% of the time. While that was substantially above the rate for the presidents' strong Republican opposition (4.4%), it does not approach the rate for Eisenhower's cross pressured strong supporters. Thus, evidence for two of the three 'partial support' strategies indicate that they were employed by Eisenhower. More significantly, they also provide support for the argument that minority party status for the president has predictable effects on their use.

Conclusions

Minority party presidents are much more limited in the number of opportunities and options that they have to exercise effective leadership of the Congress. They must adapt the context of their agendas, their style of leadership, and their strategies for coalition building to those constraints.

The findings reported here generally support the expectations about how minority party presidents should adapt themselves. First, the results reflect Eisenhower's more moderate and passive demeanor. Compared to Kennedy and Johnson, he was less ideologically extreme in the positions he took on roll call votes. He also gave signs of having a less aggressive agenda in terms of the number of roll call votes that were on the OCR's list of key legislation. Congressional voting patterns reflect back Eisenhower's moderate image. His own party was less inclined to give him strong, unconditional support than were northern Democrats under Kennedy-Johnson. However, that tendency was offset by the levels of support he received from the opposition party, which were much higher than those of Kennedy-Johnson.

Secondly, Eisenhower appears to have shied away from employing those strategies that work best for majority party presidents. In particular, congressional voting patterns give no indication that the OCR used the mobilization strategy. The risks of encouraging a countermobilization by the opposition party that would swamp his own efforts appear to have dissuaded the OCR from engaging in such high profile activity.

Third, Eisenhower seems to have used strategies that lend themselves to a minority party president. He 'stayed private' more often than did either Kennedy or Johnson. Moreover, congressional voting patterns suggest that cross pressured supporters used the 'pairing for' and 'pairing against' strategies more often than did similarly situated supporters of Kennedy and Johnson. The only hypothesis that did not generate support was the 'abstention' strategy. The evidence does not support the contention that cross pressured supporters (who felt pressure to oppose the President) would stay away from a vote rather than participate. Nonetheless, the weight of evidence does support the thrust of the argument presented.

Notes

1. Each of these strategies has applications in other voting situations, including, for example, votes that occur in committees or floor votes that are unrecorded. Thus, the behavior under study is by no means limited to the data analyzed in these articles. However, this behavior is only directly observable and so subject to analysis for roll call voting, on which members must publicly express their positions.
2. For a more complete explanation of the derivation of these expectations, see Covington (1988).
3. The characteristics of the Kennedy and Johnson records have been described elsewhere (Covington, 1986), and a more complete depiction of the Eisenhower records can be obtained from the author. Only records for the years 1957–1960 were used in this paper because it was not until 1957 that the Eisenhower administration began compiling these records in a systematic and widely-used fashion.
4. Southern Democrats were not looked upon by the Democratic presidents as part of their core coalition that could be counted upon as a reliable base of support. Rather, they formed a 'swing vote' that had to be courted as needed to create specific majorities. Therefore, they are not included in the comparison of presidential support from core supporters.

References

Covington, Cary R. 1986. Congressional Support for the President: The View from the Kennedy/Johnson White House. *Journal of Politics,* 48:717–728.
_____. 1987a. Mobilizing Congressional Support for the President: Insights from the 1960s. *Legislative Studies Quarterly,* 12:77–95.
_____. 1987b. "Staying Private": Gaining Congressional Support for Unpublicized Presidential Preferences on Roll Call Votes. *Journal of Politics,* 49:737–755.
_____. 1988. Building Presidential Coalitions Among Cross Pressured Members of Congress. *Western Political Quarterly,* 41:
Edwards, George C. III. 1980. *Presidential Influence in Congress.* San Francisco: W.H. Freeman & Company.
Greenstein, Fred. 1982. *The Hidden-Hand Presidency.* New York: Basic Books.
Jones, Charles O. 1983. Presidential Negotiation with Congress, in Anthony King (ed.), *Both Ends of the Avenue.* Washington, D.C.: American Enterprise Institute.
O'Brien, Lawrence. 1974. *No Final Victories.* New York: Doubleday.
Sinclair, Barbara. 1983. *Majority Leadership in the U.S. House.* Baltimore: Johns Hopkins University Press.
Wayne, Stephen J. 1978. *The Legislative Presidency.* New York: Harper & Row.

Chapter 9

So Many Cases, So Little Time: Judges as Decision Makers

Timothy M. Hagle

The judicial branch is a coequal part of the United States government, and yet it has escaped the type of scientific scrutiny given to the executive and legislative branches. This is not to say the judicial branch has lacked all scrutiny, only that it has traditionally been viewed from a perspective different from the other two branches of government. The executive and legislative branches are seen as political entities, but judges and the judicial branch have fostered the idea that they are nonpolitical arbiters of the law.

In *Marbury v. Madison,* the landmark United States Supreme Court case which established judicial review under the United States Constitution, Chief Justice John Marshall rhetorically asked who should determine the meaning of the Constitution. He answered this question by arguing that members of the other two branches were too involved in the nasty business of politics and only judges could be truly nonpolitical arbiters of the law. This argument by Chief Justice Marshall was not the beginning of what is generally known as the "cult of the robe," but it is a classic example in American jurisprudence.

Following Marshall's reasoning, students of the judiciary have traditionally concentrated on individual cases. It is assumed that each case is decided on the basis of cases which precede it. Although it is acknowledged that each case is different from any other in many ways, past cases are still examined to find the general principles which are then applied to the present dispute.

This reliance on precedent (known in legal terms as *stare decisis*) and its accompanying detailed examination of each case has caused legal scholars, as one observer put it, to miss the the forest for the trees. To better understand the workings of the judiciary, one must step back from the cases, remaining cognizant of the details, but not to such a degree that they inhibit the ability to see the greater whole.

Judges are subject to human cognitive limitations. They must process voluminous amounts of material before arriving at a decision. They are constrained by the judicial system which places demands on the judges as to the form and content of their decisions. To cope with all of this, judges must adopt strategies and shortcuts designed to allow them to process the information necessary for a decision. In this chapter, we consider the ways in which judges actually process information and arrive at decisions.

Rationality in Decision Making

The term "rational" actor usually refers to an actor who chooses actions which maximize the probability of obtaining desired goals. The rational decision maker, however, does not literally make calculations in order to arrive at a decision. In addition, one cannot assume that all actors will make the same choices even if their preferences are the same. The ultimate goals sought are not necessarily the same; risks actors are willing to take may vary; the amount of information available may be great or small; errors in calculation may be made.

One assumption of the comprehensive rational actor model (though not always explicitly stated) is that the rational actor will effectively examine all available alternatives and choose the alternative which produces an anticipated outcome closest to the actor's indicated preferences. This is the approach claimed for cost-benefit analysis. The comprehensive, cost-benefit method of decision making can be applied to the individual decision maker who must make everyday decisions such as whether to purchase a new car, where to vacation, or what to fix for dinner. It also can be applied to group or institutional decision makers, such as Congress or the Supreme Court. Either way, the rational actor must take into account all the relevant alternatives and the positive and/or negative consequences associated with each, before making a decision.

Exhaustiveness in the actor's search for information or alternatives is the key feature of the comprehensive rational actor model. The actor considers *all* alternatives and their consequences, then selects the one which comes closest to fulfilling the actor's preferences. (Because of the unrealistic nature of this assumption, another version of this model has been advanced which requires only "bounded rationality," which will be taken up later.)

Another factor which concerns the rational decision maker, is whether the consequences of the alternative chosen are certain or only probable. Discussions of decision making often differentiate between decision making under certainty and decision making under risk. Decision making under risk may be more complex because of the calculations of probabilities and expected values of each possible alternative, but the decision maker is still expected to perform these calculations to find the alternative which maximizes utility.

Obviously, the description of the comprehensive rational actor presented here is an ideal rather than a model of real world behavior. That decision makers engage in goal-directed behavior surely is true, but the assumptions about *how* a specific course of action is selected are questionable.

Human Limitations

Observers have noted four principal barriers to the comprehensive method of decision making. The first is the problem of control; decision makers normally cannot control all the elements of a problem. The second is that of unintended results; even if the various actors react as predicted, additional unforeseen results may also occur. Third, it is often not possible to make an accurate cost-benefit analysis of the possible solutions to a problem; data commonly are missing or unavailable. Fourth, the goals of the decision-maker may not be known or adequately identified. This is even more likely in collective decision making where goals often must be negotiated.

In other words, a number of the rules and assumptions commonly associated with rationality are not applicable in uncontrolled situations where adequate information may not be available to allow sufficient opportunity to make decisions in a comprehensive manner. A much less structured form of rationality is necessary to effectively examine decision making under uncertainty and risk.

Even if it were possible to overcome the various limitations of the rational actor model noted above, there are limits to human cognitive capacity which further restrict the level of comprehensiveness which may be attained. Simply put, humans have limited ability to process information. Even when the rational actor is only making one decision at a time, these cognitive limitations severely limit the scope of factors, alternatives, and consequences which can be considered. These limitations are not avoided when the decision maker under examination is composed of a group of individuals (such as the Supreme Court). If a group decision must be made, the limitations may compound the difficulty of finding the preferred course of action since individuals may differ on goals as well as means.

In spite of the pretensions of the "cult of the robe," it is clear that courts are composed of humans with human limitations. Americans are litigious and court caseloads have been steadily on the rise, the United States Supreme Court included. The increase in the workload of the Court has put a great deal of pressure on the justices and has led Justice Blackmun to comment, "One, therefore, to a large degree, relies on experience and an innate and hopefully already developed proper judicial reaction" (Ripple 1980:175).

This statement by Justice Blackmun implies something that should be obvious to those who study the judiciary in general and the Supreme Court in particular: it is not humanly possible for the justices to comprehensively assimilate all the information presented to them. The United States Supreme Court annually examines and rules on well over five thousand petitions submitted to them for review. Of the approximately two hundred cases granted full review each year the justices must read the briefs of both sides and any amicus curiae ("friend of the Court") briefs which are permitted. In addition, the justices may need to review past precedents before they begin the task of writing their own opinions. Each justice has a number of law clerks who do much of the initial reading, research, and possibly even writing, but this fact serves to affirm the contention that the justices cannot do it all themselves. They must and do find ways to cut down the amount of information they need to process, and this is the topic of the next section.

Cognitive-Cybernetic Decision Making

We have seen that the more rigorous versions of the rational actor model do not take into consideration the frailties of humans or the inadequacies of the decisional environment. Most theories of individual choice contain some notion of comprehensive rationality, but even the less stringent one call for more comprehensiveness than is realistically possible. Given this rejection of the comprehensive rational choice model on empirical grounds, we must find another model which more accurately describes human decision making.

Human Learning

Empirical studies of decision making find that when a problem is encountered the decision maker only looks far enough to solve the problem adequately and does not search for the best solution. Why would an individual or an organization adopt such a search strategy? Part of the answer lies in the human limitations that have been discussed thus far. In addition, there are often external constraints on the decision makers which do not allow for an extended search. If a football fan's television quits two hours before the Super Bowl, he has a very limited amount of time available to find a replacement, and will be unwilling to engage in a lengthy search. In addition to temporal constraints, searches have costs associated with them. These costs can take the form of actual monetary outlays to hire personnel or pay for necessary supplies and equipment, or simply opportunity costs associated with the time and energy lost in extending the search beyond minimal levels.

Heuristic principles are used to reduce searches to manageable proportions. For the large organization or institution these rules may take the form of standard operating procedures and explicit rules for routing and filtering information. To the individual decision maker these rules may simply be rules of thumb used in an informal way. An example of this type of informal heuristic can be found in the classroom. Even when seats are not assigned, there is a common tendency for students to sit in the same area, if not the same seat, for every class period.

This behavior can be analyzed in hierarchical fashion. On the first day of class the student is faced with an initial choice of where to sit. Requirements may include adequate visibility of the instructor and blackboards, proper distancing for hearing the instructor, not too near windows or doors or other distractions, near a friend or attractive classmate, far enough away from the front for unobtrusive naps, etc. The first step might be to divide the problem into educational and social/personal concerns. Educational concerns may be subdivided into those involving the instructor, the student, and the classroom itself. The process continues until a seat is selected. If the result is successful the problem of selection on the second day can be reduced to getting the same seat.

The preceding discussion on the adaptive strategies used by humans in the face of general and cognitive limitations should not lead one to conclude that decision makers who engage in these strategies are irrational. It is not that human decision makers are not rational, rather the models and assumptions usually associated with comprehensive rational choice theories are unrealistic in the face of the severe limitations on cognitive abilities and available resources.

Herbert Simon has made famous the principle of "bounded rationality," and describes it as follows:

> The capacity of the human mind for formulating and solving complex problems is very small compared with the size of the problems whose solution is required for objectively rational behavior in the real world—or even for a reasonable approximation to such objective rationality. (1957:198)

Under Simon's bounded rationality, also known as "satisficing," the decision maker endeavors to make a rational choice within the real world constraints—e.g., available information, cognitive capabilities, and human memory. The analysis may not be complete in the scientific sense, but is good enough. The difference here is between an open-ended search for the best and most complete explanation or choice and a search which finds an acceptable solution to the problem.

A very important implication emerges from this line of research. Simon points out that the principle of bounded rationality requires that the decision maker construct a *simplified* model of the problem in order to deal with it (1957:199). Extraneous information must be filtered out, and patterns must be identified.

In a similar way, information is filtered before it reaches the President of the United States. Clearly the President needs a great deal of information in order to make decisions, but at the same time it is not possible for him to process all of this incoming data. Generally the information is filtered through the White House staff who condense it into summaries for the President to read. If enough information is contained in the summary for the President to reach a decision he need not read additional material on the subject.

The Supreme Court also has its filters. Law clerks for the justices have the unenviable task of reading the thousands of cert petitions and drafting cert memos for their justices. These memos summarize the important points of law raised in the petition. If the justices feel they need more information to make a decision they can read the petition itself.

Cybernetic Decision Making

The strategies used by human decision makers may appear to be random or chaotic, but on closer examination patterns to the decision making activity become clear. Simon makes this point in describing the meandering path of an ant across a beach. The ant has a general sense of where his home lies, but cannot take the shortest route because of the numerous obstacles which lie in its path (1981:63–64).

Similarly, the human decision maker cannot make the best decisions, but must settle for ones which will avoid the obstacles of cognitive and environmental limitations. In studying human decision making, we must examine how decision makers deal with these limitations. A consideration of cybernetic decision making aids us in this task.

Cybernetics is a science focused on the operations of adaptive systems, human and otherwise. An ordinary household thermostat is an example of a very simple system which operates to keep a variable (room temperature) within a specified range. In cybernetics, this behavior is seen as a rudimentary form of decision making.

The comprehensive rational choice model assumes that the decision maker consciously proceeds through the steps of the model to reach a decision; it is less a model than a method. The cybernetic model is simply that: a model.

The cybernetic model is compatible with what we know about human learning, including the impossibility of comprehensive rationality, the limited capacity of human memory, and the need to cope with uncertainty and complexity. However, the cybernetic model fails to account for the uniquely adaptive abilities of the human decision maker. Hence, certain elements of cognitive theory must be used to supplement the cybernetic model.

The information processing strategies used by human decision makers involve chunking—that is, the storage of information in pattern sets—and hierarchical organization. By using these strategies, human decision makers can make seemingly complex decisions based on a limited amount of information which is within the processing capabilities of short term memory. Keying in on a small number of important elements in order to make a decision is a form of cybernetic decision making.

One can see, then, that certain regularities exist in the cognitive operations of humans, and these regularities are not dependent on the content of the information which is processed. Five important regularities deal with inferential memory, consistency, reality, simplicity, and stability.

The key point about inferential memory is that it is dominated by strong associations; weak associations decay. When the ability to recall more weakly associated elements declines, the details are inferred (rightly or wrongly) by the patterns formed by the more strongly associated elements. This inferential nature of memory can also be illustrated using material being learned for the first time. When information is lacking important details, the mind will try to fit the available information into previously learned patterns, and in so doing, infers the details.

The principle of consistency refers to constraints placed on the inferential mechanisms by the mind's effort to maintain consistency among internal belief elements. This principle can also be illustrated by optical illusions where perceptions of the size and length of objects is distorted to conform with expectations. Perceptions are also influenced by attitudes, the simplest example being the optimist who sees the glass as half full and the pessimist who sees it as half empty.

The third principle, the reality principle, asserts that stable, important features of the world around us leave reliable impressions in our minds. Despite the principles of inferential memory and consistency, if stable and important elements of the environment present themselves, the healthy human mind will record them.

The final two principles, simplicity and stability, are principles of economy. Because of cognitive limitations, information processing must be selective. It has been shown that the mind attends to and remembers important details, but pays little or no attention to what are considered unimportant details. In order to keep cognitive processing within the imposed limits, the mind attempts to keep the belief system as simple as possible. In addition, since major changes in the belief system would require great amounts of reprocessing, the mind operates to keep the system as stable as possible.

Cognitive-Cybernetic Judicial Decision Making

Comprehensive rationality in individual and group decision making finally had to be reevaluated in the face of evidence that humans can not and do not perform its complicated calculations. And so did a set of beliefs collectively known as "the cult of the robe" dominated the study of judicial decision making for many years. This set of beliefs, carefully nurtured by the members of the bench, portrays the judiciary as an august and mystical institution which must bear the burden of judgment on behalf of the populace. Let us now briefly examine these beliefs.

Harold Spaeth begins his book, *Supreme Court Policy Making: Explanation and Prediction*, with the following statement: "No aspect of American government is more suffused with myth than judicial decision making" (1979:1). There are a number of trappings to the judicial mythology. One of the most obvious is the long black robes worn by judges. Other than the military and police, no other officers of our government wear an official uniform. The length and cut of these judicial robes is reminiscent of clerical attire. The intent may be to impress upon the minds of those before the court that their fate may literally lie in the hands of the judges.

The color black is chosen to emphasize the solemnity of the office and the seriousness of the proceedings. Being in court is not unlike being in church. Attentiveness is required, dignity must be preserved, respect must be given to the judge, Truth is sought, and Justice is dispensed. In addition, witnesses must take an oath on the Bible that they will tell the truth (although today witnesses may choose to simply affirm the veracity of their testimony).

Judges preside from a raised platform, called a bench, which allows the judge to observe all that occurs in the courtroom. This bench also forces all in the courtroom, formal participants and spectators alike, to physically look up to the judge, a not-so-subtle reminder of who is in control of the proceedings. Additional reminders include requiring everyone in the courtroom to rise when the judge enters to the cry of the bailiff that court is now in session. Indeed, the business of the United States Supreme Court begins with the Marshal's cry:

> Oyez, oyez. All persons having business before the honorable, the Supreme Court of the United States, draw near and give attention. God save this Honorable Court.

Judges are addressed as "Your Honor" and referred to as the "Honorable Judge/Justice So-and-so." At all times the dignity of the court must be preserved, which means showing proper respect to the judge, whether in court or out. Differences between the judge and the court are blurred. The illusion presented is that the judge is the physical embodiment of the court, and the legal system in general. Here again, the long robes add to the illusion by hiding the sight of human bodies and presenting only a dark and shapeless mass to the observer.

For the most part, the legal system in the United States is descended from the English legal system, and many of these physical aspects of the judiciary have their roots in English legal custom. The same is true for the basic attitudes and conceptions the general citizenry holds regarding the judiciary. Some of these attitudes were religious in origin, an offshoot from the notion of divine right for kings.

Since it was these monarchs or their representatives who heard the petitions and appeals, it was believed their decisions came from God (which helps to explain the religious overtones present even in the modern judiciary) and thus required a proper showing of respect for the dispensers of divine justice. However, this attitude was not simply an extension of the fact that early judges were representatives of the Crown. Given that these early judges, as is the case with the judiciary today, held the lives and fates of the people in their hands, there was a tendency, and perhaps a desire, to look upon these judges as being superior. It is easier to place your fate in the hands of someone who has superior wisdom and an ability to find Truth and Justice than someone you consider your equal.

Judges mirrored these attitudes and adopted the belief that they were in fact dispensing divine justice. The font of their authority may not be the same, but modern American judges hold similar attitudes regarding their role. Most judges subscribe (or at least pay lip service) to the belief that they do not make policy, they merely interpret the Constitution, the foundation on which our system of government is built. If asked, most members of the judiciary would deny that they make policy. They are nothing more than a conduit, so the belief goes, an instrument to clarify, explain, and apply the policies of the Constitution in relation to actions of the other two branches of the government. As Spaeth notes, this is commonly referred to as the declaratory theory of judicial decision making (1979:3). This does not mean, however, that judges are incapable of disagreeing with the dictates of the executive or legislative branches. American judges have a higher law to which they can turn: the Constitution of the United States.

Thus constitutional interpretation is one of the major roles of the judiciary. It is the judiciary which has the last word on whether actions by the other branches are in line with constitutional mandates. This role is known as judicial review.

Although the Constitution makes no mention of who was to have the authority to interpret the document, Chief Justice John Marshall in *Marbury v. Madison* claimed this task to be the duty and privilege of the judiciary. His essential argument followed from the attitudes noted above, namely that judges were somehow more qualified to interpret the Constitution than were members of Congress or the President, all of whom were tainted from their involvement in that nasty business called politics.

This power of judicial review must not be greatly abused since the judiciary generally lacks the procedures necessary to enforce its will. If courts are viewed as mere policy makers there would be no reason to accept their view rather than that of the executive or legislative branches, and with little or no muscle to back up their policies, the courts would soon become ineffectual. Thus, courts strive to dispel any notions that they are making new policy by conjoining their decisions with the Constitution.

Courts also rely on precedent. Precedent, also known as stare decisis, is the method used by courts to justify present decisions as based on past decisions. References to past decisions show how the court is following the course it has set, and maintain stability and tradition.

Do judges have a power or gift which enables them to dispense justice? Hopefully they are more capable than the average citizen at doing what they do, but despite the cult of the robe, they are merely men and women doing their job. Do judges really base their decisions on Constitutional mandates and precedent? This question must also be answered in the negative, but requires a bit more proof.

The proof is provided in Spaeth's *Supreme Court Policy Making,* and will be summarized here. Generally there are four tactics which allow judges to say precedent is not applicable in a present case. First, they may declare the seemingly controlling material from the previous case to be *obiter dicta.* As part of their avoidance of appearing to make new policies, courts (especially the U.S. Supreme Court) usually decide only what is necessary to dispose of the case. Anything else in the opinion is superfluous, is not binding on other courts, and is called dicta. If a previous case conflicts with the desired outcome of the present case, the court may declare the troublesome passages to be dicta.

The second tactic is to distinguish the previous case. This means that the facts of the two cases (past and present) are sufficiently different that the past case is not controlling in the present case. Case analysis is the method used for determining whether a past case can be considered precedent. Essentially case analysis involves an examination of the facts of the case combined with an application of the relevant law to reach a conclusion of law (Statsky and Wernet 1977:153-156). Statsky and Wernet point out the particular importance of facts when they say, "Even a slight change in the facts can result in a totally different conclusion of law" (1977:155). Since it is the judge who decides whether the facts of a previous case are too different (as well as the interpretation of the rule of law) this is a very flexible tool for selectively choosing the precedent which best supports the desired outcome. It should be noted and emphasized that not all the facts are important. Important facts are those which have some bearing on the decision. In a search and seizure case the location of the search is important but the color of the defendant's shirt is probably not. The determination of whether a fact is important adds to a judge's ability to distinguish cases on the basis of the facts. If a fact is troublesome, it may be deemed legally unimportant.

Both of the above tactics may be employed by any court. The next two can be used only by certain courts. The reason for this distinction lies in the fact that the first two tactics do not affect the past case in any way. The next two methods permanently affect the way that a case may be used as precedent. These changes can only be made by a court with respect to its own prior decisions or those of courts inferior to it and within its jurisdiction.

The third tactic is to limit the previous case. The overall effect of the precedent remains unchanged, but a specific part of the decision no longer applies. An example used by Spaeth to illustrate this tactic comes from *Frothingham v. Mellon* where the Supreme Court banned taxpayer suits which challenged the purposes for which federal expenditures were made (1979:57–58). Later, in *Flast v. Cohen,* the Court limited *Frothingham* by carving out an exception to the previous rule.

The final tactic is the most drastic: overrule the previous case. An overruled case is no longer good law, and may not be used as precedent. (Strangely enough, precedent is often used to overrule other precedent.) A case may be overruled when two conflicting lines of cases finally come together in one case, or when changes in public attitudes and morals force a change. A well known example of the latter occurred when the Court effectively overruled *Plessy v. Ferguson* in its decision of *Brown v. Board of Education.*

Spaeth notes that the Court has overruled itself only about 100 times (1979:58). This is not surprising given the desire to maintain an aura of stability. Recent speculation as to the fate of *Roe v. Wade,* if certain members of the Court resign or die, tends to show the Court less as an institution than the group of decision makers they really are. Change the group and change the decision.

Clearly, adequate facilities exist for judges to avoid the mandatory use of precedent except in the sense of finding some past decision to support the present position. The question remains as to whether judges do decide cases in the professed manner. In answering this question, one must keep in mind the caseload of the courts. The drastic increase in the Court's workload has been noted by many. The Court itself has taken note of the increase in an informational booklet available to visitors of the Supreme Court building. In a paragraph titled "The Justices' Caseload" the following is stated:

> The Court's caseload had increased steadily, reaching a total of 5,311 cases on the docket for the Term ending July 1982. The increase has been rapid in recent years. In 1960, only 2,313 cases were on the docket, and in 1945, only 1,460. Plenary review, with oral arguments by attorneys, is granted in 180 to 200 cases per Term. Formal written opinions are delivered in 150 to 170 cases. Approximately 120 additional cases, primarily appeals, are disposed of without granting plenary review. The publication of a Term's written opinions, including concurring opinions, dissenting opinions and orders, approaches 5,000 pages. Some opinions are revised a dozen or more times before they are announced.

Unlike other organizations, the Court does not divide the labor. Each justice must deal with all the information from each case (or, as will be pointed out below, as much of the material as is necessary to come to a decision). Each justice may have three or four clerks to help with the work, but the numbers cited by the Court would seem to indicate that such a small number of people would find the task of doing all the requisite reading, research, and writing quite impossible in the time allotted prior to an initial vote either on whether to grant review or on the merits of a case. One method of lessening the burden on the justices is the practice of having law clerks prepare summaries of petitions which highlight the facts, issues, and legal arguments. Chief Justice Rehnquist notes that the justices generally cast an initial vote on the merits of a case from 48 to 72 hours after hearing oral arguments (1987:287). They are free to change their vote any time prior to the announcement of the Court's decision, but this does not happen very often.

This is further evidence that the Court must have shorthand procedures for dealing with the massive amounts of material that comes before the them. Justice Blackmun admitted as much in the statement quoted earlier on the need to rely "on experience and an innate and hopefully already developed proper judicial reaction."

Apparently Justice Brennan has also developed a proper judicial reaction. After a number of years on the Court he was able to dispose of some petitions for certiorari within a matter of seconds and had "developed a special feel for recognizing the important cases" (Woodward and Armstrong 1979:273).

Undoubtedly, both Blackmun's "judicial reaction" and Brennan's "special feel" were the result of years of training and experience using case analysis; a method which emphasizes the important facts of a situation.

The foregoing details of Court procedures and attitudes make it clear that justices do not make their decisions as maximizers under the comprehensive rational choice theory of decision making. A cognitive-cybernetic theory of decision making is more appropriate under the circumstances described.

Cybernetic systems have three characteristics: they are complex, probabilistic, and homeostatic. Let us consider the applicability of each of these characteristics to the Court.

There should be little doubt that the Court is exceedingly complex. The entire judicial system of the United States is composed of 51 court systems: 50 state court systems and the federal court system which includes the Supreme Court. Let us restrict the system to be examined in this work to the operations of the United States Supreme Court. The Supreme Court has nine primary elements; the nine justices of the Court.

A complex system is one in which the connections between the elements are highly elaborate. Certainly this describes the Court. Not only will the nine justices interact with each other at various stages in the process of handling a case, but they also interact with their law clerks (who also interact with each other) and quite often with attorneys, either face-to-face or through the briefs submitted to the Court.

The elaborateness of the communications is found in the rules which govern how and when certain interactions take place (e.g., attorneys cannot enter a justice's chambers to plead a case (see Woodward and Armstrong 1979:79–80)).

The probabilistic nature of the system is guaranteed by the presence of human decision makers. Of course, if this were not the case, the study of the law would be much simpler.

Finally, the cybernetic system must be a homeostat—that is, it must have the ability to maintain some "variable" within specified limits. In studying the decisions of the Court, the variable to be maintained will concern the particular area of the law examined, but generally it will pertain to statutory or constitutional interpretation. In the area of search and seizure the Court must maintain a balance between competing constitutional concerns: the rights of the individual versus protection of the public from criminal activity.

This ability of the homeostat is dependent on the presence of a feedback loop in the system. Feedback provides the inputs to the control device. The control device is the element of the system which makes the decision, the Court or the individual justices in judicial decision making. Feedback consists of the cases which enter the subsystem of Supreme Court decision making. Once the Court issues a decision, the decision must work its way back through the system until it reaches the litigants who must then adjust their actions in accordance with the decision. If compliance is achieved, the Court does not hear about the case again. It is only if additional problems arise, either through noncompliance or a lack of understanding of the decision, that the Court may have to deal with the problem again. When this occurs, another case must work its way to the Court for review. The particular issues of the second case inform the Court of the problems with the first decision (too inclusive, unclear, too specific, etc.) and the Court can tailor the second decision to correct these problems. In this way the Court receives feedback as to whether its decisions are keeping the relevant variables within the desired limits (i.e., whether the proper balance has been struck).

The cybernetic decision maker deals with uncertainty by focusing on a small number of incoming variables (inputs). In addition, the decision maker has a relatively small repertoire of responses and decision rules so that a decision can be easily and quickly reached once certain information is received.

Uncertainty goes hand in hand with an exceedingly complex probabilistic system like the judicial system. It has been shown that the method of case analysis emphasizes the focusing of attention on a few relevant factors. Decisional rules of the Court are quite narrow, they essentially have two choices in most cases; reverse or affirm.

The five principles of cognitive theory (inferential memory, consistency, reality, simplicity, and stability) also apply to judicial decision making. Judges use inferential memory to allow them to focus their attention on the important facts of a case. Their experience or judicial reaction supplies the general framework into which these facts may be placed. Inferential memory of the framework allows judges to focus their attention and other resources on a limited number of factors within their cognitive limits.

Consistency operates on two levels when considering the decisions of courts and judges. Like other humans, the judges operate to maintain the consistency of internal belief relationships. This implies that we can expect the decisions of judges to be consistent within a particular framework, such as a specific issue area (e.g., search and seizure) or a more general category of law (e.g., criminal procedure).

Consistency is also built into the judicial process. Although, as discussed above, courts and judges have a number of means at their disposal to avoid the necessity of following precedent, this does not give the judiciary a totally free hand. More than the other two branches of government, the judiciary must rely on the good will and respect of the people to maintain their standing. Along with the various trappings of the cult of the robe, consistency in their decision making is one of the most powerful generators of respect at their disposal. The Supreme Court's judicious use of the power to overrule previous decisions shows a recognition for the importance of consistency in their decision making.

The case analysis method keeps judicial decision making in touch with the environment in which the litigation arises. This reflects the reality principle. Judges must account for changes in the decisional environment. In order to make their decision, they must examine the facts of the situation in relation to the relevant law. A more important aspect of the reality principle is the ability of judges to adapt to radical changes in their decisional environment. The invention of electronic communications and wiretaps could not have been envisioned by the drafters of the Fourth Amendment. Nevertheless, when search and seizure issues involving wiretaps presented themselves the courts were able to adapt their decisional frameworks to include this new area of litigation.

Stability is closely related to consistency. The reality principle operates to keep judicial decision making in touch with the situational environment, but minor fluctuations in the environment are ignored. This results in the frameworks into which the important facts are placed for evaluation.

The final principle, simplicity, is an obvious one. Economy demands that judicial decision makers develop fast and simple methods of processing the voluminous amounts of information presented to them. One may observe that most judicial opinions are far from simple, especially to the layman uninitiated to the legal jargon. It must be remembered that the decision is made quite quickly and it is only the explanation of that decision which requires extensive amounts of time and verbiage.

Rohde and Spaeth (1976) and Spaeth (1979) set out the assumptions on which a theory of Supreme Court decision making is based. These assumptions fit well with cognitive-cybernetic theory and help to focus the theory on the realities of judicial decision making. Both sources describe the assumptions at length so they will only be summarized here.

The first assumption is that "actors in political situations are goal oriented . . ." (Rohde and Spaeth 1976:70). As set out above, judges are political actors. Goal orientation simply refers to the fact that the actors are not merely exhibiting random behavior; they have a goal they are trying to achieve. The goal that judges work toward is the attainment of their personal policy preferences (or their maintenance if the preferences are already embodied in the status quo).

The second assumption is that "an actor's choices will depend on the 'rules of the game'" (Rohde and Spaeth 1976:70). These rules refer to the basic structure of the system, the flow of communication, and where inputs and outputs enter and leave the system. With respect to the Supreme Court, only certain types of cases may be heard as set out in Article III of the Constitution. Rules also determine the procedure by which cases come before the Court.

Generally, the Supreme Court enjoys a fair amount of autonomy with respect to the rules of the game. Both Congress and the President must answer to an electorate on a periodic basis, whereas federal judges are essentially appointed for life.

Many state court judges must also answer to a constituency or at least higher courts. Even state supreme courts must answer to the United States Supreme Court on matters involving federal law and the U.S. Constitution. This autonomy of the Supreme Court allows it a great deal of freedom to pursue the personal policy goals of the justices.

A second category of rules relates to the particular area of the law that a case presents. For example, in cases involving search and seizure, the Fourth Amendment mandates a number of requirements before a search may be considered reasonable (Constitutional). Thus, the discussion in a search and seizure case must revolve around these requirements.

The third assumption is that "decisions are also dependent on particular situations" (Rohde and Spaeth 1976:71). The Court's decisions often require the balancing of competing interests which generally stem from the principle of "majority rule but minority rights." To strike a proper balance the Court considers a number of factors which have evolved from previous decisions. Like a designer who wishes to switch from building a kettle to a pan, when the Court makes decisions in different areas of law many of the same factors can be successfully employed. The specific manifestations of these factors in a particular area of law are the cues which the Court uses (as indicators of the factors) to strike the proper balance. Utilizing their training in case analysis, the justices examine the factual situations of cases for cues which indicate the decision which must be made in the case which best serves to advance the goals of the Court.

With these assumptions, we may examine the decisions of the Court to determine what factors influence the particular disposition of a case. These assumptions, resting on cognitive-cybernetic theory, form the "hard core" of this theory of judicial decision making (see Lakatos 1970:133–134).

Conclusion

Judicial decision making contains four essential characteristics of the cognitive-cybernetic model of decision making. The first characteristic is simplification. Simplification is desired to enable the judicial decision makers to stay abreast of their workload, but it is also a necessity imposed by human cognitive limitations.

Stable decision rules are the second characteristic. Such stable rules are a mainstay of judicial decision making. The internal belief systems of judges remain stable and decisions are made to maintain consistency. In addition, decisions in particular issue areas remain stable as part of the operative judicial process.

Third, there must be a focus on the attributes of a situation—i.e., its larger characteristics. The case analysis method and emphasis on the important facts of a case in relation to the important facts of previously decided related cases forces judicial decision makers to focus their attention on the attributes of the situation. Simplicity and economy also force this attention to be given to the gross characteristics. For example, in the area of search and seizure the fact that a search takes place in a home is a gross characteristic which is important. Whether the home is a two-room apartment or a 40-room mansion is a detail of no legal concern.

Finally, the decision maker must have a limited choice set. Again, a limited choice set is imposed by the human decision maker's cognitive limitations. However, if time and resources are available a large number of alternatives may be considered a few at a time. Judicial decision makers have neither the time nor the resources to consider many alternatives. Justices on the Supreme Court must make their decision on a case within two to three days after hearing oral argument (and they do not have the luxury of having only one case to decide at a time). In addition, the justices essentially have only two choices; reverse or affirm.

Although judicial decision makers can not and do not adhere to the comprehensive rational actor model, they are rational actors. To perform their tasks, given both cognitive and institutional limitations, judges find shortcuts for processing information and making decisions. The judicial decision making process, therefore, is best studied from a cognitive-cybernetic perspective which accounts for these limitations and adaptive strategies.

References

Brown v. Board of Education, 347 U.S. 483 (1954).
Flast v. Cohen, 395 U.S. 83 (1968).
Frothingham v. Mellon, 262 U.S. 447 (1923).
Lakatos, Imre. 1970. "Falsification and the Methodology of Scientific Research Programmes" in *Criticism and the Growth of Knowledge,* edited by Imre Lakatos and Alan Musgrave. Cambridge: Cambridge University Press.
Marbury v. Madison, 1 Cranch 137 (1803).
Plessy v. Ferguson, 163 U.S. 537 (1896).
Rehnquist, W. H. 1987. *The Supreme Court: How It Was, How It Is.* New York: Morrow

Ripple, K. F. 1980. "The Supreme Court's Workload: Some Thoughts for the Practitioner." *American Bar Association Journal,* 66:174-176.
Roe v. Wade, 410 U.S. 113 (1973).
Rohde, David W., and Harold J. Spaeth. 1976. *Supreme Court Decision Making.* San Francisco: W. H. Freeman and Company.
Simon, H. A. 1957. *Models of Man.* New York: John Wiley & Sons.
Simon, H. A. 1981. *The Sciences of the Artificial,* 2d edition. Cambridge: Massachusetts Institute of Technology Press.
Spaeth, Harold J. 1979. *Supreme Court Policy Making: Explanation and Prediction.* San Francisco: W. H. Freeman.
Statsky, William P., and R. John Wernet, Jr. 1977. *Case Analysis and Fundamentals of Legal Writing.* St. Paul:West Publishing Company.
Steinbruner, J. D. 1974. *The Cybernetic Theory of Decision.* Princeton: Princeton University Press.
Supreme Court of the United States. nd. *The Supreme Court of the United States.* Washington, D.C.: Supreme Court of the United States and the Supreme Court Historical Society, 1982+. (An informational phamplet available to visitors of the Supreme Court Building; no publishing date given)
Woodward, B., and S. Armstrong. 1979. *The Brethren.* New York: Simon and Schuster.

Chapter 10

The Politics of Administration

Douglas Madsen

A simple and useful way to describe what all governments do is to say that they formulate and execute public policy. By formulate I mean that governments decide which problems need their attention and what the nature of that attention will be. By execute I mean that governments must follow policy formulation with policy application and administration. Policies coming from "the top" do not execute themselves; they do not go into effect by some automatic process. A government must actively put them into effect, or they are very likely to wither and die. Note that all governments engage in the process of formulating and execute policy. This process, in fact, defines governing.

There are many familiar examples of this process in operation. In foreign affairs, we see some governments come to believe that other countries threaten their security. These governments respond with the formulation of national defense programs which civilian and military administrators carry out. In domestic affairs, we see some governments decide that rising unemployment is a problem that needs special attention. The government fashions a response—for example, a job re-training program, then puts it into the hands of the administrators for execution. At the local level, we see some county governments decide that uncontrolled urban sprawl is a serious problem and then respond with land-use plans and zoning rules which are to be implemented by county boards and agencies.

The conceptual distinction between formulating policy and executing policy is easy to draw. We have little trouble seeing that deciding on a policy is quite different from carrying it out. But this sometimes leads observers to believe that a similarly neat division of the process can actually be found in the real world. In fact, it cannot. The governmental process is not so tidy.

The first step in acknowledging this lack of tidiness is to confront the common misunderstanding that suggests that the conceptual distinction between policy formulation and policy execution has concrete application in the division between the legislative and executive branches of government. This mistaken point of view sees the legislature—whether it be the U.S. Congress, a state legislature, or a city council—as the policy-making body, and the administration as the policy-implementing body.[1]

Certainly elected officials do make laws. Moreover, it is equally true that their electoral connection with the citizenry makes them the legitimate agents for such law-making activities. There can be no representative democracy without that electoral connection, since this connection serves as the keystone of the popular control system which democracy represents. It is because of this electoral connection that legitimacy—that is, a sense of rightness—is accorded to the legislative process in a democracy.

But to say that elected officials make laws is not to say that they define what policy actually will be. There is a fundamental reason for the breakdown of the "elected officials as policy makers" and "administrative officials as policy executors" viewpoint. Elected officials are not omniscient. Consequently, they must usually make decisions under conditions of great uncertainty—first, uncertainty about the adequacy of the information upon which they are basing their decisions, and second, uncertainty about what the consequences of those decisions will be. Let us examine each of these problems in more detail.

Information Quality

Consider first the problem of adequacy of information. In making decisions, elected officials must rely on others for information. After all, our representatives cannot inform themselves in every policy area (or even in most such areas) that requires their vote in the course of their law-making activities. Most of the time their education and their experience before entering office provide little effective training for the decision-making roles they must take on. And given the range and complexity of the issues confronting them, elected officials cannot hope to become experts, or anything like experts, on most of the questions they face. In an attempt to reduce the immensity—indeed, the near-impossibility—of the tasks confronting them, they specialize through the committee system. Even in these reduced subject areas, however, expertise is very limited and reliance upon others—committee staff members, personal staff members, lobbyists, fellow politicians, and administrators—is necessary.

This reliance upon expert advisors raises a critical question: who is really making the laws—the legislators who cast the votes or the advisors who influence those legislators? Of course, this question cannot be answered in any general way. Circumstances vary. But for our purposes only one point need be made here: the administrators who will carry out a policy are also the very same officials who are quite likely to be influential advisors in the legislative process that creates that policy.

It should be added that legislative reliance upon administrative expertise is equally necessary when the time comes for evaluation of the consequences of past policy decisions. When elected officials need information about how well a program is working, they may seek testimony from ordinary citizens or from interest groups. But they surely will seek testimony from the administrators who have been intimately involved with that program, perhaps since its very inception. To do otherwise would plainly be irresponsible.

Once again, we see here the blurring of the administrative function. The administrator clearly does much more than simply carry out policy; he or she is closely involved in the policy-shaping and evaluation process as well. In fact, the administrator is critically important to the policy-making process. Consider the example of the U.S. Army. In the recent past there has been debate about the effectiveness of American ground forces, and that debate has had prominent representation in the Congress. When the Congress—or, more properly, its appropriate subcommittee—want information on Army readiness, to whom will it turn? By and large, Congress must turn to the Army itself, the very organization about which it wishes to make an objective judgment. In other words, it is the Army, or special units thereof, which must guide the Congress in the assessment of its performance and capabilities. Obviously, the Army is not a neutral observer. It has, both collectively and in its various components, very high stakes involved in the outcome of this evaluation. Hence, it can be expected to seek to protect itself, and even to use the occasion to promote its interests. The Army will attempt to "sell" its perspectives to the Congress (just as any other administrative unit of government would do).

Of course, the Congress is not naive on this point; it recognizes the fact that the Army has goals and will see its own needs and circumstances accordingly. But even so, the information dependency of the Congress remains, and the Army necessarily will remain the primary source of information in the evaluation process to be undertaken. Thus, the administrative unit is intimately involved in the creation of the very policies it will later be called upon to carry out.

Uncertainty about Effects

Consider next the problem of uncertainty about consequences of policy decisions. This aspect to the policy definition process is perhaps even more significant in muddying the distinction between policy makers and policy administrators than is the problem of getting adequate information. The reason lies in the character of most legislation. It is impossible for elected representatives, who as already noted cannot be experts on most of the policy questions they must address, to anticipate fully the nature of the problems administrators will face when putting public policies into effect. In other words, there is a great deal of uncertainty in any legislature about how policies will actually work. Consequently, most policy legislation will be cast in fairly general terms, and the fleshing out of those policies must be left to those who, by virtue of their direct and specialized knowledge, can make surer judgments of the likely outcomes. What this means is that the detailed versions of public policy must usually come from the administrators themselves.

Do not make the mistake of thinking this an unimportant point. Quite the opposite, the detailed administrative rules and regulations will in substantial part determine what the policy will be and who will benefit or be penalized and to what degree. In fact, the administrative part of the policy-definition process can be definitive to such a degree that the legislature itself finds the outcome surprising—sometimes far removed from what it had intended. In short, there can be no doubt that much policy-making goes on after the legislature has passed a law. Moreover, this policy-making by administrators *must* occur, given the nature of a legislature and the complexity of government.

Administrative officials, then, must make policy decisions. They must decide what a general policy will look like in its specific application. They cannot wait for legislative guidance on the specifics, for such guidance will almost never be forthcoming. But even were such guidance available, there is no reason to believe that it would be well received. Administrators, after all, are not simply neutral instruments for carrying out public programs. They have policy preferences. They have goals. They have career perspectives. And they can be expected to do their utmost to see to it that their views prevail. What this amounts to is a statement that administrators are not cogs in a machine. They are people, and like most people, they are concerned with self-promotion and self-esteem; they become attached to the causes they serve; they come to believe in the essential rightness of their mission, and they come to have strong views about how that mission should be carried out. All of this being the case, you can easily see why legislative interference with the discretionary authority of administrators would not be (and is not) well received.

Administrative Advocacy

Administrators become advocates for their agencies; and their advocacy can become quite passionate. The sense of urgency which accompanies this advocacy stems from their intimate awareness of the problems that might be solved and of the potential they believe might be realized if only "sufficient resources" were forthcoming from the legislative body. Consider the following example. Suppose you were a senior administrator in a county social welfare organization and had special responsibility for dealing with cases of child abuse. In the course of your work you regularly come into contact with heartbreaking and horrifying circumstances. Suppose further that the resources available to your agency do not permit the kind of individualized attention to cases which you believe necessary for effective therapy. What is more, you know there are many cases of abuse which, because of understaffing, you are unable to reach. Day after day these frustrations work away on you. When time comes for you to seek additional resources from the legislative body, it is unlikely that you would be reticent; and it is unlikely that you would be neutral; and most of all, it is unlikely that you would find it easy to accept any cutback, diversion, or freezing of your resource allocation. After all, you know what the problems (of your people) are like "out there"; you know what the needs are. We would expect your advocacy to be fervent; we would expect you to bitterly resist any interference with your program. Among your weapons in the struggle for greater resources would be information (get the "right" data to the legislators and to the mass media) and public support (mobilized through the mass media). Later you could possibly use your administrative rule-making authority to shape the program in the ways you believe necessary.

Imagine this kind of advocacy coming from each of the multitude of administrative units that operate in a government, and you can begin to see one of the critical problems of a representative democracy: how do elected representatives, who are dependent on other's for information and for compliance with policy, remain "on top" of the governmental process in fact as well as in name? For now, however, it is sufficient that we underscore a central point: when we say that administrators are not neutral, that they have policy preferences, and that they try to win on those preferences, what is being pointed to is the fact that in any complex governmental system, administration is (and must always be) an inherently political process. Put simply, administrators are politicians—they organize and mobilize followings, they struggle for power, they pursue policy preferences. Sometimes the administrative politician's goals are personal and narrow; other times they are programmatic and sweeping. But the key point is that the distinction between elected officials and administrators is not one between "politicians" and "neutral specialists"; rather, it is one between two different types of politicians, each of which makes public policy. In the case of the elected official, policy responsibilities are broader, expertise is more limited, and accountability to the citizenry is more enforceable. In the case of the administrative official, the opposite is true. These distinctions have very great importance for representative democracy.

Our primary concern here is with the administrative politicians of government. But it will be most useful for us now to turn to a general statement of organization theory. Such a theoretical overview will provide the broad perspective within which the more focused concerns can be placed.

Macroanalysis

There are two major ways of looking at complex organizations such as those found in government. The first is macroanalytic, the second microanalytic.[2] The perspective of macroanalysis is concerned with the organizational system as an adaptive unit. Here the organization is treated like an organism, simultaneously acting upon and being acted upon by its environment. For example, consider the Veterans Administration (VA). When it distributes educational, health, and pension benefits, it is acting upon its environment. More specifically, it is having a substantial impact upon one element of its environment: its "clientele"—those citizens who are receiving the benefits. By such action, the VA wins approval and support from that clientele. Such approval and support is likely to be communicated to elected representatives in the Congress (especially if the VA itself stirs up a campaign); the elected representatives, in turn, are perhaps more likely to vote additional budgetary resources to the VA since it seems to be doing so well. When additional resources come to the VA in this fashion, we can say that the environment is acting upon the organization. Keep in mind the fact that this interaction between an organization and its environment is a continuous process, not just an occasional event.

The term "environment," as used above, refers to all of the actors and circumstances outside the organization that influence its well-being. Among the actors might be included rival organizations, clientele groups, legislative committees, and other such groups. In addition, there are the larger social, economic, and political circumstances within which public organizations exist. Obviously, some elements of the environment are more immediately and directly important than others to an organization, but the often nebulous, large-scale factors can also have enormous impact, especially over the long run.

Organizations and Adaptation

In interacting with its environment, a public organization has many similarities to a biological organism. Organizations and organisms exist within environments fraught with threat and with opportunity. Both seek to find and exploit niches within which they can survive and flourish. For both, partly due to their own actions and partly due to outside factors, the environment can be expected to change in unpredictable ways (though the sense of unpredictability in the environment may be substantially muted both for organizations and for organisms in the short run). In this changing environment, adaptation is the key to survival.

Examples suitable to this comparison of organizations and organisms are easy to find in the private sector of American life. One can readily see that a small computer software firm, for instance, exists in an economic and technological environment fraught with danger—danger, that is, that the firm will lose out in the struggle for markets because of a failure to keep up with changing technology or to market its products effectively. Adaptation may call for modifications of the products being offered so as to gain access to a special market niche where economic security may be found. But note that any solution to environmentally-posed problems will always be temporary. The behavior of rivals, as well as a host of other environmental factors, can quickly change, threatening the firm's existence once again. There is need for continuous sensitivity to environmental change and, often, for an appropriate organizational response to such change.

Of course, not all organizations in the private sector are subject to the kind of tough competitive environment described for the software firm. In the case of a firm, or a few firms, dominating a market, the competition obviously may be muted. For example, the competitive environment to which General Motors has had to adapt since World War Two has not been until recently very threatening. Until the entrance in the last decade of foreign rivals, especially the Japanese, the environment to which GM was attentive involved not so much the behavior of other automobile producers as it did larger economic forces, raw materials prices, government anti-trust policy, tariff policy, EPA regulations, and the supply and cost of petroleum. However, the fact that rival firms were not hot on the heels of GM did not make its need for adaptation less pressing.

A commonly used example of adaptation outside both government and the profit-making sector of the society is the March of Dimes. Until the late 1950s, this charity organization raised money (very successfully) to support research on and treatment of polio. Its stated mission was to defeat polio. With the development of a vaccine against this disease in the late 1950s, its mission was accomplished. But this success carried with it the unhappy possibility of eliminating the need for the organization itself. It in no way diminishes the estimable purpose of the March of Dimes to recognize that this organization, like virtually all organizations, would not intend its own demise as a result of its success. Clearly, the organization needed to adapt to the dramatic change in the environment brought about by the vaccine discovery.[3]

The March of Dimes organization adapted by finding another worthy goal. The one it chose was fighting birth defects, a mission for which it has been raising money ever since. In other words, in the face of environmentally-posed danger to its existence, this organization did what it had to do: it found a new (and open-ended) justification for its continuance. It survived.

In the public sector, this aspect of the analogy to organisms may at first appear a bit strained. After all, it has become a part of conventional wisdom that organizational units in government never really go out of existence; they always seem to survive. This impression, however, is not entirely accurate. It is true that the complete disappearance of an established governmental organization is a rare event (most often tied to the end of a war or to a national crisis). But it is not so uncommon to see smaller public units be swallowed up by larger ones, or to see governmental reorganizations bring a number of previously autonomous units together under a single head. While such restructuring of units may not truly entail a question of survival, there still may be a very painful shift of decision-making authority to higher levels. Thus, although existence itself may not be threatened, a great deal of power may be lost; this is a fate which can substantially change the lives of affected units even if it does not mean their death.

If questions of organizational survival are at least blurred in the public sector, questions of organizational well-being are much less so. A very useful indicator of well-being is the amount of public resources that the organization is able to command. If the organization is "doing well" or is "secure" or is beyond the reach of its political enemies, its budget can be expected to reflect that condition. The rate of budgetary growth will at least match that of the government as a whole, and may even greatly exceed it. On the other hand, if the coalition of support for the organization has lost strength or if other organizations are more successful in their appeals for funding, the rate of budgetary growth may decline and possibly even reverse.

Organization and Environment

The immediate environment to which public organizations must adapt is the political marketplace. Dominating that marketplace are a number of very important actors, among them the elected chief executive, the legislature and its committees, clientele groups, other pressure groups, political parties, and so on. The struggle that goes on within that marketplace has a vital impact on the organization. Hence, it behooves the organization to do its utmost to influence the influential actors in a positive way so as to protect, and possibly to expand, its resources. We have already considered this situation briefly in the case of the Veterans Administration. In addition to the immediate environment, a public organization must also be cognizant of and responsive to changes in the larger context within which it must function. For example, the condition of the national economy is obviously relevant to the well-being of public organizations, just as it is to private ones and to individuals. There will be differential effects, with some units actually commanding a larger share of the public resources in times of economic reversal (e.g., unemployment insurance administration) but with others facing severe economic stringency. Social changes also can be important to public organizations, the coming of affirmative action programs in employment being an obvious example.

What do we mean here when we talk about "organization," or "organizational system," or simply "the system"? The definition is arbitrary; it depends on what unit we want to think about. For example, we might be interested in the strategic submarine service in the U.S. Navy. That submarine service will be "the organization" or "the system" we are to analyze. Everything outside that service—including the rest of the Navy, the rest of the Defense Department, the rest of the government, and so on—will be "environment." Once we have defined this "system" and its "environment," we can proceed with the analysis we want to make.

To offer another example, suppose we want to analyze the behavior of the organizational system called the U.S. Navy. That becomes the system of concern. Everything inside that system—including the submarine services, the Navy air force, the surface ship force, etc.—is subsumed under the general heading of "U.S. Navy"; none of these individual units is the object of the analysis. Everything outside that system (i.e., outside the U.S. Navy)—the rest of the Defense Department, the rest of government, the supplier organizations, and so on—will be "environment."

Or, with a still larger focus, consider treating "the Defense Department" as the system for analysis. Everything outside the Defense Department is "the environment." In fact, following the same conceptual approach, we could take as the system for analysis the entire government, and analyze the adaptive behavior of government in the larger environment. A graphic illustration of these alternatives in defining the system to study is given in Figure 10.1.

Where we draw the boundaries of the organizational system—that is, what we put inside this system and what we leave for the environment—depends entirely upon how we see the problem. There is no way to draw a single set of boundaries for every analysis. Moreover, even when we know what system it is that we wish to analyze, there often is some difficulty in knowing which elements

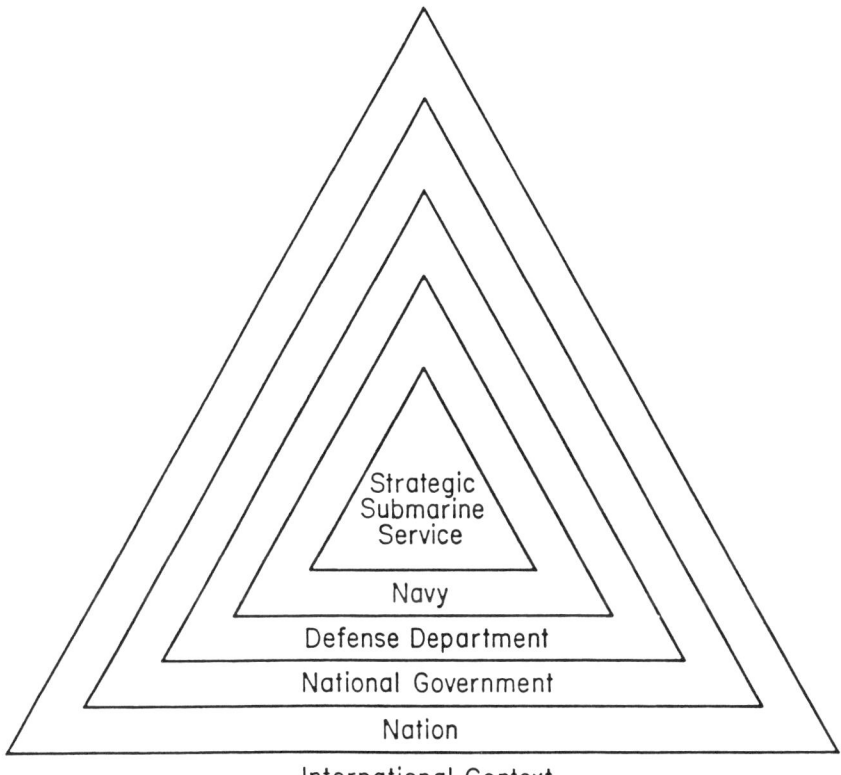

Figure 10.1. Systems Within Systems: Alternatives for Analysis

belong inside and which belong outside. For example, if the organizational system we wish to analyze is a university, it seems simple enough to decide that faculty and administrators lie inside the system—but what about students? Are students part of the university system, or are they the clientele of that system and, thus, part of the environment? And where would we locate activist alumni groups? You can see that some of these decisions are not perfectly straightforward.

Before moving on, let us consider one more example of systems-within-systems so that no misunderstanding exists about focusing on an organizational system for analysis. Remember, where one draws the boundaries of the system depends on what one wishes to analyze. Suppose you want to analyze the adaptive behavior of the political science department of a university. This department, then, becomes the system. All other university departments, the remainder of the university, and everything that exists outside it, become the environment. But you might wish to take a different focus in your analysis, such as the college of liberal arts (which includes the political science department, among many others). In this perspective the college of liberal arts is the adaptive unit, following policies which are intended to enhance its well-being in the environment it confronts. That environment would include other divisions of the university—the business college, the law college, the medical college, and so on—as well as the various actors outside the university and the larger circumstances in which all are embedded. Or, moving to a still larger focus, the analysis might take the university as a whole as the adaptive unit. Again, we can specify elements of the relevant environment within which the university must act, among them competitor colleges and universities, legislative bodies, and so on.

Note that when we take the behavior of the organizational system as our concern, we do not deal with the activities of individuals and groups within that system. Instead we focus on the interaction of the system with its environment. This is not because we believe that no important causes of the organization's behavior can be found through the investigation of processes within that system, but rather because we are taking a larger perspective in order to address different questions. In this larger way of looking at organizations we see how the system as a whole responds to different kinds of environmental stimuli, and how the system as a whole affects the environment within which it is trying to survive and flourish. We think in terms of inputs to the system and outputs from the system, without taking up questions about how the inputs flow through and the outputs emerge from that system.

Perhaps an analogy will make this clear. When we wish to analyze the behavior of individual people—whether in a formal scientific way or in an informal everyday way—we usually treat the individual actor as the behaving entity. We are concerned with how that actor responds to environmental stimuli and how the environment is changed by his or her actions. We are not likely to be concerned with the various sub-systems of that individual. (For example, we do not investigate the behavior of his neural or muscular systems.) Whatever is going on within that individual, even though it may be important to explaining behavior, is set aside as beyond our immediate concern. And this focus on the individual actor usually serves us quite well even though we remain ignorant of many of the internal mechanisms involved in producing the behavior in question. In the same way, a focus on organizational systems as behaving entities can also serve us well for many theoretical purposes.

As already noted, this larger focus for the study of organizations is called a macroanalytic perspective. It is contrasted with the study of individual actors within organizations, which is called a microanalytic perspective. Of course, the distinction between micro and macro here is relative. If we were investigating the huge organization called the Department of Defense (our macro focus), we might take as the actors within this organization the individual agencies or bureaus which, though not individual persons, nonetheless would represent micro units in this analysis. If, on the other hand, we were investigating a rural county welfare office (a macro focus, even though this unit is much smaller than our micro units in the previous analysis), the micro units here would probably be individual persons. This reflects my earlier point: where we draw the boundaries around a system (the macro unit) depends on what we want to analyze. Once the boundaries are drawn, the components within the system are micro units. In other words, in an analysis what is macro and what is micro depend on how we look at things.

Microanalysis

Microanalysis of organizations brings us to consider the behavior of individuals or groups within the system of interest. In the macroanalytic perspective it was sufficient simply to proceed with the assumption that an organization is an adaptive system. But here we are interested in the internal processes through which that adaptation takes place. Who actually makes the decisions that lead to adaptation? How are these decisions carried out? How is the information base for decision-making created and validated? These are the kinds of questions that microanalysis poses.

Goals: Organizational and Personal

A useful point of departure in gaining an understanding of this approach to organizations is the statement by James March, a leading student of organizations, that individual people have goals, but collectivities (like organizations) do not. What is meant here is that individual people are the fundamental building blocks of all collective units, be these units simple groups or complex organizations. If we reduce the systems viewpoint discussed earlier to its simplest terms, we are dealing with the individual person, the most fundamental adaptive unit in any social, economic, or political context. This means that it is only through a combination of individual people's goals that a collective goal emerges. This is a fundamental point.

However, do not misunderstand: March is not saying that organizations do not offer general statements as to their intentions. Instead he is focusing on what organizations actually do (rather than what they say they will do) and more specifically, on where the decisions come from which determine that behavior. He is saying that such decisions come from all members of the collectivity, and through a combination of these decisions the organizational direction—that is, its goal in a concrete behavioral sense—emerges. Of course, we all know this with respect to our own personal lives; even though we may be members of a group or organization, we still continue to have personal goals of our own, goals which we pursue both inside and outside the group or organizational context. The general point that follows, then, is that people, even when they seem wholly committed to an organization, are operating on the basis of personal goals. It is where those personal goals overlap that the basis for collective action exists. But remember that any overlap is always partial and always subject to change. Hence, there is a dynamic to organizational goal setting which simply reflects March's point: individuals have the goals, and it is only through the amalgamation of individual goals that an organizational goal emerges.

Since the fundamental units of organizations are individuals, the discovery that organizations strive to survive means that the individuals in an organization have in the main agreed upon this goal—that is, their personal goals overlap here to yield the organizational perspective. Usually the agreement on survival is implicit, but from time to time we see members explicitly confronting a threat to an organization's existence by taking dramatic actions (such as substantially cutting their own pay) in order to keep the organization going.

Although it may be relatively easy to get agreement from organization members on the need for organizational survival, the question of "survival for what?" is much harder to work out. One can go one step further and get agreement on a goal like "maximizing profits" in a private organization or "serving the public interest" in a public one, but the all-important matter of how remains. It obviously is much simpler to get agreement on vague and general statements of purpose that have no clear operational implications than to get such agreement on specific and operational ones which do. And noble-sounding goals are always easy to endorse.

Thus, the official statement of purpose for most governmental units will amount to little more than one or another version of "serving the public interest." We might, for example, expect to see a public education administrative unit state its official purpose as seeing to it that all citizens have access to the best education available anywhere. Or a public housing organization may state that its goal is that all citizens live in decent housing. Or a public health organization might have the goal of seeing to it that all Americans enjoy good health. All of these goals sound worthy—and that is exactly the purpose of such "advertised" goals. They justify the organization to its environment—that is, they help convince the citizenry and its representatives of the importance of the organization itself.[4] But note carefully that we cannot tell from such statements of purpose what the organizations will in fact be doing. Again, the question is how. How will education be provided? How will decent housing be made available? How will public health be improved? It is here at the operational level of goal setting that the personal goals of individual organization members will be involved in the process that determines which activities the organization will actually pursue.

It could be reasonably argued, of course, that the concrete actions taken by an organization do not tell us what the agreed-upon goal of that organization is, but rather what the agreed-upon means to that goal are. In this argument, the goal is service to the public interest, and the means are the specific actions to be undertaken to accomplish this goal. We could also take this argument one step further and say that the goal of the organization is survival, and service to the public interest is only the means through which that end will be achieved. But however we approach this, the point is that when an organization gets to the operational version of its statement of ends or means, conflict is likely to emerge. It is not hard to understand why this should be so. The operational statement gives the first relatively clear indication of who will and who will not benefit (both inside and outside the organization) by what the organization plans to do. As noted earlier, there are egos and careers involved here; beyond that, there are programmatic concerns and values.

Perhaps an illustration will help at this point. Consider the case of the U.S. Forest Service. Let's suppose you were part of the conservation movement that was strong on campuses during the late 1960s. You decided to join the Forest Service during that period, attracted by the opportunity to help conserve the nation's natural resources and wilderness areas. You found it easy to embrace the Forest Service's advertised purpose—"to manage the nation's forests in the interests of the American people" (or words to that effect). To you, that statement of purpose translated clearly and directly into conservation, and you were all for that. Moreover, let's suppose that the Forest Service leadership was also inclined toward conservation—perhaps not as much as you would have liked, but still basically on "the right side."

In the 1970s, however, two features of the national economy changed. First, housing costs soared, and private housing started becoming prohibitively expensive for many Americans. Second, the nation's balance of payments with Japan deteriorated drastically. The first development set off cries to make housing affordable again. These cries came from prospective home owners who had been forced out of the market. They also came from contractors and workers who, with the downturn of the housing starts, were forced out of work. One way to help, it was argued, would be to bring down the cost of lumber and wood products. And the way to do that would be to harvest more of the national forests. If the harvests from the national forests were much larger (and carried out efficiently through clear-cutting), the argument continued, the lumber market would reflect this surge in supplies, and prices would come down. Homes would be more affordable, housing starts would increase, jobs would be restored, and so forth.

The second change, the negative balance of payments with Japan, also inspired a call for large harvests from the national forests. Japan is a major customer for North American lumber and wood products. The more we could sell to Japan, it was argued, the closer we could come to a zero trade deficit. Hence, the well-being of the national economy would be enhanced by harvesting the national forests and selling the wood to Japan.

These new pressures on the Forest Service could well result in a new definition for the 1980s of what it means to "manage the national forests in the interests of the American people." But that would not mean that you had changed your orientation. With your commitment to conservation and wilderness preservation, you might be expected to fight in every way you could to sidetrack these new pressures. Moreover, you would no doubt find it difficult to work with those of your colleagues who "sold out" to the commercial point of view. One way to attempt to advance your views as to the Forest Service's proper purpose would be to get the right kind of information to the top, where key decisions will be made. Another would be to quietly do your utmost in your own day-to-day work to sidetrack any harvesting inclinations that might emerge from the top. In any case, you would keep fighting as long as there was any chance for you to make a difference.[5]

Organizational Goals, Bargaining, and Conflict

This example illustrates the point that individual people have goals of their own. It also shows how those goals may be maintained in the face of organizational directives which are in conflict with them. But how do such conflicts get resolved, or at least resolved to the extent that an organizational direction is established? If every participant has goals of his own, how are those goals brought into a coherent whole? The answer is that in decisions about the concrete policies an organization will follow, agreement is reached and conflict resolved through a political process. What is involved is bargaining and trading among the influential members and groups within the organization until an alliance is formed that has within it sufficient power to impose its concrete policy views on the rest of the organization. In other words, this bargaining process brings into existence a dominant coalition, the members of which for reasons of their own come to embrace a particular statement of what the organization actually will do.

Of course, not all participants in an organization have the same amount of influence in this process. Key members of the organization are highly influential, perhaps by virtue of the authority which attaches to their organizational roles, perhaps by virtue of their indispensability, or perhaps both. Moreover, the weight of an individual player in this bargaining game can be very substantially enhanced if he or she speaks for many others, as might be the case with sub-unit heads or with union leaders.

As the bargaining proceeds, each player may be thought of as having an agenda which lists the set of operational activities he or she wants the organization to carry out. But no player can get everything he wants. Each will have to be prepared to give and take, sacrificing some activities in order to get other players to support his remaining preferences. Needless to say, some players are more successful than others. In short, this is a mutual "back scratching" process up to the point where an alliance of sufficient power emerges. This dominant coalition will then guide organizational life for a time.

It is important to recognize, however, that this political process never ends. A dominant coalition emerges in a particular set of circumstances, environmental and internal. When those circumstances are altered, this alliance may be weakened and even fall apart. For example, changes in internal circumstances, such as the departure of key members from the organization or the adoption of new technology, can undermine the stability of the dominant coalition. And changes in the environment, as when rival organizations achieve great success or when larger economic circumstances turn sour, can have the same effect. In sum, in this conflict-resolving political process, there is continual activity that, at least in the short run, determines the operational direction of the organization and, hence, its adaptive strategies in the larger environment.

Not all conflict within an organization can be resolved through this political process. There will be those who completely lose out in this process, after all, and although some of them will go along with the outcome (perhaps waiting for more propitious circumstances to renew their struggle), others may find the organizational direction unacceptable. When those most unhappy leave the organization, conflict levels, of course, decline. Other dissidents often will be isolated within the organization or possibly be fired. Those members who feel only mildly unhappy with the organizational direction can often be persuaded to go along, at least in the short run. But for those on the losing side who are of great value to the organizational effort—that is, those who although outside the dominant coalition are nonetheless indispensable to the organization—there may be a need to offer special inducements, such as material benefits and special prerogatives, to keep them from leaving and to keep their performance levels high.

Those in charge of an organization also attempt to control internal conflict by careful recruitment and by socialization of new members. Finding "the right people" means more than simply locating individuals with appropriate skills, especially in the higher echelons of the organization. Perspective on the organization and its mission must be correct. The proper spirit must be present. Once such people are identified and hired, they are brought into further congruence with the organization through a variety of formal and informal socialization methods. In a sense, they are asked to embrace the organizational "creed." The result should be new members who identify with, and who are committed to, the organizational goals being maintained by the dominant coalition. Of course, one must remember that all of these selection and shaping efforts are highly imperfect; in fact, the agents socializing new members often do not pull in the same direction. Still, such efforts do help to reduce potential conflict within the organization, at least in the short run.

With a dominant coalition firmly in place in an organization, one still cannot assume that it is possible to control fully the organization's internal activities and output. It is one thing to be theoretically in charge, to be theoretically able to set the organizational course; it is another to have decisions actually carried out. Here we come back to the problem discussed earlier: how to be on top in fact as well as in name. The first part of this problem is information dependence: where do the organization's "rulers" get the reliable information they need to make decisions? The second part is compliance: how do leaders get others to do their bidding?

A crucial—and inevitable—problem is distortion in information channels. As information flows from the top of an organization downward, one kind of distortion is random. It is well illustrated by the children's game, "Tell It To Your Neighbor," where a message is started through a chain of children, and each one passes it on to the next until the message has reached the last child. Comparison of the message that was started through this chain and the message that emerges at the end usually shows them to be very different, if indeed the final message is not sheer gibberish. Distortion here is accidental and unpatterned. The second kind of distortion is systematic—that is, the bias that occurs in the passage of information from one link in the organizational network to the next goes in the direction of the interests of those doing the passing. This may be inadvertent or deliberate. If deliberate, it often will be undertaken in the name of the public interest, or decency, or justice, or good policy.

I do not mean to suggest that more personal motives—ego, career, etc.— are unimportant. But you will miss the point here if you assign all or even most information distortion to such motives.[6] Remember in this context that organizational members have goals of their own; they have policies that they truly believe in; they have clienteles they wish to help. It does not take any assumption of low integrity in the civil service to explain the massive amount of information shaping and distortion that goes on in a government organization. Indeed, quite the opposite: our focus can be on high purposes, noble callings, and selfless endeavors. Think of our earlier illustration of the conservationist in the Forest Service.

Hierarchy and Independence

Getting good and timely information is one of the great problems of organizational management. It is obviously critical to effective decision-making, and hence, to organizational adaptation. However, even if good information is available and effective decisions are made, no good can come from these decisions if the organization members charged with carrying them out are unwilling to comply. Organization managers must have effective control systems if intended behaviors are to be forthcoming from subordinates in reliable fashion. Once again, this returns us to the question of conflict. A fundamental requirement in gaining compliance is that the members in the various strata of the organization be willing to give that compliance. That will not always be the case. Of course, it is sometimes true that decisions are so little understood and so poorly spelled out that compliance is impossible. But setting that circumstance aside, we are here concerned with the possibility of willful non-compliance of the type mentioned earlier in our Forest Service illustration.

Some of the ways organization managers try to cope with such "independence" have already been noted: selective recruitment, careful socialization, special inducements for compliance, and so on. In addition, there is the regular use of rewards (promotions, pay increases, praise, medals, or whatever) and punishments (the absence of rewards, or even demotions and firings) to gain sufficient levels of compliance. The effective use of rewards and punishments presupposes an organizational structure in which supervision is sufficiently close so as to permit timely assessment of good or bad performances by organization members. Put differently, it presupposes the presence of hierarchy. And, in fact, hierarchical structure is the norm in both private and public organizations, with each stratum monitoring and evaluating the performance of that below it so that in summary (and somewhat idealized) form, the organization can be thought of as a large triangular structure such as that shown in Figure 10.2.

There may be variations in the structure represented in Figure 10.2. For example, the base may be narrower for some organizations and wider for others. And some divisions of an organization may not fit neatly into this triangle of power and authority. Moreover, such a structure surely does not reflect the informal influence paths within an organization. But for our purposes it will be useful to think of organizations in such triangular terms, with each stratum having greater authority and greater supervisory responsibility than the one beneath

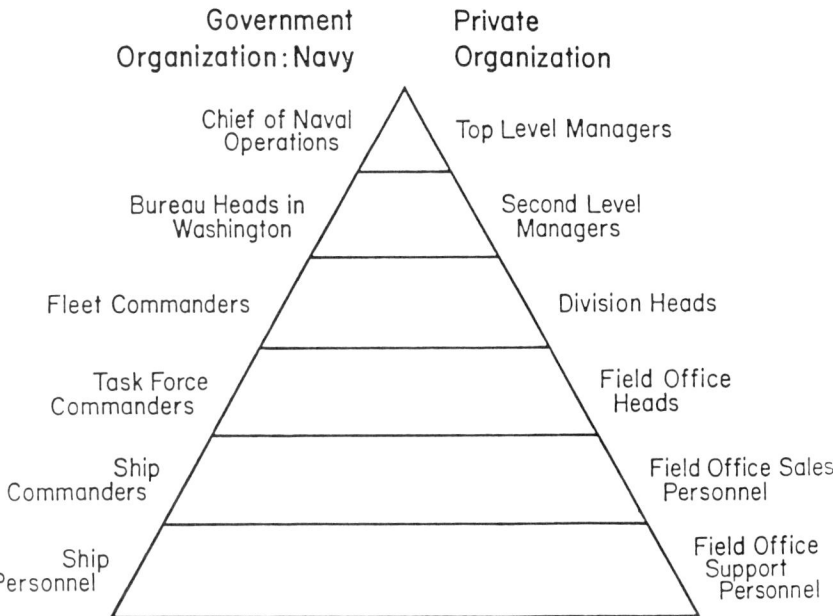

Figure 10.2. Hierarchical Organizational Structures

it. Thus, the monitoring and enforcing of compliance within the organization aggregates upward to the peak of the structure.[7]

While the hierarchical structure of an organization plainly promotes compliant behavior from organization members, it does not ensure it. As we all should know, supervision can be a difficult art, and monitoring the behavior of organization members is imperfect at best. What is more, there are important informal aspects of organizational life which influence both those doing the monitoring and those being monitored. Group norms are important. Larger contextual circumstances can be significant factors as well.

A summary perspective on the constraints operating on individual behaviors within an organization is found in the notion of the organizational role system. This perspective argues that organizational roles are like roles in a play; they are intended to be performed pretty much the same way no matter who the actor may be. In a play the constraints upon the role performance include the story line, the required dialogue, and the performances of the other actors. In an organization the constraints are the nature of the work, and the activities and expectations of those surrounding the organization member in the role. Constraining factors in the nature of the work include the flow of that work, something normally beyond the control of the role performer.[8] In addition, there is the character of the work itself, which in lower level roles is more fixed or programmed and in higher level roles is more discretionary.

The ways in which the performances of other organizational actors constrain the behavior of a role player are a bit more complicated. What is involved is the myriad interactions between that player and those with whom he or she works. These interactions, of course, are related to the nature of the work, and they help to impose the work flow. But beyond that, they act both formally and informally to limit the range of "acceptable" actions a role player may engage in. There is the general view that one must do things "the right way." And one must behave "properly" in non-work activities on the job as well. A great deal of social pressure can be brought to bear by fellow workers to enforce these expectations; and as already noted, management in a more formal way also acts to enforce role behavior. (But we should not assume that the pressure exerted by management and that exerted by fellow workers always goes in the same direction.)

Let's take a concrete example of how role performance is enforced in an organization. Suppose you had been working for several years in the juvenile division of an urban police department. With your partner you had been dealing with cases of juvenile delinquency of one kind or another. You had during these years worked out a standard way of proceeding, one which had evolved in the course of handling hundreds of cases, and one which you and your partner believed to be both efficient and effective. Now let's suppose that your partner is transferred and that you have been assigned a new partner. The police department has recruited and trained this new person to be right for the job. But the novice has a lot to learn. You begin the socialization process with the goal of producing a new partner who is as much as possible like the one you had worked with before. You explain your standard procedures, and if necessary, enforce them through unofficial and perhaps even official means. You convey a way of looking at the job and the organization. Others in the juvenile division also "work on" the new partner, shaping the newcomer to fit in. What is being sought here is a replacement for and like your old partner. The organization is also looking for much the same thing (assuming that the old partner was an effective worker).

This process of shaping role structures goes on at all levels in all organizations. The role structure gives the organization its patterned behavior; in turn, patterned behavior helps the dominant coalition gain compliance. In other words, the predictability of behavior within the organization is directly related to the strength of its role system.

However, your own experience probably tells you that no organization is left entirely unchanged by new personnel. Role constraints are sure to be imperfect. Thus, change in an organization, to greater or lesser degree, comes with change in its members. If the member change comes in the lower echelons where roles are substantially programmed, then the resulting change in the organizational functioning may be minimal. But if the member change comes at the top (e.g., in the dominant coalition), where roles permit much more discretionary behavior, then the change in organizational functioning can be very great indeed. Finally, if an organization faces a large number of personnel changes at one time, even in the lower echelons, there may be substantial modification of organizational functions; here, the power of the role structure is simply not sufficient to cope with the recruitment and socialization requirements.

Information and control are major foci in microanalysis. Moreover, they are the key problems of management. They are problems partly because of human error but perhaps more because of the fact that individual people, as I have often pointed out here, have goals of their own. Thus, the dominant coalition within an organization must continuously strive to enforce its will so that its definition of organizational purpose will be a description of what the organization actually does. This problem never goes away.

A final point: sometimes the human nervous system is used as a model of the information/control problems and processes for organizations. There clearly are parallels. For example, in the human nervous system information flows from sensors (touch, smell, taste, vision, etc.) to decision-making centers in the brain; so, too, in organizations—information about the environment flows from those who are responsible for assessing that environment to those who are responsible for fashioning policies to cope with it. Another example: in human nervous systems, the simpler and more routine problems are dealt with at lower levels of the brain, whereas the complex and novel problems involve higher cortical centers. Similarly, in organizations, the simple and routine problems are solved in sub-units, but the complex and novel ones involve top management. But, it seems to me, there is one fundamental difference between organizations and the human nervous system. The individual neurons of the nervous system are not in business for themselves; they do not have careers to defend; they do not have egos; they do not become committed to particular decisional outcomes and shape their information accordingly.[9] Hence, the political problems of organizations have no counterpart in the human nervous system.

Notes

1. At the state or national level, the governor or president is usually grouped with the legislators in this argument since, like them, he or she is an elected official; hence, the true distinction being drawn here is usually one between elected officials and non-elected officials. This is the distinction we will emphasize.
2. Although our main concern is with public organizations, you will see that these perspectives are for the most part equally suited to the examination of large private organizations.
3. If you think about this in personal and concrete terms, the meaning and importance of survival here will become quite clear: suppose that you had worked for the March of Dimes for 20 years, that you were good at your job, that you found the work satisfying, and that the chances of finding similar employment elsewhere were not good. Obviously, you would not want to see the March of Dimes go out of business, even though you were wholly committed to the fight against polio.
4. This public interest claim also may be well-received by the organization's members; after all, it is satisfying to be associated with a worthy purpose.
5. Ronald Reagan in his first term, encountered a similar phenomenon in environmental protection. Ordered by President Reagan to desist from unnecessary and obnoxious regulation of private industry—which, in effect, meant all regulation—the Environmental Protection Agency (EPA) proceeded to increase almost every aspect of its regulatory activity, both in frequency and severity.
6. Such a view may lead to the idea that to correct the problem all that is needed is civil servants of higher integrity. That argument, which we will take up later, does not deal with the more serious problem.
7. And just as there can be systems within systems, as noted in the earlier discussion of macroanalysis, there also can be triangles of authority within triangles, as with sub-units of organizations.
8. This is most pronounced in assembly line work, but it is also a major influence on other types of work as well. Consider, for example, the work flow for a college professor as established by the academic schedule.
9. But here is the level of analysis issue again, perhaps with a vengeance. Dawkins (1976) argues that all biological entities, including us, may be understood as survival machines that exist for the primary purpose of protecting and perpetuating their "selfish genes."

References

Dawkins, Richard. 1976. The Selfish Gene. (New York: Oxford University Press).

Part 4

The Public Policy Outcome

Chapter 11

Inside Games, Outside Games, and the Common Defense: Congress and National Defense

James M. Lindsay

Article I, Section 8 of the Constitution of the United States of America grants to Congress the power "to provide for the common defense," "to raise and support armies," and "to provide and maintain a navy." Although Congress' power to provide for the common defense is well-established, *how* Congress decides defense issues changed dramatically in the five decades after World War II. In the 1950s and 1960s Congress generally altered few Department of Defense (DoD) requests and Congress routinely disposed of the annual defense authorization and appropriations bills with little debate and few floor amendments. In contrast, in the 1980s extensive changes in budget line items, lengthy floor debates, and a blizzard of floor amendments were the norm for DoD bills.

Three developments account for the growth in Congress' interest in defense issues. First, the rise of the annual authorization process increased the *opportunities* for legislators to intervene in defense issues. Second, the increased political volatility of defense policy in the 1970s and 1980s expanded the *incentives* legislators have to address defense issues. Third, the congressional reforms of the 1970s eroded the institutional constraints on the behavior of members of Congress. This gave lawmakers greater *freedom* to participate in the defense debate.

These changes in opportunities, incentives and freedom in turn changed the nature of congressional decision making. In the 1950s and 1960s, congressional decision-making was an "inside game."

The most senior members, and especially the chairs, of the defense committees—the Armed Services Committees and the Defense Appropriations Subcommittees—dominated Congress' handling of defense policy. In the 1970s, the congressional reform movement dispersed power on Capitol Hill and strengthened the subcommittee system within the Armed Services Committees. This produced a decentralized variant of the inside game where more committee members participated in decision-making but the defense committees continued to dominate the congressional defense debate. In the 1980s, an "outside game" emerged in Congress. The defense committees remained the major players but their parent chambers circumscribed their freedom of action.

Overview of Congress and Defense Policy

In broad terms, Congress has the power to do three things on defense policy. First, Congress can *approve* the defense programs the executive proposes. It may do this either because it agrees with the administration's defense plans or because it chooses not to involve itself in defense policy. Second, Congress can *modify* the programs the executive requests. At one extreme, Congress can refuse to fund a program, and, at the other extreme, it can direct the Pentagon to initiate a program. Between these two poles, Congress can order DoD to revise elements of a program while still accepting its main outlines. Third, Congress can *focus attention* on issues in defense policy. It can direct the administration to review programs and to study potential deficiencies in the force structure as well as possible remedies. Also, media coverage of congressional hearings and debates can inform the broader public of the issues at stake.

The main vehicle Congress has to influence defense policy is the defense budget. Today the annual defense budget process on Capitol Hill consists of three stages. In the first or budget resolution cycle, Congress assesses national priorities and sets an overall ceiling on defense spending. By statute, Congress should adopt a budget resolution by May 15 each year. During the second or authorization cycle, Congress authorizes individual programs and establishes expenditure ceilings for these programs. Ostensibly, at this stage defense goals and priorities are matched with the programs designed to achieve them. In the last or appropriation cycle, Congress sets the actual funding levels for defense programs. This final cycle should be completed by October 1, the start of the fiscal year.

Two aspects of the defense budget process merit emphasis. First, the fact that Congress' main tool to influence defense policy is the budget process underscores the dominance of DoD in setting the policy agenda. DoD prepares the requests for programs; Congress may choose to revise DoD's plans, but legislators are not responsible for drafting their own defense budget. As a result, Congress' actions on the defense budget generally involve oversight rather than the drafting of legislation. Second, the authorization and appropriation cycles are the most important stages of the budget process for individual weapons programs. The budget cycle establishes the total level of defense spending. It does not deal with individual programs. In contrast, the authorization and appropriation cycles determine the *composition* of defense spending. In these two cycles Congress reviews the individual programs or line items in the defense budget.

By virtually any empirical indicator one examines congressional involvement in defense policy grew dramatically in the five decades after the end of World War II and especially in the 1980s. One aspect of growing congressional intervention in defense policy was the shift by the defense committees in the 1970s and 1980s to more detailed reviews of DoD requests. Changes in the nature of defense committee hearings illustrate the shift. A former assistant secretary of defense writes that in the 1950s and 1960s "Few committee members attend[ed] defense budget hearings. Few, if any prepare[d] for the hearings. Few regard[ed] the hearings as a crucial part of the legislative process." As late as 1969 the Services commonly supplied committee members with lists of questions to ask at the hearings. [This practice fell into disuse after one defense committee member drank too much at lunch and read both the supplied question and answer.] This attitude explains why in 1968 the Senate Appropriations Defense Committee (SADS) could complete its review of the multi-billion dollar antiballistic missile (ABM) program in a morning. The laissez faire attitudes the defense committees displayed disappeared in the mid-1970s as all the defense committees began to hold more and longer hearings on defense requests that included testimony for the first time from civilian defense experts. Indeed, by the 1980s some committee members believed the pendulum had swung too far in the other direction; they believed the defense committees were being swamped by testimony.

The other aspect of growing congressional intervention on defense policy took place on the floor of the House and Senate. During the 1950s and 1960s floor challenges to the defense committees were rare. Typically the annual defense authorization bills passed after less than a day of floor debate. On those rare occasion when nonmembers challenged the recommendations of the defense committees, those willing to oppose the defense committees seldom numbered more than a handful. Floor debate rose sharply in 1969, stimulated largely by congressional disillusionment over the Vietnam War, and remained at this level before dropping off somewhat in the mid-1970s. In the 1980s floor activity again soared. By the end of the decade the House and Senate typically spent two weeks debating various facets of the defense authorization bill. Indeed, legislators began to offer so many amendments that by the late 1980s the defense committees had to resort to a variety of formal and informal steps to limit the number of amendments so that Congress could get on to other business.

The increased committee and floor activity meant that Congress became much more likely to alter DoD's requests. Some simple statistics illustrate this point. In 1969 Congress changed 180 line-item requests in the defense authorization bill and 650 requests in the appropriations bill. In 1975 these figures stood at 222 and 1,032. In 1986 Congress changed 1,343 line items in the authorization bill and 2,079 changes in the appropriations bill. This represents a seven-fold increase in changes to the defense authorization bill and a threefold increase in changes to the appropriations bill. Other congressional directions to DoD also have jumped. In 1969 Congress requested 36 reports from the Pentagon, directed 18 other actions, and changed 64 provisions in the law. By comparison, in 1985 Congress requested 680 reports (an increase of 1779 percent), mandated 571 other directions (3072 percent), and made 236 changes in the law (269 percent).

Why did Congress' interest the defense budget increase so much? One major reason was the rise of the annual authorization process. In the 1950s the Armed Services Committees examined individual programs only in the case of military construction, which constituted roughly three percent of the defense budget. For the remaining 97 percent of the budget the Armed Services Committees provided so-called lump-sum authorizations. This legislation was no more specific than "the Secretary of the Air Force may procure guided missiles and 24,000 serviceable aircraft." In 1959, however, Congress passed legislation that stipulated that all appropriations after 1960 for the procurement of aircraft, missiles, and naval vessels had to be preceded by specific annual authorizations. Over the next two decades Congress gradually extended the annual line-item authorization to the entire defense budget.

The growth of the annual authorization process partly reflects the Armed Services Committees' efforts to gain legislative power. In the 1950s the Defense Appropriations Subcommittees were the pre-eminent congressional actors on defense policy. The Armed Services Committees exercised less power because their lump-sum authorizations generally far exceeded DoD requests. DoD was far more solicitous of the Defense Appropriations Subcommittees because the Subcommittees examined individual programs and on occasion changed Pentagon requests. Members of the Armed Services committees therefore reasoned that if they began to review programs on a line-item basis then they would have a greater say in determining defense policy.

The Armed Services Committees also fought to extend the authorization process to limit the power of the Office of the Secretary of Defense (OSD). In the 1960s Secretary of Defense Robert McNamara implemented a series of management reforms designed to improve defense planning by concentrating more power in the civilian staff members of OSD. The Services bitterly opposed McNamara's reform package because the changes curtailed their traditional autonomy. Members of the Armed Services Committees strongly supported the Services and denounced what they saw as "pointy-headed bureaucrats" in OSD. The Armed Services Committees found annual line-item authorizations a useful tool for keeping watch over OSD and for providing opportunities to solicit the advice of the professional military.

The rise of the authorization process in turn stimulated the Defense Appropriations Subcommittees to increase their scrutiny of the defense budget. In part, this increased activity was automatic. Under House and Senate rules, appropriations cannot exceed authorizations, so funding cuts in the authorization cycle necessitate cuts by the Defense Appropriations Subcommittees. The rise of the authorization process also gave the Defense Appropriations Subcommittees an incentive to take a more activist role on defense policy. If the Subcommittees simply ratified authorization decisions, then the Armed Services Committees would become the major congressional actor on defense issues.

The emergence of annual line item authorizations means that Congress now has a twin-track decision-making process on the defense budget. The authorization and appropriations cycles now cover the same terrain, so Congress essentially decides defense requests twice each year. Although the degree of coordination and conflict between these two tracks varies at times, their growth expanded the opportunities for congressional intervention in defense policy.

The 1950s and 1960s—The Inside Game

The major congressional actors on defense policy during the 1950s and 1960s were the senior members of the defense committees, and especially the chairs of these committees. By virtue of congressional rules, these chairs had the power to create subcommittees, set committee agendas, choose committee staff, and manage defense bills on the floor. Moreover, congressional norms held that junior members would see their service as an apprenticeship and defer to committee leaders. These rules and norms produced an "inside game" in Congress, a closed decision-making style with relatively few participants. As a result, the senior members of the defense committees generally could command the support of Congress for their positions on defense matters.

The power of the committee chair was most obvious in the House Armed Services Committee (HASC), where Carl Vinson (D-Ga.) and his successor, L. Mendel Rivers (D-S.C.), ran the committees as their personal baronies. Both hearings and markups of the annual defense authorization bills were done in full committee, where Vinson and Rivers dominated deliberations. There were four standing subcommittees but they lacked formal jurisdictions and simply were numbered one through four. House rules gave the committee chair discretion in assigning legislation to subcommittees—discretion Vinson and Rivers often used to promote or bury legislation—which meant the subcommittees generally did the bidding of the chair. Junior members were expected to serve lengthy apprenticeships, sometimes as long as 10 years, before they were allowed to play a major role in committee business. Rep. Robert Leggett (D-Calif.) complained in 1969:

> But we have another thing on our committee [HASC]. It is called the policy committee . . . I have been on the committee only 4 1/2 years. I do not know who the members of the policy committee are . . . I have never seen a scratch of the pen before our committee authorizing what the policy committee does. I know that on the day of our committee markup it was reported to us

that the policy committee had recommended such and such with respect to all these various systems, but I have never heard one member of the policy committee . . . relate what was happening, relate an argument, or relate some of the democracy that has taken place on that very important committee.

When Leggett became too outspoken in his criticism, Rep. Rivers took to the floor to threaten to block defense programs intended for Leggett's district. Rivers was not reprimanded for this breach of House etiquette, implicitly demonstrating the power he wielded as committee chair.

The House Appropriations Defense Subcommittee (HADS) operated in a less autocratic fashion. Being a subcommittee itself, the chair controlled no subcommittee slots, and George Mahon (D-Texas), who chaired the subcommittee throughout the 1950s and 1960s, was less heavy-handed than his counterparts on HASC. Still, Mahon and the most senior members dominated the committee's deliberations. The subcommittee was small (generally 11 members) and there was little turnover among the members; of the five ranking Democrats on the subcommittee in 1961, four still sat on the subcommittee in 1969. By tradition, representatives were appointed to HADS only after they had served several terms in the House and on other Appropriations subcommittees and had demonstrated strong pro-defense views.

The Senate defense committees, like their House counterparts, were run from the top down. Sen. Richard Russell (D-Ga.), who chaired both SASC and SADS for most of the 1960s, not only dominated the Senate defense committees, he was widely considered the most powerful man in the Senate. As chair Sen. Russell possessed a wide range of formal powers to direct the operations of the committee. In the case of SASC, the full committee marked up all defense legislation, and none of the subcommittees had standing responsibility for any element of the authorization bill or any major aspect of defense policy. As in the House, the norms of apprenticeship and deference to the committee chair were strong. According to Sen. Thomas McIntyre (D-N.H.), who joined SASC in 1964: "Russell and the senior members would sit way down at one end of the table and the junior members would sit at the other end. I'm partially deaf in my right ear and I couldn't even hear what the hell was going on. Finally one day I spoke up and asked Russell if he would mind talking louder so we could hear what decisions were being made!"

None of the defense committees made extensive changes to DoD budget requests in the 1960s. Defense committee members saw their task as representing DoD's interests in Congress rather than overseeing defense programs. As Rivers explained HASC's role: "You must remember this is the most important committee in this Congress. This is the only voice, official voice, the military has in the House of Representatives." When the White House and the Services split on defense programs the defense committees typically sided with the Services. The defense committees also seldom faced challenges from the floor. Most members willingly deferred to defense committee judgment largely because the Cold War had forged a consensus on defense policy. The strength of this consensus discouraged members from dissenting. As Sen. J. W. Fulbright (D-Ark.), longtime chair of the Senate Foreign Relations Committee, admitted: "I must confess that I have not really exerted myself as I might have in an effort to control the military . . . Actually, I have been under the feeling that it was useless and utterly futile, that nothing could be done, for example, to cut an appropriation for the Department of Defense no matter what I did."

The degree of coordination between the defense committees, however, differed markedly in the House and the Senate. In the House the two defense committees worked in isolation from one another. There was no membership overlap (traditionally members of HADS have no other committee assignments), and members of HADS generally did not read HASC's hearings or reports. In the Senate, however, Russell and several other senators sat on both committees. SADS also had three *ex officio* members from SASC with voting rights at the subcommittee level (although not in the full Appropriations Committee). This "interlocking directorate" in the Senate gave the twin authorization-appropriations process an informal coordinating mechanism and limited the amount of committee conflict the inside game produced.

The 1970s—The Decentralized Inside Game

The major change in congressional decision-making on defense issues in the 1970s was the rise of the subcommittee system within the Armed Services Committees. Although this change came at the expense of the power of the chair, the locus of influence remained within the defense committees. Non-committee members displayed increased interest in defense matters in the early 1970s but their influence over defense legislation remained low and indirect. The result was the emergence of a decentralized version of the inside game.

The dispersal of power within the Armed Services Committees, part of a broader trend in Congress, reflected both internal and external pressures. Many legislators, especially in the House, chafed against the tremendous power of the chairs. They hoped not only to increase their say in policy-making, but to increase the potential for gaining political credit with constituents through committee work. Their cause was aided by the arrival in the late 1960s and early 1970s of new, more individualist legislators who were unwilling to enter into an apprenticeship while more senior members managed the business of Congress. These legislators loudly criticized the concentration of power in the hands of senior representatives and senators.

The House adopted two sets of reforms in the 1970s that affected HASC. The Legislative Reorganization Act of 1970 (which also applied to the Senate) required committees to make public all recorded votes, placed limits on proxy voting, empowered a majority of committee members to call meetings, and encouraged committees to hold open hearings. Even more important reforms came in 1973 when the House Democratic Caucus adopted the Subcommittee Bill of Rights. These new rules stripped the committee chairs of their power to make subcommittee assignments. Committee members won the right to bid for subcommittee chairs, in the order of their committee seniority, as well as the right to at least one choice subcommittee assignment. The Subcommittee Bill of Rights also mandated that subcommittees have formal jurisdictions, adequate budgets, authorization to hold hearings, and a staff selected by the subcommittee chair.

Despite these changes, F. Edward Hebert (D-La.), who became chair of HASC upon Rivers' death, continued to run the committee in an autocratic manner. He frequently violated procedural rules and opposed the mood in the House to trim defense spending. House Democrats had become less tolerant of autocratic chairs, however, and in January 1975 the Democratic Caucus removed Hebert and two other committee chairs. The Caucus chose Melvin Price (D-Ill.), the next ranking member of HASC, to be Hebert's successor. The selection of Price suggests that House Democrats were opposed more to Hebert's style and personality than to his defense views. [Hebert hurt his chances of being reconfirmed as chair of HASC when he repeatedly referred to freshmen members as "boys" and "girls" during the Caucus' deliberations.] Price also was pro-defense—he had repeatedly voted against amendments to cut defense spending—but he had a reputation for fairness.

Price accepted the reduction of the role of the committee chair and shared legislative responsibility with the subcommittee chairs. He democratized committee procedures, assigned staff to the subcommittees on a permanent basis, and made legislative referrals automatic. Hearings and markups of the annual defense authorization bill were done in the subcommittees, and Price was less involved in the work of the subcommittees than his two predecessors. Price remained the single most powerful member of HASC, but the subcommittee chairmen as a group equalled Price in power.

The Senate adopted several reforms in the 1970s that encouraged committee decentralization. The Legislative Reorganization Act of 1970 limited future senators to only one seat on the Senate's top four committees—Appropriations, Armed Services, Finance and Foreign Relations. This reform enabled junior senators to gain seats on the most prestigious committees earlier in their careers. In 1975 the Senate increased the size of the legislative staff that junior senators could hire for their committee work. The Senate adopted its most important reforms in 1977 when it prohibited senators from chairing more than one subcommittee per committee and limited senators to three subcommittee seats per committee. The 1977 reforms also changed the procedures for selecting subcommittee assignments. Under the new rules each member selected one subcommittee seat before the next ranking member chose. Previously, committee members chose all their subcommittee assignments within the committee, in order of their seniority before the next ranking member chose, a selection process that ensured that junior senators received the least prestigious subcommittee assignments.

Informal changes, however, played the greatest role in the decentralization of SASC. The most important informal change came with Sen. John Stennis' (D-Miss.) ascension to the committee chair. The chair of the committee from 1969 to 1980, Stennis was more willing than Russell to allow other senators to participate in committee business. In 1971, Stennis created subcommittees on Research and Development and on Tactical Air Power, and gave them authority to mark up those parts of the DoD budget. He also created subcommittees to address other aspects of defense policy. Even when subcommittee chairs opposed committee decisions on the floor Stennis did not use his power to subvert the subcommittee structure. The arrival of new, more assertive senators to SASC reinforced Stennis' willingness to give other committee members increased responsibility.

The growth of the subcommittee system was greater in the House than in the Senate because of the more wide-ranging nature of the House's Subcommittee Bill of Rights. By 1979, HASC's subcommittees marked up the entire annual defense authorization bill and they had the right to schedule hearings on virtually any subject they chose. Moreover, in the 96th Congress (1979-1980), HASC referred 99 percent of its legislation to the relevant subcommittee, as compared to 12 percent during the 91st Congress (1969-1971). In contrast, SASC continued to mark up the procurement account, with the exception of requests for tactical aircraft, in the full committee. The chair of SASC also retained the power to schedule hearings and meetings, and the committee staff remained more centralized than in the House. Finally, SASC's small size meant that most of its subcommittees included nearly half of the full committee members.

The rise of the subcommittee system strengthened the ability of the Armed Services Committees to intervene in defense policy. This new ability was enhanced by the increase in committee staff size—HASC's staff grew from 37 in 1970 to 45 in 1978, while SASC's staff rose from 19 to 30. The increased floor debates in the early 1970s further stimulated the Armed Services Committees. Stennis' decision to revamp SASC was reinforced by the fact that he became chair at a time when the defense committees were besieged with criticism that they merely rubberstamped the administration's defense budget. To remain credible the defense committees had to establish that they were more than rubberstamps.

Why did floor activity increase in the 1970s? The reason was the Vietnam war. Vietnam broke the national consensus on defense policy and thereby broadened the range of acceptable debate. For the first time since Pearl Harbor members could openly challenge the basic assumptions of defense policy without appearing subversive. For many members criticism of U.S. defense policy even became politically profitable. Vietnam also made many members skeptical of the quality of the decisions coming out of DoD. As former Senate staff member Alton Frye notes, many members came to believe "that military judgments on new weapons systems were likely to be no better than what they considered their [the Services'] proven misjudgments on the course of the war." Skepticism about DoD decision making was reinforced by repeated revelations that major weapons systems (in particular the C-5 transport plane) were running far over budget or failed to work as advertised.

Although the Armed Services Committees had to be more sensitive to the likely floor reaction than was the case in the 1960s, they retained their influence over defense policy. For the most part, floor activity in the 1970s focused on a small (albeit important) number of issues and the Armed Services Committees generally defended their recommendations for weapons programs. Excluding committee and technical amendments, the House adopted only eight percent (5 of 60) of the amendments that sought to change the dollar amounts HASC had recommended for programs in the procurement and research and development accounts. The figure was higher in the Senate, standing at 19 percent (10 of 53), which reflects the less restricted nature of debate in the upper chamber.

The congressional reforms of the 1970s did not have a major impact on the Defense Appropriations Subcommittees. The major change in the operation of these subcommittees during the 1970s—their increased scrutiny of the defense budget—was prompted by the expansion of the authorization process and the rise in floor activity. Moreover, like the Armed Services Committees, the Defense Appropriations Subcommittees generally defended their dollar recommendations for programs in the procurement and research and development accounts. Excluding committee and technical amendments, the House adopted only three percent (1 of 32) of these amendments and the Senate adopted 42 percent (11 of 26). Although the figure for the Senate is relatively high, members of the defense committees offered nine of the successful Senate amendments.

The 1980s—The Outside Game

The major change in congressional decision-making on defense policy in the 1980s was the emergence of the outside game. This new decision-making style merits the description "outside" in two ways. First, unlike the preceding decades, much of the congressional activity on defense policy took place in the public arena, and, thus, was highly visible. Second, much of this activity bypassed the traditional channels of power within the defense committees. The emergence of the outside game owed to the rise of the authorization process, the growth of legislative "individualism," and the increased politicization of defense issues.

One aspect of the outside game was the explosion of floor activity in Congress. The average number of floor amendments the Senate considered on the annual defense authorization bill nearly tripled in the 1980s while the number of amendments debated in the House nearly quadrupled. The other aspect of the outside game was the tremendous growth in congressional activity off the floor. On the one hand, there was much more activity by individual legislators. Whereas in the 1960s critics of DoD were a minority, in the 1980s many legislators (both hawks and doves) took to criticizing the Pentagon. On the other hand, there was more activity by groups of legislators on defense issues. One bicameral example of this was the formation in 1981 of the Military Reform Caucus, a loosely organized, bipartisan coalition of legislators interested in broad changes in U.S. defense policy.

In the House, the most important group activity was that of the Democratic Caucus. The Caucus first emerged as a power on defense issues following the congressional decision in May 1983 to approve flight testing of the MX missile. House Democrats who opposed the decision used their strength in the Caucus to force the House Democratic leadership into uniform opposition to the production of MX. Representatives who held leadership positions or aspired to them apparently believed that the Caucus would oppose their future candidacies unless they opposed MX. This success emboldened the caucus to challenge HASC. Many Democrats believed that HASC was too hawkish and too ready to concede House positions in conference negotiations with SASC. In 1984 the Caucus effectively stripped HASC of the power to negotiate with SASC on key issues; the Caucus forced HASC to accept dozens of special delegates to the House-Senate conference on the authorization bill. [Traditionally the defense committees appoint conferees from among committee members.] The Caucus reimposed the restriction in succeeding years.

The Caucus action that gained the most attention came in 1985 when it voted to replace the ailing Rep. Price with Rep. Les Aspin (D-Wis.) as the chair of HASC. In violation of the cherished norm of seniority, the Caucus passed over the most senior Democrats on HASC, all hawks, to make Aspin chair. The choice sent the unmistakable signal that House Democrats wanted the chair of HASC to be closer to the mainstream of the Democratic Party. After removing Price, the caucus kept close tabs on Aspin's performance as chair. It quickly voiced displeasure with his handling of several defense issues. When Aspin failed to reassure his critics the Caucus in January 1987 removed him as chair. The Caucus eventually reappointed Aspin as chair buy only after letting him spend two weeks in political limbo and making him publicly confess his shortcomings on the floor of the House.

The House Democratic Caucus has no analogue in the Senate, where activity has been more individualistic. For example, after Sen. Charles Grassley (R-Iowa) made national headlines by exposing abuses in the Pentagon's pricing of spare parts, many senators rushed to find horror stories of their own. Still other senators publish their own suggested defense budgets. This activity is not limited to senators who seek to cut defense spending. Conservative senators often challenged the Reagan administration on a range of arms control and defense issues. The failure of the Senate to produce an analog to the House Democratic Caucus reflects the more individualistic nature of life in the Senate. As a senior Senate staffer puts it, "There's a lot more of an ego problem over here, and a bit less of a willingness to fall in behind a leader. They're bigger players over here. They make louder sounds when they walk. Some senator wants to offer an amendment and another doesn't like some of the language or says he wants to offer it."

Why did the outside game emerge? Part of the answer lies in the expansion of the authorization process, which dramatically increased the opportunities for members to alter defense programs. More decisions meant more legislators were likely to find an issue important to themselves or their constituents. At the same time, the congressional reforms of the 1970s loosened the constraints on legislative behavior and ushered in legislative "individualism." In the 1980s, legislators could debate defense issues with less fear of retribution by congressional and committee leaders.

The expansion of the authorization process and the rise of legislative individualism enabled legislators to address defense issues for reasons of "good policy." This was most evident in the frequent battles in the 1980s over strategic weapons policy where representatives and senators challenged both the defense committees and the president on a wide range of issues. Such floor challenges were rare in the 1960s (the ABM debate in the Senate being the primary exception). At the same time, junior members of the defense committees managed to establish reputations as influential "players" on policy issues early in their careers. This achievement was next to impossible to accomplish when the inside game dominated in the 1950s and 1960s.

The increase in opportunities and the decline in legislative constraints also enabled more legislators to use defense requests for "pork barrel" purposes. Of course, a pork barrel component to defense budgets is as old as the republic. What was new in the 1980s, however, was the *extent* of pork barreling. When the inside game lived legislators had to cultivate the support of the senior members of the defense committees if they wanted new funds and jobs for their constituents. Cultivating this support was inherently time consuming and success was by no means guaranteed. In the 1980s, however, the ability of defense committee leaders to control pork barreling diminished. Junior committee members won greater influence on the mark-up of the authorization and appropriations bills. Other legislators used floor amendments to gain pork barrel benefits for their constituents because, as Sen. Sam Nunn (D-Ga.) points out, "both the House and Senate tend to accept floor amendments rather than to take them on and defeat them." At the same time, the Reagan administration's emphasis on defense over social spending encouraged members to scour the defense budget for pork barrel opportunities. Rep. Pat Schroeder (D-Colo.), a member of HASC, noted that "If you want anything for your district . . . the only place were there is any money at all is in the Armed Services Committee bill."

The third factor contributing to the emergence of the outside game was the increased political volatility of defense policy in the 1980s. The politicization of defense issues owed in part to the increased partisanship on defense issues following the Vietnam War. In the 1950s and 1960s divisions over defense policy often cut *across* party lines. For example, during the ABM debate of 1969, the anti-ABM coalition was led by a Democrat (Philip Hart) and a Republican (Sen. John Sherman Cooper) and the pro-ABM forces were led by a Democrat (Sen. Russell). When the liberal wing of the Republican Party and the conservative wing of the Democratic Party collapsed in the 1970s, cleavages on defense policy came to fall *along* party lines. The result was that defense debates became partisan battles. The Reagan presidency further fueled this partisanship by coupling sharp increases in defense spending with attempts to eliminate social programs. This spurred lengthy and acrimonious debates in Congress over both the composition of the defense budget and its relative share of federal expenditures.

The politicization of defense policy expanded the electoral incentives for members of Congress to address defense issues. In the 1980s the number, size and strength of both defense and peace lobbies jumped dramatically. These groups sought to mobilize constituents to lobby legislators to vote for or against particular weapons programs. With the growth of peace and defense lobbies, there were tangible electoral benefits, in the form of financial contributions and constituent support, to legislators who championed one defense cause or another. Legislators also had to worry about potential electoral penalties for choosing the wrong side of a defense issues. Defense and peace lobbies both tried to defeat legislators who opposed the group's favored position.

The political volatility of defense policy also made defense is sues fertile ground for members seeking to enhance their reputations, and, in turn, their electability. The temptation to use defense issues for "political grandstanding" was especially great on the floor, where amendments targeting real or imagined ills in the Pentagon became another means of campaigning. Sen. Nunn contends that, "there is much greater public relations value in a floor amendment—irrespective of its value—than there is in proceeding with responsible suggestions through the committee process." Similarly, former Sen. Gaylord Nelson (D-Wis.) argues that, "the floor is being used as an instrument of political campaigning far more than it ever has before." The clearest example was the controversy in the mid-1980s over spare parts pricing for defense programs. When the first stories of overpricing drew national media attention, members rushed to expose other examples. As one observer wrote at the time, "It made little difference that the sum of all the spare parts and tool overcharges did not approach the roundoff error of major programs such as the B-1. The stories played well at home." As a result, the Senate considered 11 amendments on DoD procurement policies and the House 24 amendments during the debate on the fiscal year 1986 defense authorization bill.

Impact of the Outside Game

The emergence of the outside game made the defense debate on Capitol Hill more representative of the views of members of Congress. The Armed Services Committees continued to be more conservative than their parent bodies, and, thus, the outside game aired views held by few members of the defense committees. Moreover, to the extent that Congress mirrors the attitudes of the American public, the debate in Congress became more representative of the body politic. Both of these were important developments. After all, one of Congress' primary functions is to articulate the views of the American public.

The increased representativeness of the outside game meant that Congress came to debate a wider range of defense issues than was true in the 1960s or even the 1970s. In 1989 alone Congress debated MX, Midgetman, the Strategic Defense Initiative and the B-2 ("Stealth") Bomber among other issues. Of course, both hawks and doves criticized these debates, arguing either that Congress is endangering the U.S. defense posture (hawks), failing to cancel dangerous weapons systems (doves), or misunderstanding the fundamental issues involved (both). These complaints notwithstanding, Congress in the 1980s attempted to grapple with at least some major defense issues.

The floor debates circumscribed the actions of the defense committees. This was most evident in the congressional debate over the MX missile, where the committee system was effectively abandoned. A report commissioned by Congress on the MX debate concluded:

> The major avenues of congressional influence [on MX] were almost entirely separate from committee and party structures. Although some of the principal actors served on committees and subcommittees relevant to defense and arms control issues . . . the pressure brought to bear on the administration came not from the standing committee but from a bipartisan and ultimately bicameral group of representatives and senators who had different amounts of seniority on different committees.

Although the MX was an extreme example of how the power of the defense committees was curbed, it was not unique. For example, the pressure to limit tests of antisatellite weapons, to reduce spending on the Strategic Defense Initiative, and to reform the defense procurement process all originated outside the defense committees.

The defense committees also were less able in the outside game to protect their dollar recommendations for weapons programs. On numerous occasions, and especially with MX, the defense committees found themselves overruled on the floor. Successful floor amendments had an impact on defense committee decision making that went beyond the immediate issue at stake. Congress operates heavily on the principle of "anticipated reactions," that is, actors often modify their behavior to take into account how others are likely to act. Michael West, a member of the HASC staff, writes: "The Hill is totally success-oriented in measuring power and influence. . . . Whatever else the committee and its staff accomplish, they must draw up legislation that will be approved. Defeats on the floor for whatever reason must be avoided like the plague." Because defense committee decisions met strong opposition in the 1980s, opposition the defense committees could not always defeat, for the first time in the postwar era the committees had strong incentives to incorporate floor views into the legislation they reported to the full House and Senate.

The defense committees, however, remained the most powerful congressional actors on defense issues. The reason for this is that the defense committees are the only congressional actors that have the time, staff and jurisdiction to pore over the annual defense budget in depth. Nonmembers mounted floor challenges but the size of the defense budget precluded the floor debate from addressing most of the decisions the defense committees made. Other committees occasionally tried to wrest "turf" away from the defense committees but they lack jurisdiction over the defense bill. Moreover, members of the defense committees still carried extra weight in congressional debates because many legislators see them as "experts" on defense policy. Rep. Aspin observed:

> Senators like Barry Goldwater (R-Ariz.) and Howard W. Cannon (D-Nevada), who are both pilots and staunch airpower advocates, regale their colleagues with stories about fighter planes they have test flown replete with the jawbreaking jargon of the profession. Other members sit in awed silence, unable to respond because they lack the expertise and the jargon.

Nonetheless, the outside game ended the hegemony of the defense committees and made them more accountable to Congress as a whole.

What is the half-life of the outside game? The answer to this question depends ultimately on what happens internationally. The outside game developed in the context of relatively low tensions between the U.S. and the Soviet Union. Although U.S.-Soviet relations had tense moments in the 1980s, most notably at the start of the decade when the Soviet Union invaded Afghanistan, they never reached the heights of tension common in the 1960s. Should superpower tensions return to (and stay at) levels comparable to those which prevailed in the 1950s, the World War II precedent no doubt would convince most members to give the president great leeway on defense policy. Indeed, in 1980 and 1981 many doves resigned themselves to the political inevitability of higher levels of defense spending over the short term. By the same token, the dramatic changes that occurred in Eastern Europe and the Soviet Union at the end of the 1980s made it likely that Congress will become even more willing to challenge the president on defense policy.

Conclusions

Does Congress' involvement in defense policy advance the common good? The answer to this question all too often depends on one's views of the policies of the current administration. Hawks who in the late 1970s applauded Congress for revising President Carter's programs lambasted Congress in the 1980s for obstructing Reagan's policies. Doves expressed opposite sentiments. Leaving aside politically-motivated assessments, it is important to recognize two things in assessing Congress' increased role in defense policy. One is that the inside game should not be idealized simply because it was more orderly than the outside game. The inside game had its own costs. The other point is that for all its disorder, the outside game means a more representative debate in Congress. For a political system that prides itself on representation, the importance of open debate should not be underestimated.

The most common indictment of Congress is that it is inefficient. Critics complain that Congress takes too long to make decisions and that it frequently changes its mind. As one commentator complained in 1984, "By my count there have been thirty-six 'test votes' in the House and Senate on the MX missile since Reagan took office, most of them necessitated by some whorl of the budget process. These test votes have been accompanied by tension, packed press galleries, ringing debate—all the drama of decision, but no decision." The first year of the Carter administration was also the last time Congress managed to pass the annual defense appropriations bill before the start of the last fiscal year (October 1). While chair of SASC, Sen. John Tower (R-Texas) complained that the defense committees wasted too much time on turf battles: "Our committee spends a large portion of its time trying to fend off competition from other committees and monitoring what other committees are doing." Critics contend that such inefficiency hampers DoD's ability to plan which in turn prevents defense contractors from scheduling efficient use of their production lines. The result is defense waste.

Complaints about congressional inefficiency have merit—Congress *is* inefficient. But that is the nature of the place. Congress is a *political* institution and not a bureaucratic one. As Stanley Heginbotham writes:

> Congress invariably appears inept and irresponsible from the perspective of anyone who thinks of it as a bureaucracy that can formulate policies, manage operations, or even systematically assess and review programs. Congress does not have the structure of bureaucracy, it is institutionally incapable of doing what bureaucracies do, and it is unrealistic to expect otherwise.

Absent total passivity Congress will always be inefficient compared to the executive branch. Moreover, critics exaggerate how much congressional inefficiency hurts DoD's planning ability. Fiscal constraints dictate most budget cuts and often Congress follows DoD's recommendations on which programs to cut. And when Congress blocks a major weapons program it may prevent considerable sums of money from being wasted on a weapons system of questionable value.

Efficiency is also only one, and by no means the most important, standard for judging government. Congress was a more efficient decision maker during the 1950s and 1960s than it is today. But efficient government is not the same as wise government. The inside game processed defense issues quickly but it neglected oversight. Congress repeatedly failed to question DoD about new weapons. What resulted was weapons programs like the C-5A that suffered massive cost overruns. In other instances the inside game rubberstamped DoD decisions that in retrospect look questionable. This was most serious with the multiple independently-targetable reentry vehicle (MIRV) program. When the Soviets followed the U.S. lead and deployed MIRVs, the U.S. ICBM missile force suddenly became vulnerable to a first-strike. Even Secretary of State Henry Kissinger, who ardently backed developing MIRVs, later admitted "I wish I had thought through the implications of a MIRVed world more thoughtfully in 1969 and 1970 than I did." The great failing of the inside game was that it never forced the administration to think through its policy proposals.

A second complaint about Congress' increased role in defense policy contends that Congress is ill-suited to oversee defense programs. The guardianship argument holds that members should defer to executive branch expertise because they lack the qualifications needed to judge defense programs. As description the guardianship argument is unassailable: few members are trained as engineers, scientists or defense strategists, whereas many DoD officials have devoted much of their adult lives to mastering the intricacies of defense policy.

The guardianship argument, however, suffers two serious flaws. One is that it claims superior technical expertise for the executive even though bureaucracies fall short (sometimes very short) of rational decision making. Studies of decision making within DoD repeatedly find that politics often influence Service decisions on acquisition issues. To take just one example, the Trident submarine assumed its mammoth dimensions primarily because Admiral Hyman Rickover wanted a platform for a new reactor he had devised and not because of military requirements. Politics also shapes White House decisions. Again, to take one example among many, President Nixon asked Congress in 1972 to increase spending on strategic programs to win Pentagon support for the SALT treaty because the Secretary of Defense and the Joint Chiefs of Staff had made a new strategic modernization program the price of their support of the treaty.

The other flaw in the guardianship argument is that evaluating defense policy requires far more than technical judgments. As Samuel Huntington noted several decades ago, "The more important the policy issue is, the less important becomes detailed technical information and the more relevant become broad judgments on goals and values, i.e., political judgments, where presumably the congressman's competence is greatest." Despite its arcane jargon, defense policy is not about science. It is about politics. That is why 40 years of debate have not answered a question as fundamental as what deters the Soviet Union. It is also why members can play the game of "pick your scientist" as world famous scientists line up on every side of controversial defense issues.

The third criticism levelled against Congress contends that Congress' activism limits the president's negotiating leverage. The bargaining chip argument does not raise constitutional issues. To quote Justice Robert H. Jackson, "Congress alone controls the raising of the revenues and their appropriation and may determine in what manner and by what means they shall be spent for military and naval procurement." Arguments for bargaining chips hinge instead on assessments about negotiating effectiveness, that is, proponents believe the president would be better able to negotiate if Congress stayed out of sensitive acquisition matters. Intuition suggests the bargaining chip argument has merit. Congress frequently resembles a rabble rather than an assembly, it cannot act in secret, and it often fails to act at all. The presidency is well-suited in comparison to act secretly and decisively. Moreover, the Soviet Union would seem to have an incentive to bargain only when the U.S. possesses or is developing weapons that threaten key Soviet assets. After all, if the Soviet Union has nothing to fear, why should it negotiate?

Despite the intuitive appeal of the bargaining chip argument the supporting evidence is mixed. Not all negotiators accept the notion that successful arms control talks depend upon accumulating weapons to trade. Gerard Smith concluded from his stint as chief U.S. negotiator of SALT I that President Nixon's bargaining chip strategy actually hampered negotiations, and that "if restraining measures are not taken early in the development of new weapons systems, control becomes much more difficult." Former U.S. ambassador to Moscow Averill Harriman echoed Smith's views. Harriman believed that "the bargaining chip theory should be abandoned. It is utterly discredited."

Skepticism about bargaining chips has several roots. One is that the theory assumes Soviet leaders will negotiate from a position of inferiority. Yet just the opposite may be true; weakness may drive them to redouble development efforts. The theory also assumes the Soviets tailor their bargaining positions to political events in the U.S. But Soviet leaders may be responding (as American presidents often do) to internal forces rather external ones. Last, programs advertised as bargaining chips often do not get bargained away. Secretary of State Kissinger, for instance, pushed for the development of cruise missiles, over air force objections, to enhance U.S. leverage in arms control talks with the Soviets. When the air force later prevented him from cashing in the cruise missile chip, Kissinger could only lament, "How was I to know the military would come to love it?" The possibility that bargaining chips will not be traded means the bargaining chip strategy may force members to choose between funding a weapon of dubious value or being accused of sabotaging the administration's arms control policy.

Today no compelling evidence exists that Congress' involvement in defense policy hurts the public interest. But can anything be said for congressional activism? Yes. The American political system is based on the democratic idea, the belief that policy made by the many is better than the policy made by the one. When Congress participates in the policy process it counters the (often hidden) parochialism of the executive branch. Challenges from Capitol Hill, be they led by doves or hawks, force the executive branch to justify its programs. Debate does not guarantee better policies, but it does force the president to build public support for his policies and it reduces the possibility that an administration will commit to an important policy without considering the potential ramifications. Moreover, Congress is even-handed in its activism. Hawks may protest that Congress blocked President Reagan's defense proposals, but President Carter received as much if not more "advice" from Congress.

In short, Congress enriches the defense policy debate because it airs diverse public views. That is the brilliance of American democracy. It does not guarantee that Congress will choose wisely. But the Constitution does not mandate wisdom. The freedom to make mistakes is part and parcel of democratic government. Critics of Congress should take this point to heart.

Chapter 12

Trade Policy: Government Action in the Face of International Commercial Rivalry[1]

John A.C. Conybeare

Governments are held responsible by their citizens for national economic well being. In pursuing that well being, governments formulate few policies more important than those which deal with international commercial rivalries. Intervention in trade has always been an object of state policy and is well documented back to ancient times. Conflict over trade has been endemic in the international system at least since the late Middle Ages, as the number of sovereign entities increased and trade expanded along the major international trade routes. These normal conflicts have sometimes escalated to the point that they become trade wars.

In the heartland of the country, this international competition is perhaps most visible in agriculture, where gains and losses of markets are the subject of frequent news stories. As those news stories make clear, international commercial relations involve high stakes for all Americans and can lead to very serious conflicts.

How the U.S. government deals with those conflicts bears directly upon immediate and future economic prospects for Americans. This chapter takes up bilateral trade conflict. The approach involves examination of the income-maximizing behavior of a rational national actor within the context of an international trade-taxing game ("game" here being used in its competitive or conflictual sense). The starting point is a simple model from the pure theory of trade. The model assumes that rational state actors seek to maximize their national incomes through trade restrictions. The trade model is then set out in the form of simple game structure, following which is given a description and analysis of a short but serious agricultural trade war between the U.S. and the European Economic Community (EEC).

Theories of Bilateral Trade Wars

Theories of trade all agree on a single premise: trade occurs because there are national income gains to be derived from specializing in the production and export of commodities in which the country has a comparative advantage. Trade begins when the price of the same good differs across countries. The gains from that trade will depend on how much prices change when trade occurs. If one country is sufficiently large, the trading prices will be determined by its domestic markets, so that the price of the small country's export will rise until it equals the domestic price of that good in the large country, and the price of the small country's import good will fall until its matches the price of the same good in the large country. The pure theory of trade suggests that most of the gains from trade will accrue to smaller countries because the terms of trade are determined by domestic prices in the larger countries; hence a small country will experience a large increase in the price of its export when trade begins, the large country perhaps none at all.

Under certain competitive conditions, free international trade will maximize world income in the aggregate. Unfortunately, what is good for the world is not necessarily the best outcome for any one country. The traditional economic approach to trade wars is to focus on bilateral, income maximizing tariff conflicts. A country may improve its income by imposing a tariff on imports and/or taxing its exports. Unilateral trade restrictions may improve the country's terms of trade (i.e., the ratio of its export prices to its import prices), and hence raise its income. Other countries may, however, retaliate with their own optimal tariffs, and in the ensuing rounds of retaliation and counter-retaliation both countries may be made worse off.

Large countries facing small countries are much more likely to improve their income with a trade tax, even if the small country retaliates. The size factor operates in much the same way that it does when there is asymmetry between firms in a market; the larger the firm relative to the rest of the market, the more likely it is to be able be able to reap monopolistic profits by manipulating the overall market price and quantity supplied. Large country demand should be more sensitive to the price for products of a small country than small country demand to the price for the products of the large country, due to the large country's wider range of substitutes. A small country is likely to be more dependent on a particular import from a large country, and therefore less likely to reduce its demand for that product if the large country imposes a price raising tax on the good. On the supply side, the smaller country often cannot afford to reduce its sales to the large country or cannot find alternative markets. Moreover, the small country is likely to be insignificant in determining the world price of a commodity. In the extreme case, it may face fixed terms of trade, again causing the gains from a tariff to disappear. In that case, the price received by foreigners for the import remains constant, and the only effect of the tariff is to raise the domestic price to consumers. The very small country will only lower its national income by imposing a tariff on a much larger country.

In summary, the gains from a tariff war are likely to be directly proportional to the countries' relative sizes. Since size is the predictor of income gains in a tariff war, it is also the key variable for predicting war outcomes. Some small countries have recognized this limitation on their freedom of action, and have opted for free trade policies. However, size is not a perfect proxy for the elasticity conditions that make a country highly vulnerable in a trade war. Other factors may also create similar elasticity factors that produce the same kinds of vulnerability. A high degree of commodity and geographic concentration of trade, for example, may produce the same elasticity conditions as small size. One case is late nineteenth century Russia, vanquished in a tariff war with Germany. Despite its national income near to that of Germany, agriculture was the major part of Russia's national income, and its exports were heavily concentrated on Germany, producing both the demand and supply elasticity conditions that made Russia a "small" country in the sense of being weak and vulnerable in a tariff war with Germany.

Two equal size countries engaging in a tariff war are likely to make each other mutually worse off in the final outcome, even though each may individually make some gains until retaliation occurs. As the disparity in size increases, the ability of the large country to extract gains from the small country or hurt it with retaliation increases; the ability of the smaller country to gain from a tariff or hurt the large country by retaliation diminishes. The extreme case would be where the small country cannot change its terms of trade, will only lower its national income by imposing a tariff, and may not even be able to hurt the large country by retaliation (i.e., the large country may gain from a tariff in spite of retaliation). This conclusion is relevant to and inconsistent with the contention of some theorists that hegemonic powers will or ought to prefer free trade. Two very small countries in a tariff war will not even make pre-retaliation gains from a tariff, since they are both price takers on world markets, cannot change their terms of trade, and will make immediate income losses by initiating a tariff. A corollary of the above is that a large country will lose and a small country will gain from an unreciprocated reduction in tariffs, a point which has some importance for contemporary negotiations in the General Agreement on Trade and Tariffs (GATT).

Trade Wars and Other State Economic Objectives

A difficulty with the economic theory of tariff wars might be that it presumes the state actor is maximizing national income. An alternative objective could be revenue, sought either for state expenditure or because tariff revenues may be disbursed to private beneficiaries. Revenue tariffs were common until the late nineteenth century, when most western countries shifted the primary burden of taxation on to income taxes. They are still prevalent in developing countries, where trade taxes accounted for an average of 29% of government revenue.

Still another objective might be improvement in the balance of trade, central to mercantilist theory and revived in the twentieth century by the Keynesians. A favorable balance of trade, the mercantilists believed, would enhance a country's wealth and power. The classical economists' disputed that, but Keynes reintroduced some of the mercantilist conclusions with his assumption that prices and wages may be inflexible downwards, in which case an economy could settle at a less than full employment equilibrium. A balance of trade surplus therefore may effect a sustained increase in national income and reduce unemployment, "exporting" unemployment to the rest of the world. A significant part of the competitive protection policies of developed countries today are at least implicitly Keynesian in their nominal purpose.

Closely related to these employment rationales are those which are subsumed under the term industrial organization. This includes the well known "infant industry" and national defense arguments for protecting certain industries. The former involves the argument that a country must protect its new industries, at least until they can get on their feet and compete in the international arena. The latter argues that some industries are so important to a nation's security (the steel industry, for example) that they cannot be allowed to fail. These industrial organization objectives may also be related to particular goals of interest groups.

The key point here is that these alternative goals that might be pursued by states are still broadly consistent with income maximization and produce similar outcomes. Revenue seeking will produce an optimal tariff higher than an income maximizing tariff, but theoretically close enough that they would be empirically difficult to distinguish. Moreover, a revenue maximizing tariff war will be structurally identical to an income maximizing tariff war. A Keynesian unemployment exporting strategy of protection has as its ultimate goal the maximization of income. Even if the intermediate objective is an improvement in the balance of trade, this is but a means to increase national income, since the balance of trade has no intrinsic value by itself. Tariff policies related to industrial organization will in most cases produce bargaining incentives similar to that of the income maximizing tariff war. The generalizations about asymmetric trade wars also still hold true, since in a balance of trade war, the large can obviously inflict far more damage than can the small.

It is therefore reasonable to follow the analytic aspects of trade war through a model of income maximizing tariff wars. This is true, first, because the competitive dynamics of inter-state interactions over other economic objectives (e.g., revenue, balance of trade, promoting specific industrial sectors) are structurally similar in the actors' preferences over outcomes. Secondly, the final objective in many cases is still maximization of national income, and at the very least, income losses must be used to place some value on the objectives being sought, so as to make them comparable to alternative goals.

Basic Game Structures

Games are classified by the configuration of payoffs, which in turn imply certain dominant strategies. The first distinction that needs to be made is between constant and variable sum games. The "sum" of the game is the total payoff to all players for any given combination of strategies. A market share game between firms is a good example of a constant sum game, since the sum of their market shares is always 100%. A game over changes in market shares would be a zero sum game. These are games of pure conflict where little cooperation is possible, since the gain of one must be the loss of the other. Mercantilism offered a view of world trade that was essentially constant sum, since nations were seen as competing for a static volume of trade.

In international trade rivalries, market share games often involve more than two actors, in which case we may have a more conceptually interesting problem, since a subset of these actors may cooperate in order to reduce the market shares of the other actors. This is known in the game literature as the "minimum winning coalition." An example is the contemporary conflict over shares of the U.S. domestic steel market. Japan and the EEC clearly have a strong interest in coalescing in order to reduce the share of developing countries in the U.S. steel market, given the U.S. policy objective (proclaimed in 1984) of limiting foreign producers to under 20% of the U.S. market.

Variable sum games offer opportunities for cooperation even when there are only two players. The basic forms will be explained in terms of two states (X, Y) which may choose cooperation (C, not imposing a tariff) or defection (D, imposing a tariff), producing four possible outcomes: C_xC_y, D_xD_y, C_xD_y and D_xC_y. When discussing a single actor only, apart from any specific bilateral game matrix, the designations of outcomes may be used without subscripts, with the relevant actor being first in the designation and the other player being second. Hence, DC will refer to a strategy of unilateral exploitation—i.e., unreciprocated defection, while the other player cooperates; CD will refer to allowing oneself to be exploited—unrequited cooperation, while the other defects; and CC and DD to mutual cooperation or defection.

Classifying the games according to the players' preference ranking of payoffs produces three common games and associated strategies: unconditional non-cooperation, attempting to pick the opposite choice to that of the opponent, and conditional cooperation. The most well known game is the symmetric Prisoners' Dilemma. This is so-named because of its applicability to the following situation: two suspects have been arrested for a crime. The police are questioning each separately, hoping for a confession. The best hope for both jointly is to remain silent, in which case each will be sentenced to only 60 days in jail. However, if one confesses and the other does not, the confessor will go free and the other will spend 10 years in jail. Thus, it seems that confession would be a good idea. The problem comes if both confess; then both will be sentenced to eight years in jail. Obviously, the ideal joint outcome is not the ideal for either of them

TABLE 12.1
Payoffs in a Prisoners' Dilemma Trade War*

	Country X: Tariff (D_x)	No Tariff (C_x)
Country Y:		
Tariff (D_y)	2,2	1,4
No tariff (C_y)	4,1	3,3

*The rank ordering of the payoffs is 4 (most desirable) > 3 > 2 > 1 (least desirable)

considered alone. No matter what his partner does, each will be better off confessing. But this thinking will produce two confessions and eight years in jail for each—at least if the game is played only once (i.e., not iterated). The key feature of the single play Prisoners' Dilemma is that each actor's best strategy is to confess (i.e., not cooperate with the other player), regardless of what he thinks the other player will do.

The parallel to trade conflict is given in Table 1 above. Player X has the preference ordering $D_xC_y > C_xC_y > D_xD_y > C_xD_y$, and Y has its own counterpart to that ordering. In a static context, the dominant strategy for X and Y is to impose a tariff regardless of their conjectures about the behavior of the other state, and the game defaults to the inferior outcome of D_xD_y. This game has been widely used to model international conflicts, including tariff wars. There is a closely related game known as Deadlock. This game has the same preference ordering as Prisoners' Dilemma, but with the ranking of CC and DD reversed (viz., the overall ranking for a player is then DC>DD> CC> CD). The dominant strategy is the same (defection), but Deadlock and Prisoners' Dilemma differ when played more than once, since the latter may tend to become cooperative, whereas the former will not.

The Effects Of Time

Trade games cannot be treated as if they were static, with all the moves occurring simultaneously. A general theory of bilateral trade wars must presume that trade games are invariably iterated, in the sense that moves occur sequentially and players may have the opportunity to communicate, observe each others' behavior, change their own behavior and possibly contrive enforceable agreements. This iteration may occur both within games and between serially played games.

There is a large body of theoretical and empirical evidence suggesting that some sequentially played games should develop cooperative patterns of interaction, when one can retaliate against the defector. In the Prisoners' Dilemma game, the defector may be punished in the following game, inflicting a jointly lower payoff on both parties. Unfortunately, iteration will not generate cooperation in the Deadlock game, since both parties *prefer* mutual defection to mutual cooperation.

Iteration may also be relevant to moves within games, with the same kinds of cooperation-inducing effects. Given the length of the time lags that often occur in trade conflicts, one might expect to observe some cooperation even in single play trade games. Some examples may be found in the recent conflicts between the US and steel exporting countries, in which U.S. threats and or unilateral action afforded steel exporting countries the opportunity to cooperate in the light of their knowledge of U.S. policy.

Contingent retaliation may take many forms. Strategies in a trade war may reactive, as in retaliatory trade restrictions, or they may be anticipatory, as with "hostage taking." Where agreements lack a reliable mechanism for legal enforcement (such as in international trade relations), we may observe hostage-taking (an irreversible, nonsalvageable advance commitment) for the purpose of making the agreement self-enforcing. Current U.S. anti-dumping policy, for example, requires importers suspected of dumping to post a bond to cover the value of any penalty duties that may be assessed from the date that the investigation began.

The effects of iteration are easily observable in both the norms and strategies of international trade practices. The General Agreement on Trade and Tariffs (GATT) has internalized norms of both reciprocity and retaliation. Hence GATT incorporates both exhortations to observe reciprocity and justifiable retaliation as incentives to cooperate. In addition to reciprocity and retaliation being well established international norms, they may also be adopted as a coercive strategy. There have recently been many advocates within the U.S. of a new trade strategy incorporating tit-for-tat principles of aggressive reciprocity.

Discussion of the effects of time raises an analytic question relevant to trade conflicts which are carried on for a great many years. More generally, if all trade relations are iterated, and if iteration induces cooperation (assuming that political leaders do not have very short time horizons), why would one ever observe trade wars lasting more than a short time? In the case of trade wars, there are at least four categories of answer: (1) the static structure of the game may by itself be unconducive to cooperation when iterated (e.g., Deadlock); (2) time may introduce factors that inhibit cooperation (e.g., by generating destructive feuds); (3) cognitive and informational difficulties may make contingent retaliation problematic (e.g., misperceiving a Prisoners' Dilemma as some other type of game where retaliation may be inappropriate); and (4) large numbers of actors may introduce problems that reduce cooperation (e.g., by making it difficult to punish a defector without also punishing too many other cooperators).

Three Hypotheses on Trade Wars

The preceding discussion of trade theory, bilateral game structures and iteration has set in place enough theoretical background to enable me to make three predictions about bilateral trade wars:

1. Two large countries will be in a symmetric Prisoners' Dilemma trade war, where each has the dominant strategy of defection, leaving both with lower incomes at DD than they could have had at CC. As the game is iterated, strategies of contingent retaliation should induce cooperation, and the game should gradually move back to CC. Though the above discussion of iteration suggested some factors that may inhibit this tendency, it is a reasonable first approximation of what one should expect to observe. Historically, the most important modification of this hypothesis occurs when one introduces more than two actors, since strategies of contingent retaliation may no longer be sufficient to ensure cooperation. In fact, the introduction of large numbers into the large country Prisoners' Dilemma will not usually have a lasting effect on the game, since actors will take steps to bilateralize the problem.
2. Two small countries will be in a trade conflict where each hurts itself by imposing a tariff, either unilaterally or in retaliation. This produces a symmetric game where mutual defection (DD) is least preferred, mutual cooperation (CC) most preferred, and allowing oneself to be exploited (CD) is preferred to unilateral defection (DC). The result should

be no trade war at all, or at least an outcome at the low end of the conflict continuum.
3. A severely asymmetric conflict between a large and a small power should end at the large power's DC outcome, where it exploits the smaller country. Iteration is unlikely to change this outcome.

It is inevitable that these three hypotheses, which use size as the primary predictor of outcomes, will need to be modified in their application to the cases. Among the more important reasons for this is the common linkage of political issues to trade wars. Such linkage does not appear amenable to any a priori generalization as to effects on outcomes, cooperative or otherwise. Analysis of linkage must by default be a largely empirical question.

This concludes the theoretical background and analytic structure. Starting with the initial assumption that states in trade wars seek to enhance their economic welfare, I have explained the basic types of game structure that, when combined with the iterated nature of all trade games, yield three determinate predictions about bilateral trade wars. With these predictions in place, I now turn to the case of the Chicken War between the US and the EEC during the early 1960s, as an example of a Prisoners' Dilemma type trade conflict.

The Chicken War

The Chicken War was fought over trade restrictions initiated by the European Economic Community against the U.S.[2] Since the two powers were both large and roughly equal in size, one may safely predict a Prisoners' Dilemma game structure. The EEC should have expected to make welfare gains by taxing imports from the U.S., as should the U.S. have expected to gain from taxing imports from the EEC. The outcome in a static Prisoners' Dilemma game would have been mutual defection. Given the iterated nature of all trade games, one may also expect that strategies of contingent retaliation should have pushed the game back toward mutual cooperation. This did not occur; both chose to defect and maintain their strategies of non-cooperation with each other.

Hence the principal analytic question is why the U.S. and EEC became locked into a pattern of mutual defection. Three answers are suggested here. First, the EEC preference structure shifted, as a result of a linkage of the trade game to the EEC's need for internal unity, to that described as Deadlock (viz., DC>DD>CC>CD), making the joint structure of payoffs close to a constant sum game, generating more severe conflict because there was little opportunity for mutual gain. Second, both sides misperceived the payoffs to the other side and made inappropriate attempts to convey commitment to defection. Finally, the operation of international mediation through the General Agreement on Trade and Tariffs (GATT) may have provided incentives to keep the outcome at one of mutual defection. Though GATT encapsulated the conflict, preventing it spilling over into other issues and poisoning future trade relations, it also removed much of the need to cooperate on the issues of the Chicken War itself.

A Short Chronology

The Chicken War was a result of the formation of the EEC and, more specifically, its scheme for protecting its agricultural sector, the Common Agricultural Policy (CAP). U.S. reservations about the implications of CAP for U.S. farm exports were set aside in the immediate period following the Treaty of Rome, (which established the EEC in 1958) in the interest of not delaying either the formation of the EEC or the completion of the Dillon Round of negotiations under the auspices of the GATT.

In January 1962 the EEC's Council of Ministers agreed upon the basic policies to be incorporated into CAP, the major one affecting the U.S. being the decision to protect agriculture by way of price supports implemented through buffer stocks, and variable levies (import duties) to raise the price of imports up to or above EEC price levels. One of the first commodities on which these policies were put into operation was poultry meat. Regulation 22, effective from July 1962, virtually stopped the rapid build up of U.S. exports of frozen chickens to the EEC market, and particularly to West Germany, to the benefit of intra-EEC producers (mainly in Holland and France). The U.S. quickly voiced strong objections, on the grounds that Regulation 22 would "treble" the magnitude of EEC barriers to U.S. chicken exports, arguing that these tariffs were "bound" under GATT, and could not be increased (or "unbound") without compensation under GATT's article 14, paragraph six.

The war took place in three overlapping phases. The first phase lasted until June 1963, and centered primarily on a debate over the degree of EEC discrimination against U.S. chicken exports. Wearying of these negotiations, the U.S. then requested compensation under an agreement reached during the Dillon Round. These discussions also proved unfruitful, as they could not produce agreement on the total compensation to be exacted. The third phase formally began in September 1963, when both sides agreed to submit the matter to a special GATT tribunal, which found U.S. claims to be justified, but scaled down the U.S. damage claim from $46 million to $26 million, much closer to the EEC's own estimate of $19 million. The U.S. then implemented the GATT finding with penalty duties on certain commodities for which the most recalcitrant EEC members were the principal suppliers to the U.S. In the terms of the game structures outlined above, the situation clearly ended up at DD, or mutual non-cooperation.

The U.S. Position

I have already suggested that the structure of U.S. policy preferences, deduced from the theory of income maximizing tariff wars, would have been that of Prisoners' Dilemma. There were at least four supporting elements that reinforced this preference structure. The first was the strength of American poultry producers in urging a combative strategy upon the political leadership. The position of the poultry industry was, not surprisingly, that Regulation 22 had to be completely abolished and that this should be the unalterable goal of U.S. policy.

Talbot (1978: 42) curiously suggests that the influence of farmers was not great: "United States policy decisions in the Chicken War were not, to a substantial degree, built on the domestic interests of American farmers." Yet in other places he points out that the poultry industry had strong Congressional advocates (1978: 95) and was able to send a delegation (including four state governors) to present the industry case directly to President Kennedy (1978: 71). He also notes that the administration needed farm support in order to pass the Trade Expansion Act of 1962, giving the President authority to enter the next round of GATT negotiations, the Kennedy Round (1978: 133).

Supporting the interests of U.S. poultry producers, the Department of Agriculture was the principal actor within the U.S. government pushing for a direct confrontation with the EEC, outweighing the more conciliatory stands taken by the State Department. President Kennedy, though he initially treated the dispute with what his Speech writer Sorenson referred to as "mock despair," eventually supported the tough stand taken by the Department of Agriculture in negotiations with the EEC.

A third factor was that the poultry issue had some importance in its own right, irrespective of the domestic backing it received. The production of chickens, like other farm commodities, suffered from over-production and falling prices, and a thriving export market was seen as the only easy solution.

Hence the initial U.S. demand during the early phases of the war was for a guarantee of the existing U.S. share of the market at the time of the formation of the EEC, and at the very least, a significant reduction in the proposed level of protection. Ironically, it was the U.S. that had insisted in the 1950s that domestic agricultural programs be exempted from the strictures of GATT. Nevertheless, as the dispute got under way, Secretary of Agriculture Freeman delivered a forceful message to the EEC that "We are not going to stand by and allow our historical market to be taken away" (quoted in Talbot 1978: 74).

Finally, there was more to the Chicken War than chickens. Walker (1964: 672) suggests that:

> the loss of a few million chickens was hardly catastrophic—when account is taken additionally of the fact that the reduced volume is still above the 1958–1961 average; that the German market is of peripheral importance to the American poultry industry as a whole; and that the long-range outlook there was not rosy, even had the old duty regime continued, considering the likelihood that the Europeans would soon master the technology and reacquire a competitive edge on their own side of the Atlantic. The wider importance of the chicken issue for the U.S. must be found elsewhere.

As I noted above, the U.S. did not vigorously challenge the EEC's agricultural proposals during the formative period of the EEC, from 1958 to 1961. The establishment of the EEC was seen as politically important, particularly since it was hoped that the EEC would replace a declining Britain as the principal ally of the U.S. (Talbot 1978: 57). Also at stake was the completion of the Dillon Round of tariff negotiations, under the auspices of GATT. Unable to secure EEC agreement to preserve its historic share of EEC agricultural markets, the U.S. allowed the Dillon Round to conclude under a "standstill agreement" in March 1962, by which the U.S. reserved its negotiating rights on agricultural matters as they stood in September 1960. This agreement covered all agricultural commodities that were to be subject to the variable levy system, and was based on GATT's article 14(6), requiring compensation for the "unbinding" of tariffs.

Although the wider resonance of the chicken issue initially encouraged U.S. restraint, it soon became a powerful incentive for a more belligerent U.S. policy. First, chickens were to be the first of many agricultural goods to be subject to CAP's variable levy, threatening agricultural exports to the EEC worth $1.2 billion in 1961. The EEC was the largest single market for U.S. agricultural exports. These exports were useful not only for the balance of payments, but also in reducing the costs of U.S. domestic farm subsidies. Second, there was the "still larger question of effective trade promotion tactics generally: the degree of forceful diligence with which the government ought to promote American trade interests wherever found, in this day of worry over the U.S. balance of payments" (Walker 1964: 672). Congress expected effective action in this regard, and strengthened the President's retaliatory powers during the passage of the Trade Expansion Act of 1962. The structure of U.S. preferences thus seems fairly clear.

The most preferred outcome would have been for the EEC to abandon agricultural protection, leaving the U.S. free to pursue its own protectionist proclivities. However, the iterated nature of trade games made this first preference unattainable, even if only because the EEC had made it clear that it would retaliate against U.S. protection. In March 1962 the U.S. sheet glass, carpet and rug industries received escape clause protection from EEC exports allegedly causing serious injury. The EEC promptly retaliated against U.S. chemical products (see Talbot 1978: 71). The best outcome the U.S. could hope for was mutual restraint in protection, obviously superior to the mutual trade barriers that would exist if the U.S. retaliated against EEC chicken tariffs. Least desirable would be to allow EEC policies to go unchallenged.

In short, the formal U.S. diplomatic position appears to have been premised on the (not necessarily conscious or explicit) judgement that the situation was analogous to an iterated Prisoners' Dilemma game in which the U.S. could only secure EEC restraint (i.e., the outcome of mutual cooperation) by credibly threatening and implementing retaliation. The difficulty with this strategy, as I shall discuss below, is that it assumed that the EEC also faced a Prisoners' Dilemma payoff structure.

The EEC Position

As a first cut at the imputation of goals to the EEC, one must presume that it too faced the Prisoners' Dilemma structure predicted by the theory of the optimal tariff war. However, in this case, the structure of economic payoffs was modified by internal political pressures. Like the U.S., the EEC had a strong agricultural lobby favoring greater protection of the EEC poultry industry, particularly in France, the largest producer.

The ramifications of Regulation 22 extended beyond merely increasing the degree of EEC self-sufficiency in poultry. Much more important was the widely accepted principal that the CAP was the foundation stone for the EEC itself. The basic CAP regulations were complicated and time consuming to negotiate, and the EEC was reluctant to reopen the issues even if only because of the huge transaction costs of the complicated logrolling agreements (based on the unanimity principle) necessary to construct the scheme.

As the negotiations with the U.S. progressed, the incentives for the EEC to refuse all modification of Regulation 22 increased. If it abandoned Regulation 22, the rest of the CAP would unravel and with it (or so many Europeans believed) the EEC. French President De Gaulle's veto of British entry in January 1963 made it even more vital to keep the rest of the EEC together, which meant continuing with the CAP, since he also emphasized that France would not stay in the EEC without a satisfactory agricultural policy that included high levels of protection. As Talbot (1978: 133) put it: "There could not be an EEC without France, and French agricultural interests would not cooperate unless agriculture was accorded special treatment within the Community." Regulation 22 became a symbol of the need for EEC unity in the face of a common adversary.

What does all this suggest about the structure of EEC preferences in the Chicken War? The EEC's most preferred outcome was obviously unilateral defection, where the U.S. would allow agricultural protection to proceed without retaliation. The most interesting question is whether the EEC preferred mutual cooperation (no EEC agricultural protection and no U.S. retaliation) to mutual defection (protection and retaliation).

Though there may have been a time early in the period when the EEC might have preferred the former, the increasingly unassailable linkage between Regulation 22, the rest of the CAP and the existence of the EEC made the preference for mutual defection over mutual cooperation overwhelmingly convincing to the major EEC decision-makers. The political benefits of a unified EEC outweighed the economic costs that could be imposed by U.S. retaliation.

Hence the EEC had the preference ordering of a Deadlock game (i.e., Prisoners'' Dilemma, but with DD>CC). With one actor (the EEC) playing a strategy of unconditional defection, and the other (the U.S.) playing a Prisoners' Dilemma strategy of conditional, retaliatory defection, the outcome of mutual defection would seem inevitable. The unlikelihood of cooperation becomes manifest when one examines the actual course of the bargaining between the EEC and the U.S.

Bargaining Tactics

The negotiations progressed (or rather, degenerated) through three stages: bargaining over the exact level of EEC protection of its poultry market, which then moved into increasingly acrimonious discussion of the magnitude of damages claimed by the U.S., along with some thinly veiled threats of linkage to larger games, and finally to the resolution phase when both sides agreed to GATT mediation. The process of negotiation in all three phases helped push the outcome to mutual, sustained defection.

The first phase of bargaining over levels of protection revealed the lack of any Pareto optimal bargaining set, that is to say, any solutions that both sides could agree to on the basis of making at least one of them better off without making the other worse off. The problem centered on access to the German market, which had previously been protected by a 15% tariff on imported poultry, in addition to a subsidy of 15%. Regulation 22 proposed to raise this level of protection by first establishing a sluice gate price for imported poultry, purportedly an estimate of foreign production costs, to which would be added a supplementary levy equal to the difference between the sluice gate price and the price of the foreign import, to which would then be added several ad valorem duties totalling 12.5%, and an equalization fee to offset the higher cost of feed grains within the EEC.

From June 1962 until September 1963, negotiations focused on the value of the sluice gate price, variable levy and equalization fees. Although the EEC lowered the sluice gate price (in April 1963), the variable levy (in November 1962 and January 1963) and the equalization fee (June 1963), it also raised them at other times during this period. The sluice gate price was raised in May 1963 and the levy in

June 1963. At this point, negotiations ground to a halt. Concessions created too many divisions within the EEC, and the U.S. finally despaired of getting anything near to the 25% ad valorem tariff that it proposed as an alternative to Regulation 22. By September 1963 the most the EEC could offer was a 10% reduction in the variable levy, which the U.S. countered with a demand for a 30% reduction. The U.S. had already formally requested compensation under the Dillon Round agreement (June 1963), and had begun hearings on proposals for retaliation.

Once the possibilities for altering Regulation 22 had been exhausted, and with them the patience of both sides, the discussions became more tense and acrimonious. In the same month that the U.S. requested a return to the Dillon Round protocol, a Senate Concurrent Resolution urged a firm stand by the U.S. By the end of July 1963 the U.S. declared that it would begin to consider on which imports concessions would be withdrawn in order to exact its claim of $46 million damages. The EEC claimed that only damages of $19 million were justifiable and threatened counter-retaliation to the amount of $27 million. All this occurred during the relatively brief period of June to September 1963.

In the course of this second phase both sides hinted at linkages to larger games. In August 1963 the French delegation to the Council of Ministers was reported to have threatened to cause difficulties at the coming Kennedy Round of GATT talks, if concessions were made to the U.S.; and President de Gaulle held a press conference in which he extolled the virtues of autarky (Talbot 1978: 98–9). On the U.S. side, mention was made of U.S. troop levels in Western Europe (Talbot 1978: 102). These threats had little credibility, partly because the magnitude of the threatened actions seemed disproportionately large, and more important, because such threats indicated considerable misperception of the opponent's payoff structure.

The essence of this second phase appears to have been the concerted attempts by both sides to convey a credible commitment not to cooperate and not to give in to the demands of the other party, both by hinting at linkages and by threatening counter-retaliation (in the case of the EEC). The obvious question to ask of such a strategy is what it could be expected to achieve, given the payoffs of Deadlock and Prisoners' Dilemma to the EEC and the U.S., respectively. If the EEC faced a Deadlock payoff, its strategy of defection should have been unconditional, and not contingent upon an estimated probability of U.S. retaliation. If it saw the U.S. as facing a Prisoners' Dilemma payoff structure, it should also have seen that conveying commitment to defection would only encourage the U.S. to also defect.

If the EEC convinced the U.S. that it would only choose defection, then defection would also be the only sensible move for the U.S. One explanation for this apparently irrational expression of resolve is that the EEC misperceived U.S. payoffs, thinking incorrectly that the U.S. was facing a completely different game (known as Chicken) in which EEC commitment to defection might force the U.S. to cooperate.

For the U.S. to demonstrate immovability also seems to have been a misplaced act of resolve. The constant U.S. emphasis on its next move (e.g., demanding the rights it claimed to preserve under the Dillon Round, and drawing up a retaliatory list of commodities) indicates that U.S. negotiators saw the game as an internally iterated Prisoners' Dilemma in which cooperation might be achieved by holding retaliation in reserve while waiting for the other party's move. The U.S. failed to see that the EEC payoff structure was not Prisoners' Dilemma, as the EEC failed to see that the U.S. preference ordering was Prisoners' Dilemma.

Both sides grossly underestimated the other's incentives to defect, most probably because they did not perceive the strength of domestic agricultural interests, both in the electoral systems and in their access to the institutions of government. Neither perceived the highly uncooperative nature of a Prisoners' Dilemma versus Deadlock game in which parties with relatively equal power (at least within the issue area) were fighting over stakes that were very close to constant sum in their configuration.

The denouement phase of the Chicken War began as early as April 1963, when the U.S. voiced hopes of GATT involvement in the dispute. It officially proposed GATT mediation in September, and the EEC accepted, despite its worries that GATT might be partial toward the U.S. view of the case. Reluctance to accept mediation is a predictable result of a Deadlock payoff structure (i.e, there is no reason to negotiate if you prefer a DD to CC). Why then, did the EEC accept mediation at all?

Perhaps it was because of uncertainty over what the U.S. might then feel driven to do in order to change the EEC's payoff structure, possibly considering options that hitherto had had little credibility (e.g., a linkage to NATO troop levels). A further escalation in the conflict might also have threatened to crack EEC unity against the

U.S., particularly since one member (West Germany) would have been highly vulnerable had the U.S. chosen to raise the stakes.

The GATT panel's finding, that the U.S. had a just grievance and was entitled to $26 million damages, was accepted by both parties. The U.S. raised tariffs on expensive brandy (hurting France), potato starch and dexedrine (hurting Holland) and on light trucks (hurting Germany). Though some hints of European counter-retaliation were made, the EEC was apparently happy to refocus its decision-making energies on its own internal disputes. The principal upon which this decision was based (viz., that suspension of concessions must be on a "Most Favored Nation" (MFN) basis, and not by imposing penalty tariffs on particular countries) was later challenged by an importer of Spanish brandy, but upheld by the U.S. Court of Customs and Patent Appeals.

Paradoxically, taking the dispute to GATT ensured that the conflict ended in a deadlock. Though it helped to contain and isolate the problem within the narrower confines of the process norms of the GATT regime, and so in a larger and longer term sense might be considered a "cooperative" outcome, mediation also reduced the chances of a mutually higher payoff within the shorter term, narrow structure of the chicken issue itself. This occurred first of all because GATT removed the iterativeness of the game by specifying an exact monetary amount of damages that could be requited in a single round of retaliatory withdrawal of concessions by the U.S. The possible cooperation inducing effects of many rounds of retaliation and counter-retaliation by parties using contingent strategies of retaliation (such as tit-for-tat) were thereby relinquished.

The analytic focus on iteration suggests another way in which GATT reduced cooperation—by precluding the kinds of longer term linkages to larger games (e.g., future trade matters or non-trade issues) which might have significantly reduced the incentives to defect for one or both parties. The U.S., for example, could not, once the dispute was with GATT, threaten a review of its NATO commitment. Had it done so, this would might have changed the EEC's payoff structure into one resembling Chicken, and made the EEC more cooperative, especially if the U.S. preference ordering remained (and was recognized by the EEC as being) that of Prisoners' Dilemma. The EEC might, of course, have counter-linked the Chicken War to the Kennedy Round, possibly giving the U.S. a Chicken payoff structure. Both parties might then have backed off and reached another solution. While all this is pure speculation, one may still conclude with some conviction that GATT did preclude the occurrence of events which might have reduced the gains from defection.

Thus, an assessment of the effect of GATT on the Chicken War ultimately turns on one's definition of cooperation. GATT reduced cooperation within the narrow confines of the chicken issue, by encapsulating the conflict and isolating it from further iteration and linkage effects that might have increased the incentive to seek an outcome with higher joint economic payoffs. Yet GATT also might be considered to have helped cooperation insofar as it prevented these additional effects hurting longer term trade and other foreign policy interests.

Chickens and Other Animals

The Chicken War pattern was repeated in a conflict over the EEC's application of the sluice gate price and variable levies to turkey meat. U.S. tariffs on brandy had been lowered in 1974 in an attempt to induce European concessions during the Tokyo Round of GATT negotiations. However, in July 1974 the EEC greatly increased levies on imported turkeys.

Negotiations carried on through 1975 and 1976, in much the same manner as they had in the Chicken War; that is to say, bargaining centered on alterations in the level of EEC restrictions. Both sides claimed to have made concessions: the U.S. had in 1974 reduced the incidence of the Chicken War's retaliatory tariff on brandy, and the EEC held back automatic increases in turkey levies during 1975 and 1976. Again, as in the Chicken War, negotiations proved fruitless, and the U.S. eventually retaliated in November 1976 with increases in brandy duties. The EEC replied by increasing the levies on turkeys. The Turkey War appears to have had much the same payoff structure as did the Chicken War. The U.S. strategy was one of contingent retaliation, while the EEC had a unilateral preference for defection, again because of internal EEC politics. Hence the Deadlock—Prisoners' Dilemma game ending at DD.

Disputes of this type have become somewhat more cooperative in outcome, as the EEC's commitment to the consequences of CAP have come into question. The U.S. imposed penalty duties of 40% on EEC pasta in 1985, retaliating for EEC tariff preferences in favor of Mediterranean citrus fruits, and the EEC retaliated against U.S. lemons and walnuts. A truce was finally proclaimed in August 1986, with both sides removing their penalty tariffs.

A similar issue arose in 1986, when the U.S. threatened quotas (and the EEC threatened counter-retaliation) on some two dozen EEC exports (including wine, cheese and pork), unless compensated for the new EEC trade restrictions on grain products, which accompanied the entry of Spain and Portugal into the EEC. In July 1986, the EEC agreed to compensate for the loss of U.S. grain exports.

More cooperation has been achieved where EEC agricultural export interests are directly affected by retaliation—removing the public good incentive for EEC agriculture to demand protection irrespective of U.S. retaliation. In 1975, the U.S. forced the EEC to reduce export subsidies on cheese, by threatening a countervailing duty. These are more symmetric Prisoners' Dilemma situations where the EEC derives no great benefits from the game ending in mutual defection.

The more recent dispute, beginning in 1982, between the EEC and the U.S. over agricultural export subsidies in third markets is similar in nature, since each can quickly remove much of the benefit to the other from defection, by way of retaliatory defection (i.e., raising its own export subsidies). The war began with President Reagan's decision in January 1983 to make $250 million available to subsidize farm exports, at the same time announcing a large sale of subsidized flour to Egypt, long one of the EEC's best markets. One intent of the U.S. was to force the EEC to allow the issue of export subsidies to be discussed within GATT, having already filed complaints with GATT over EEC export subsidies on flour, pasta, poultry and sugar. The EEC retaliated with a subsidized wheat sale to China in February 1983. In 1985, the U.S. announced a subsidized wheat sale to Algeria, a traditionally French market. Two billion dollars was made available to the Bonus Incentive Commodity Export Program, for the subsidization of agricultural exports to countries where the U.S. has lost markets through unfair foreign competition. The recent concern of both sides to reduce their farm subsidy costs should help dampen their enthusiasm for this battle.

Analogous disputes have occurred within the EEC. One of these is the chronic conflict between France and Britain over the use by both parties of health regulations to restrict imports of agricultural goods from the other. France has typically restricted the import of British lamb (most recently in September 1984), ostensibly because of the use of pesticides and hormone treatments. Britain, for its part, restricts imports of French poultry and heat-treated milk, also on spurious health grounds.

It is not clear whether the Anglo-French game is Prisoners' Dilemma or Deadlock, that is to say, whether or not the domestic political support benefits outweigh the economic welfare losses. This is partly because it is not clear how much these conflicts are genuinely interactive, and how much they are simply temporally coincident responses to domestic forces. It is also difficult to identify a payoff structure because a third party (the EEC Court of Justice) has usually intervened in order to force a cooperative solution. Third party intervention also occurred in the Chicken War, but not until the dispute had dragged on long enough for the payoff structure to be readily apparent. In any case, GATT intervention did not alter the final outcome in the Chicken War (U.S. retaliation), but merely specified and sanctified the exact amount of punishment to be inflicted. In the Anglo-French wars the EEC Court declared both restrictions invalid, and forced a cooperative solution, making both parties economically (if not electorally) better off.

Conclusion

The Chicken War was selected in order to illustrate some of the problems of cooperation in a simple, short, yet still internally iterated game, where mutual defection is the result. The discussion has identified three reasons for the outcome: the Prisoners' Dilemma (for the U.S.) versus Deadlock (for the EEC) structure of payoffs (including the near constant sum nature of the payoffs), misperception and institutional variables. These factors necessarily altered the a priori prediction that an optimal tariff war between two large size powers should move initially to mutual defection, but subsequently evolve into an agreement to cooperate.

Both parties' efforts to convey commitment to unconditional (in the case of the EEC) or conditional (in the case of the U.S.) defection merely served to increase the incentives for the other side to also defect, suggesting that each misperceived the game payoff to the other side. The U.S. thought the game was an iterated, mutual Prisoners' Dilemma in which the EEC could be induced to cooperate by a commitment to retaliate. The EEC thought that the U.S. could be "chickened" out of its resolve to retaliate.

Finally, GATT mediation isolated the dispute both temporally and spatially, reducing the iterativeness or potential linkages that might have been conducive to restraint, and might in this case have modified the EEC's propensity to see the game as Deadlock. Hence the game was cooperative only in the sense that some other consequences outside of the particular issue were avoided, but uncooperative in terms of the economic payoffs of the Chicken War itself.

Notes

1. The material for this chapter has been summarized from John Conybeare, Trade Wars (New York: Columbia University Press, 1987).
2. Most of the historical background for the following discussion of the Chicken War was obtained from Ross Talbot, The Chicken War (Ames: Iowa State University Press, 1978).

References

Conybeare, John A.C. 1987. Trade Wars. New York: Columbia University Press.
Talbot, Ross. 1978. The Chicken War. Ames: Iowa State University Press.
Walker, Herman. 1964. "Dispute Settlement: The Chicken War." American Journal of International Law. No. 58, July.

Chapter 13

Agriculture Policy and Policy Making

G. R. Boynton

Drought and a depressed international market are the two principal threats to the prosperity of U.S. agriculture. Both have hit the agricultural community in the 1980s—with a vengeance. The drought of 1983 was followed by the "overvalued" dollar and the consequent un-competitiveness of U.S. agricultural products on the international market. Then, just as the agricultural community was beginning to return to a measure of prosperity the drought of 1988 hit.

Despite drought, a rocky road in the international market, and the Reagan administration which wanted to get the government "off the back" of farmers by having no agricultural program, agricultural policy in the 1980s remains essentially unchanged. The agricultural policy of the 1980s, enacted in the two authorization acts of 1981 and 1985, has the same basic structure as the legislation passed in the early 1970s. Given the propensity of Congress to react to crises—such as drought and depressed markets—with legislation aimed at solving the crisis of the moment, continuity in policy "across crises" is a puzzle.

This paper looks back to the 1960–1973 period to understand agricultural policy and policy making. The argument of the paper is that policy and policy making interact reaching what can be understood as an equilibrium in the 1970s that has been reproduced ever since. The paper focuses on the Senate Agriculture Committee.[1] The policy making of the committee is characterized as a constrained search through a policy space without having "ahead of time" a clear understanding of what the law would become as a result of the search. This characterization is consistent with Herbert Simon's conception of procedural rationality and is consistent with the information available about the committee.

The picture emerging from this research is that of a committee paying careful attention to the detailed working of the law, and, over a thirteen year period, adapting the law to function throughout the boom-bust cycle that characterizes economic conditions in agriculture. Agricultural legislation is elaborate with intricate interactions between provisions. The committee develops a rather precise understanding of these interactions during the thirteen years studied. The result is a law that adjusts to both boom and bust—homeostatically maintaining farm income and adjusting the cost to taxpayers. It is this feature that has given the law staying power. Congress and various administrations have, justifiably, been accused of "throwing money" at some problems without attending to how the program is working or what would make it work better. That is not what one sees here.

The Framework of Analysis

Law making may be understood as a process, operating through time, of putting together provisions to constitute a law. The first point emphasized in this framework for analysis is the historical continuity of legislating. For example, an agricultural authorization act was passed in each of the years 1965, 1970, 1973, 1977, 1981, and 1985. Much of the legislation passed by Congress each year is re-authorization and re-appropriation with modifications and additions or amendments to legislation that is already "on the books." A system with this character will go to an equilibrium over time, if one exists, and that is the conclusion of the research reported here. The law, as of 1973, is an equilibrium for this policy making process.[2]

Herbert Simon, in a paper addressed to economists, lists the features of a decision making process that need to be examined.

> Economics without psychological and sociological research to determine the givens of the decision-making situation, the focus of attention, the problem representation, and the processes used to identify alternatives, estimate consequences, and choose among possibilities—such economics is a one-bladed scissors.[3]

Procedural rationality, as explicated by Herbert Simon, serves as the basis for unpacking the functional relationships of this framework of analysis.

Simon's list is a larger agenda than a single paper. Two of the processes on his list are examined in this paper: 1) problem representation, and 2) the processes used to estimate consequences of policy alternatives. The problem representation adopted by the committee serves to limit the policy space searched. The committee's problem representation does not go unchallenged; the Farm Bureau and Republican administrations regularly challenge this problem representation. But the committee's representation of the problem is a constant through the entire period which is its importance in producing the equilibrium. The way the committee estimates the consequences of policy alternatives proposed by witnesses shows in a particularly clear way the interaction of process and policy. The provisions of the legislation at (t-1) becomes the calculating routine for the committee when assessing proposals for change. These two processes are the focus of the paper because they seem particularly important in the equilibrating of policy and policy making through the period.[4]

The paper is organized to show how these two routines operate to produce and maintain the equilibrium which is the structure of the law from 1973 to present. The process being explained occurs through time, and a chronological account would have been one straightforward way to describe it. But the paper is analytical rather than chronological; it describes the law and two features of the process. There are, however, a number of historical references that are difficult to understand without some chronological account of "what" was happening "when" during the period. The next section gives a very brief chronology to provide a context for these references. The third section describes the representation of the problem adopted by the committee and shows how it reduces the space searched by the committee. The fourth section describes the operation of the law. This is the law as of 1973; it is the result of 13 years of change and adaptation. Then in the fifth section I present evidence that the law at (t-1) is the calculating routine used by the committee in estimating the consequences of policy alternatives suggested to them. The final section of the paper asks what it means to characterize the process as 'procedural rationality.'

Brief Chronology

One legacy of the Eisenhower administration was warehouses bursting at the seams with wheat and feed grain surpluses, the law that produced the surpluses, and grain farmers who were no longer willing to accept the mandatory programs that had characterized much of U.S. agricultural policy since the 1930's. The agriculture committees, Congress, and three administrations struggled with this problem for 13 years, 1960–73, attempting to bring prosperity to the agricultural community.

Agricultural legislation is organized by commodities—corn and feed grains, cotton, rice, wheat, dairy products and other smaller programs.[5] Before 1965 each of the commodity programs was handled in separate legislation. The provisions of the legislation were different for each commodity and the "current" financial condition of each commodity was different. This paper will focus on the changes in the corn and feed grains program and the wheat program. In 1960 the laws for these two commodities were quite different. By 1973 they had become very similar, and this basic structure is then generalized to operate for the other programs—except for the dairy program.

In 1960 the Kennedy administration found large surpluses, production exceeding demand for corn, feed grains, and for wheat, and a depressed market price. In 1962 a mandatory program for wheat passed Congress but was rejected by the wheat growers. The administration and Congress then passed legislation for a voluntary program modeled very roughly on the program for corn and feed grains. In 1965 the major commodity programs were brought together for the first time in a single law. In 1965 and 1970 there was much argument about setting the amount to be loaned per bushel and the value of the different certificates of the programs. During this period the Commodity Credit Corporation was taking much of the wheat and corn grown by farmers and re-selling it. By 1970 the surpluses had been substantially reduced and the market was recovering. In 1972 the Soviet Union purchased large quantities of U.S. wheat, corn, and feed grains, completely wiping out the surpluses. By 1973 most corn, feed grains, and wheat was being sold in the market as demand was strong and prices were high. The target price, which had been adopted for the wheat program between 1970 and 1973, was made a part of the legislation for most of the other commodities.

During the 1960s the emphasis was on how to protect farm income when prices were depressed and how to handle surpluses. In the 1970s the emphasis turned to adjusting the law so there were no payments to farmers when agriculture was prospering while still retaining the features of the law that protected farmers when the next "bust" arrived.

The Problem Representation Adopted by the Senate Agriculture Committee

How a problem is understood is critically important in finding a solution. How human beings proceed depends, in large measure, on how they understand or represent a problem.[6]

There are five constants in the committee's representation of the problem that faces them. They are:

1. The law should contain provisions to protect farm income when there is a precipitous drop in demand—even during periods when demand and prices are high.
2. Bringing supply into line with demand is accomplished by controlling supply rather than increasing demand.
3. Voluntary rather than mandatory programs.
4. U.S. agriculture should participate in the international market rather than producing only for the U.S. market.
5. The programs should be designed to minimize the cost to the government as there is a limit on what Congress as a whole will spend on agriculture.

Before describing the committee's understanding of these points it is important to see how these constants influence consideration of the provisions to be included in the legislation. These are not provisions of legislation, but the next section describes the coordination between provisions of legislation that is necessary for the law to work within these constraints.

If one of these constants was changed it would have quite dramatic effects on the entire agricultural program. To illustrate this, one constant will be considered changed and the implication for a single provision of the legislation will be considered. An argument can be made for restricting U.S. agriculture to the U.S. market. The U.S. market is much more stable than the international market; the ups and downs generally associated with the agricultural economy would be smoothed out. Sticking to the U.S. market was suggested by some witnesses in 1965, during that period of farm recession, and was even more strongly argued for in the middle 1980s by the American Farm Movement. How would this change effect the legislation? The legislation worked out by the committee involves reducing excess production by restricting the number of acres that a farmer can plant in a given commodity. When demand goes back up farmers are then permitted to increase the acreage planted in the commodity. This provision promotes increasing bushels per acre even when demand is down because income support is based on the total number of bushels produced. This provision "makes sense" only if you think the long term trend is growth in demand—which it has been for the international market. For example, the amount of wheat produced in the U.S. almost tripled between the 1960s and the 1980s, and most of the increase was due to increasing the number of bushels produced per acre. But U.S. demand for wheat has remained almost constant.

The general point is that these five points define a set of alternatives with a minimum of 32 combinatorial possibilities. The committee, by restricting its consideration to one point in this 32 point space, rules out a vast number of possibilities for the legislation they are fashioning. The rest of this section describes how the committee understood each of these constants.

Boom and Bust

The starting point in the Committee's representation of their problem is "boom and bust." The history of U.S. agriculture, as understood by the Committee, is oscillation between good times and bad times.

By 1973 the government-held surpluses of the 1960's had been sold off. International demand was growing rapidly. But the committee was not prepared to give up on bust as the principal problem they faced. The following conversation between Senators Humphrey and Young is indicative of the position of the entire Committee.

> Senator Humphrey. If we expand production as much as recommended by the administration do farmers need better guarantees against lower prices?
>
> Witness. Yes
>
> Sen. Humphrey. Well, I want to emphasize this, Mr. Chairman. I happen to believe that we are going to have to produce more, a great deal more, this year and maybe for years to come. In fact, I think we ought to look forward to that. But the experience that members of this committee have had—I have been on this committee off and on since 1949—is that every time we have asked our farmers to open up and produce, almost without exception, something has gone amiss . . .
>
> And what happened was the farmer went down the tube, the prices collapsed and the surpluses gathered. The Government

costs on surpluses went up and, basically, what really happened was liquidation of thousands of farms . . .

Sen. Young. I quoted the wheat figures in 1953. They were higher then than they are now. That year, the Secretary of Agriculture, Secretary Bensen, asked farmers to increase wheat production . . . But I remember very well that the Secretary of Agriculture then asked farmers to increase production.

Sen. Humphrey. And prices went down.[7]

World demand was picking up, and the Secretary of Agriculture was urging farmers to expand production. Supplying the demand was good for farmers as well as for the nation's balance of trade. The Committee, however, wanted to make sure there was protection for farmers when the "inevitable" bust came—as it did in the 1980's.

Supply and Demand

In the Committee's representation of the problem, demand is taken as a given. Demand for U.S. commodities fluctuates with weather patterns that increase or decrease the output of other producing nations. It fluctuates with political decisions to increase or decrease output in the same nations. Demand fluctuates with political decisions by importing nations such as India or the Soviet Union. Demand fluctuates with changes in technology; the substitution of man-made fibers for cotton, for example. Few of the factors affecting demand are under the control of the Committee. The Committee, the Department of Agriculture, and U.S. farmers may try to estimate demand to adapt to it, but they could influence demand only marginally. They were "in charge of" school lunch programs, Public Law 480 and food stamps. They did, in 1973, attempt to make sure the Department of Agriculture was well organized to take advantage of export markets. But these were modest influences on the total market demand.

The commodity programs are primarily designed to balance supply and demand by controlling supply. Increasing demand is a policy space largely unexplored.

A Voluntary Program

The principal organization of agricultural policy from the 1930's through the 1950's was mandatory programs. A referendum of all producers was held when one authorizing law expired and another was passed. If two-thirds of the producers voted for the program then quotas for production were established and farm income was supported with a nonrecourse loan.[8] The programs for wheat, cotton, rice and tobacco were all organized this way. Corn and the feed grains were the major exception; the growers had not accepted a mandatory program.

Two events brought change in the agricultural program. One was the rapid buildup of wheat, corn and feed grain surpluses at the end of the Eisenhower administration. This "disaster" shifted the focus of attention of the Committee to these two commodities. The other was rejection of a mandatory program by wheat growers early in the 1960's. Devising a voluntary program which would promote prosperity for the family farmer became the focal point of Committee activity for the thirteen years from 1960 through 1973. When the Committee found a satisfactory "solution" they shifted the remaining mandatory programs.

The search of the Committee during this period was primarily a search through the options available for a voluntary program.

The International Market

Wheat is sold in an international market. In 1965 sixty percent of the wheat grown in the U.S. was exported. By 1970 exports had increased to two-thirds of the U.S. crop. During the 1960's corn and feed grains grown in the U.S. were used primarily in the U.S. But during the early 1970's that began to change, and corn and feed grains became an export commodity. These commodities could not be sold in the international market if the agricultural program raised the price above the international market price as it had in the 1950s. The means used to support prosperity for wheat and feed grain farmers could not simultaneously price their product out of the market.

The desire to sell wheat and feed grains in the international market ruled out a number of "solutions" the Committee might have explored. There was almost no interest in farming only for the U.S. market during this period.

Limits on What We Can "Sell" to our Congressional Colleagues

There are limits on what Congress will invest in promoting the prosperity of family farmers. The members of the Committee keep reminding witnesses that changing demography limits what farmers, and the Committee, can expect.

> The Chairman. One thing that has concerned me in the last 4 or 5 years, is the shift of population from the farm, from country to the city. When I first came here, as I recall, about 22 or 23 percent of the people lived on the farms, they earned their living there. Today, it is about 7 1/2 percent. That shift is being reflected in the House of Representatives. We have a lot of Congressmen who represent city folks entirely. Of course, city folks don't like these payments being made to the farmers. You see it all around. What concerns me is the fact that many of these programs are becoming more and more costly. That cost is reflected either in taxes or in prices, you know. My fear is that if we are depending on the Government too much and make these programs cost too much there may be a reaction by the Congressmen who represent the cityfolks in the House of Representatives.
>
> Mr. Smith. Certainly.
>
> The Chairman. We have discussed that around this table quite often and that is a big concern to me.[9]

The search from 1960 through 1973 was a search for provisions for the program that would reduce the cost and still protect farm income.

The Committee's Representation of Their Legislative Problem in the Discussion of the Wheat Program

If the proposals discussed by the Committee are examined it is clear that the Committee is, for the most part, operating from this one starting point; the other thirty-one are largely unexplored by the Committee. Figure 13.1 presents a hierarchically organized count of proposals discussed for the wheat program in 1965. Each time a provision is discussed, whether it is in the law or is a proposal for changing the law, it was counted and placed in one of the categories used in the figure. The percentages add "up." Forty-six percent of the proposals discussed were about income support. That 46 percent can be added to the 43 percent for production control, and that plus 4 percent general discussion of a two price program equals the 93 percent in the box "two price."

Provisions that would work under a mandatory program are only 5.5 percent of the total while 92.5 percent of the provisions discussed

278 *The Public Policy Outcome*

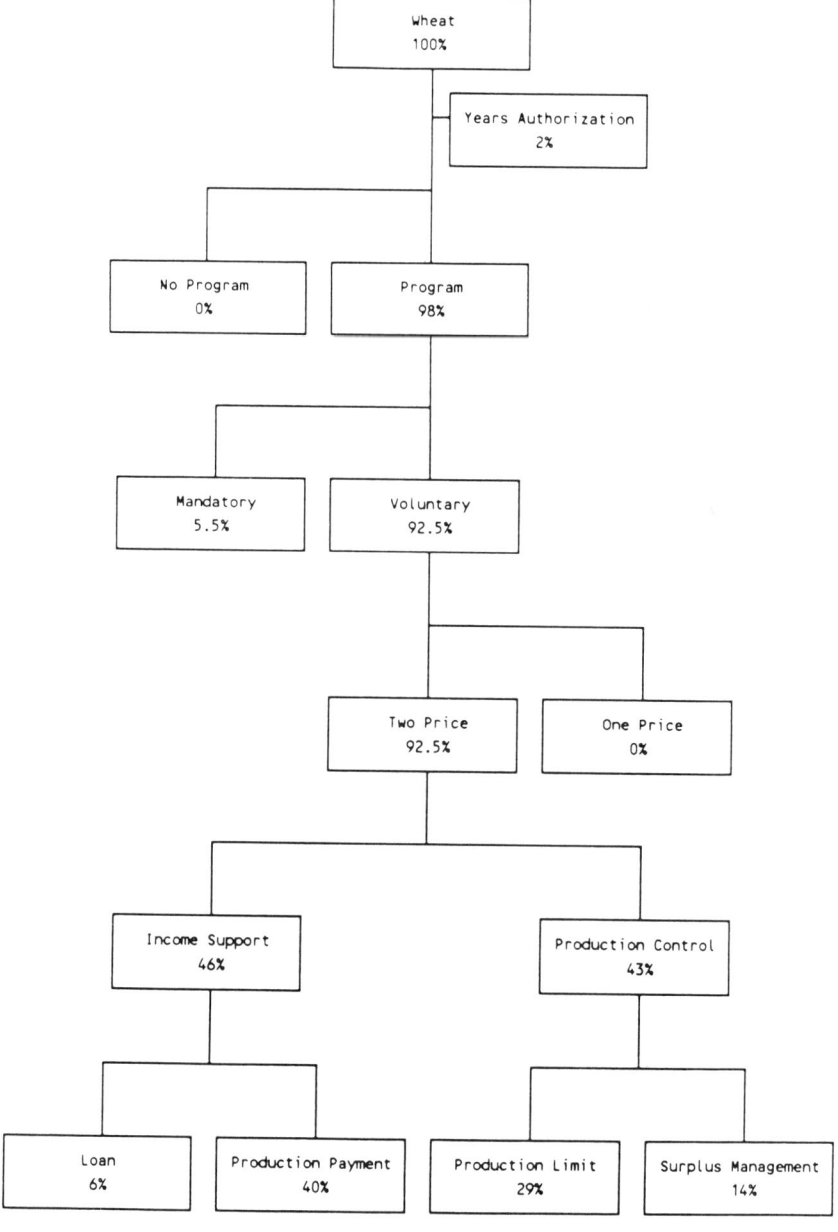

Figure 13.1. Provisions considered wheat program

Agriculture Policy and Policy Making 279

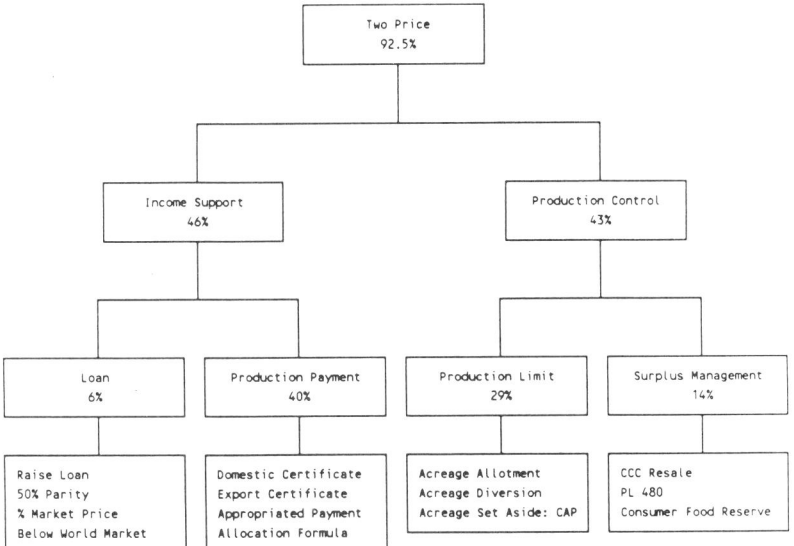

Figure 13.2. Specific provisions

are for a voluntary program. The emphasis on income support and production control is consistent with protecting farmers against bust. The discussion of the provisions related to the international market are found in figure 13.2. Figure 13.2 carries the "tree" down to the level of specific provisions discussed. The international character of the program, as revealed in the discussion of provisions, is: 1) the loan needs to be below the world market price; 2) the export certificate was used to generate income for farmers for wheat sold abroad at world market prices; and 3) PL 480 is discussed primarily as a means of reducing wheat surpluses. The limit on what the program can cost does not show up as a separate provision. How much the program will cost is a function of the provisions adopted. But "limits" is a point made over and over in the hearings.

The point is: This is a distinctive understanding of their legislative task. Other ways of representing the problem were available; starting at any one of the 31 other points in this space would have produced discussion of very different proposals. As they developed a distinctive representation of their problem they narrowed the search for a solution.

The Homeostatic Quality of the 1973 Law

The last section described five constraints within which the committee operated in fashioning agricultural policy. This section describes the law that was produced, operating under those constraints, which has been reproduced in all subsequent agricultural authorization legislation. The claim is that the structure of the legislation described in this section is an equilibrium for agricultural policy making operating within these five constraints.

The five principal components of the program are described next.

The Nonrecourse Loan or Price Support

When a farmer harvests a crop it may be used as collateral for a loan from the government. If the farmer sells the crop in the market for more than the loan the loan will be re-paid with carrying charges, and the farmer will receive the higher price obtained in the market. If the wheat or corn cannot be sold for more than the loan then the government keeps the collateral and the farmer keeps the loan. The loan is called a nonrecourse loan because turning the commodity/collateral over to the government does not have a negative impact on farmers' credit rating.

The important feature of this provision of the law is that it sets the lower bound for the market. Prices will not fall below, or much below, the per bushel value of the loan. If the market price is likely to fall below the loan value most farmers will participate in the government program, and they will turn their crop over to the government if the loan is worth more than the market when they are ready to sell. For this reason the nonrecourse loan has usually been called a price support.

One of the changes between the 1950's and the 1960's was a substantial drop in price supports. The loan for wheat, for example, dropped from $2.00 a bushel to $1.25 a bushel, and the Committee held it there through 1973 letting the moderate inflation of the period push it further toward the cost of production.

Commodity Credit Corporation Resale Price

When there is a surplus and the Commodity Credit Corporation is taking over a substantial percentage of the annual production there is also an upper bound on the market. The U.S. Government, through the Commodity Credit Corporation, becomes the owner of large stocks of the commodity which is sold when the price rises. When the market price reached 105 percent of the price the CCC had paid, the government stocks could be sold on the open market. This was changed to 115 percent in 1970 as the surpluses declined.

If the government is holding more than a year's supply of a commodity, as it did wheat for much of the 1960's, the government can supply more than any difference between demand and what is being produced "this year" by farmers. For most of the 1960's the market price for wheat and corn fluctuated only between the value of the loan and 105 percent of the loan because the surpluses held by the government were "hanging over the market;" as farmers and the Committee were wont to characterize the situation.

When the government had sold most of its stock, the remaining surplus had a much less dramatic effect on market price. But it took an entire decade for the government to sell the surpluses they had purchased at the end of the 1950's. And prices were substantially constrained by this action.

One of the features of this provision is that the government gets back most of what it has "lost" on defaulted loans. There is an "opportunity cost"; the government could be doing something else with the money. However, most of the cost of price supports is returned to the government via the resale of the crop.

Reducing Production

The program reduces production three ways. The means of calculating how each would work and thus the names change during the period. But the "basic idea" behind each is re-produced in each authorization act.

The first is a conservation reserve. This was based on a survey of land use taken at the end of the 1950's. At that time the agricultural program encouraged farmers to produce as much as they could. Thus, this was probably a reasonable estimate of land that would not be in production under most conditions. If a farmer participated in the program a certain part of the land could not be planted to conserve the productive value of the land.

Second, to participate in the program farmers established an historical base of producing a crop. If there was a surplus farmers had to plant less than the full base when participating in the program. In the first half of the 1960's, for example, participants in the corn program had to plant 20 percent fewer acres in corn than their base.

The third provision allowed the Secretary of Agriculture to make set aside payments to further reduce production. Farmers would be paid to divert land from production of the crop in surplus. The payment was less than the loan because farmers had very modest expenses on this land.

Target Price or Income Support

If price supports are reduced to approximately the cost of production as part of the mechanism of inducing participation then farmers will obtain very little income from the price support. But farmers have to have money to live on. The solution was income support. Initially this took the form of certificates which were financed quite differently for wheat and corn. Each farmer participating in the program received a certificate, for each bushel produced, which was redeemed for cash.

The major innovation of the 1973 law was the target price. The target price is a price per bushel the Committee determines is necessary to provide farmers with adequate income. When the market price is less than the target price the farmer is given a deficiency payment which is the difference between the market price and the target price. If the market price is greater than the target price there is no deficiency payment, and the cost of the program to the government is only the cost of administration. The deficiency payment "automatically" adjusts annually as the market price increases and decreases.

The target price and deficiency payments provide a means for the government to "smoothly" withdraw from support of agriculture when market prices are good as well as support farm income when market prices fall. It lets the law "adjust to" both boom and bust.

Annual Adjustment

Authorization bills lasted for from three to five years during this period. They also contained a large number of parameters which were to be adjusted for annual variation in supply and demand. The Secretary of Agriculture was given the responsibility for making these annual adjustments, and in the legislation the Committee set boundaries on the adjustments. When times were bad or when the Committee did not trust the administration they set narrower bounds. When agriculture was booming in the 1970's they gave the Secretary more latitude.

Summary

The committee wanted to promote farm income within five constraints. The provisions of legislation for doing that have been described. By 1973 the law had become:

The program is voluntary; farmers participate only when it is to their advantage.

When agriculture is booming no farmers participate, and no tax revenues are used.

Participation is induced by a combination of spreading the surpluses over time and transferring income from the rest of the society to agriculture when agriculture is not booming.

The nonrecourse loan, price supports, is a way of spreading the effects of surpluses over time. The surpluses the government takes "this year" it will sell next year and the next year. That means production must be reduced, and lower income for farmers.

The deficiency payment and the payment for voluntarily setting aside acres are income transfer. The deficiency payment supplements farmer income to a level the Committee and Congress determine it should not fall below. The voluntary set aside reduces the surplus more quickly than the nonrecourse loan alone by paying farmers not to plant. It shortens the time over which the surplus must be spread.

This form of income protection was within the guidelines of GATT. And the price support is normally set at or below the international market price.

Within its own limits, the law promotes efficiency in agriculture. In almost all circumstances the more efficient farmers will benefit more than the less efficient. Greater efficiency might have resulted from some other law, but this law is not designed to "stand in the way" of efficiency in agriculture.

The law is a homeostatic mechanism in not letting farmers' income fall below the target price, reducing production when there were surpluses and letting production expand as surpluses declined, and varying the cost of achieving that goal directly with the distance between the market price and the goal. The "lower bound" of prosperity for the family farmer is the target price. How it is achieved, through boom and bust, is the law.

How the Committee Computed Benefit to Farmers

The paper has described five commitments of the committee which shape the law. The law that resulted from their actions has been described, and it has been shown to fit within these five constraints. But the constraints are only "boundaries." They do not fully determine what the law will become. How the committee, working within these constraints, moves from the disparate collection of independent laws of 1960 to the law described in the previous section—now applied with only modest variations to all the commodities—is the subject of this section. The section shows how the history of the period and the way the committee computes benefit to farm income interact to produce the legislation.

The Importance of History

The sequence of laws governing the wheat and feed grain programs took a sharp turn in the early 1960's. Thereafter it was a history of refinement or adjusting the law to changed circumstances.[10] The importance of the refinements lies in the circumstances to which the law was being adjusted.

In 1965 the committee held hearings to discuss with the Secretary of Agriculture and approximately 100 witnesses how the law was working and how it could be improved. They did the same in 1970 and 1973. For the most part these were not "in principle" assessments of the law. They were very concrete; what was happening to farmers that year? The importance of the history of the period for the development of the law is that between 1960 and 1973 farmers and the Committee went through an entire boom and bust cycle. The focus of most of the 1960s was on bust. How do you handle the surplus and maintain farm income—were the questions that dominated the hearings. Adjustments made to the law were made to improve the way it handled these problems. By 1970, and even more strongly in 1973, demand was growing. The problem became adapting a law designed to support farm income during bust to the changed circumstance of boom. How to reduce the cost that had been built into the program in the 1960s without losing the income protection features of the law was the important focus of attention. This was the problem that the target price-deficiency payment was designed to solve.

History provided the opportunity to—or forced—the committee to work through adjustments in the law through an entire boom and bust cycle. In making these historically "driven" adjustments the committee works through the full range of possibilities of the boom bust cycle for this organization of the legislation. And in working through this full range reaches an equilibrium.

How the Committee Computes the Consequences of Recommendations

The historical description of the market conditions to which the law was being adjusted gives a macro perspective on the process. This section describes the adjustment from a micro perspective.

Here is the problem for members of the committee. They receive a large number of recommendations for changes in the law. How are they to sort out the "good" ideas from the not so good ideas? It is clear from the hearings that they do this sorting and that they do it rather easily. One of the ways they do it has already been described. If the recommendation challenges any one of their "commitments" then they present arguments to the witness about the infeasibility of the recommendation. But that is only part of the story. The committee is also able to compute the effects of the recommendation for farmers. They can calculate "what's in it" for farmers. This calculation is used to estimate how farmers will respond to the proposal and the consequences of the actions they estimate the farmers will take for the operation of the recommended provision in the context of all the components of the legislation.

Two examples of these "computations" are given in this section. They are intended to illustrate two points: One, that the committee does make these calculations or, more precisely, that what they say only makes sense if they are understood to be making such calculations. Two, that their computing routines are updated as they learn about the operation of the law. Then the routines used by the committee are discussed.

Participation in the Cropland Adjustment Program

In 1960 the U.S. government owned record amounts of feed grains and wheat. Reducing production while these surpluses were sold in the market became a central focus for agricultural policy for almost a decade. In 1965 the Secretary of Agriculture recommended re-authorizing, amending, and re-naming the Soil Bank program. He believed long term land retirement contracts, 5 and 10 years, would attract farmers at a lower cost than the annual diversion program. The members of the Committee do their calculations and come up with a different answer.

> Senator Young. I think it would be going too far if we required the operator to put his entire acreage of allotment crops into the program before he could retire any other crop acreage. Farmers in my area just could not go into such a program. On the other hand if a producer had to take out a percentage of his total allotment equal to the percentage of the land he is retiring is of his total cropland, it would be all right . . . This would be equitable. A farmer could live with this kind of a program. Otherwise I think it would be useless to put such a program on the statute books. You probably would get all the poor land signed up under such a program and little else . . .
>
> The Chairman. . . . But this statement of yours, that you are making to us today about the first acres to go in are these allotments, I agree with Senator Young there that the chances are that you might be able to set aside very few acres under that, particularly if the farmer desires to keep on growing wheat or corn or whatever he is permitted to grow on these allotment acres.[11]

The Committee was in favor of a long term retirement program that would help reduce production, but they "computed" that the financial arrangements proposed by the Secretary "would get all the poor land signed up under such a program and little else." Farmers would not find it financially beneficial to participate in the program by their calculation. If farmers would not participate then the provision recommended by the Secretary would not make an important contribution to reducing production.

The Cropland Adjustment Program was included in the bill reported by the Committee, but it had quite different provisions for payment. They are provisions the Committee believed farmers would find attractive.[12]

Setting the Value of the Nonrecourse Loan

One of the facets of the law the committee has to work out is what the value of the loan should be. The value of the loan is directly related to participation. In 1965 the Committee knew the nonrecourse loan had to be held down for the law to work the way they wanted it to work. When raising the loan was proposed this was the reaction:

> Mr. Heinkel. No. I think our farmers would be inclined to favor raising the loan rate rather than the price support payment.
>
> Senator Mondale. If you raise the price support payment, don't you improve the percentage for compliance at the same time you improve the income for the complier?
>
> Mr. Heinkel. Yes. I don't mean we oppose it. It does get greater compliance and you keep this grain from going into storage and that holds down costs.[13]

The effect of raising the loan rate is lower participation in the program, agree Senator Mondale and the witness. The effect of raising the "price support payment"[14] is greater compliance. The Committee was attempting to achieve reduced production, and they preferred improving farmers' income by increasing the "price support payment."

By 1973 the Committee had shifted from not raising the loan to setting the loan at the cost of production.

> Senator Clark. You feel, all of you, that the support prices ought to be held at about the cost of production?
>
> Mr. Van Pelt. This would sure give you something to fall back on if you have a support price there. So you have the option then of storing that wheat on the farm and this is why I feel it is really important . . .
>
> Senator Clark. There have been several witnesses here, as I understand it, who have said that the support price ought to be increased because of the increased cost of farming and various

items and it ought to keep pace with inflationary increases and so forth. You don't support that concept as I understand it . . .

Mr. Moomaw. Just let us live another year. In case of another huge crop worldwide, just let us live another year and have a chance to do something a little differently then.[15]

A lower loan and a higher certificate (or target price) to induce participation is a vague standard. After 13 years of working with the voluntary program the committee has figured out that 'lower' means cost of production if they want to maximize participation. The point to be noted is that the committee has shifted from a vague standard to a more precise standard in their calculations about how farmers will respond to how this provision of the law is written—and farmers see the logic in this more specific standard.

Updating the Computing Routine and Approaching the Equilibrium

It is possible to build a computing routine that gives the same answers as do the committee members. It can compute, for recommendations made to the committee, the same answer about benefit to farmers that the committee uses in discussing the provision with the witness. That would seem rather surprising except there are two reasons to expect it. First, reading the committee hearings it is clear that they have to be doing something very much like this, and it is equally clear that they are consistent in their computations. Second, when cognitive scientists have attempted to build computer programs that can plan they find they have to build in routines like this. Their work suggests it would be implausible for a computing routine to be missing.[16]

What is important at this point is the way the routine is updated. In each hearing the computing routine is based on the extant law. Being better than the extant law is the way the recommendations are tested and the test the recommendation must pass. Then with the next hearing the computing routine is updated to reflect the changes that were made to the law. Since much of the discussion is about setting rates of payment for loans, set aside payments, etc. the process takes on the character of searching for a set of values that will satisfy all the constraints and do a better job than the last law in helping farmers. By 1973 they had figured out how to make the cost flexible, where the loan had to be set to induce participation in a voluntary program, and how to compute all the other parameters once these two are fixed. And this is the way they arrived at the equilibrium—the law that is still in place.

The Procedural Rationality of the Senate Agriculture Committee

The paper has relied heavily on Herbert Simon's ideas in its exposition because they seemed appropriate to the task of describing the actions of this committee. Given this starting point, one question remains. By what criteria should procedural rationality be assessed? If the optimal solution was known the answer would be easy. We would choose the procedures if they produced the optimal solution. But if the optimal solution could be computed there would be no need for procedural rationality. In principle, the criteria must be something other than: "The optimal solution" has been achieved. Simon's answer has always been that the decisions of human problem solvers produce "satisfactory" rather than optimal outcomes—or they change their minds and try something else. This section will examine the standard by which satisfaction is established in the Committee.

The standard of the Committee was: the law is (or is not) doing what it was supposed to do. Witnesses argued for their suggestions on the grounds that the provisions would improve the prosperity of family farmers. Members of the Committee had a large fund of historical experience, as well as the computing routines described in the last section, they called on in evaluating the claims of the witnesses—accepting some and rejecting others.[17] When the law produced the expected outcomes the Committee expressed satisfaction—the provision was retained. When the law did not work they changed it.

It should be noted that "works" was not an a-political standard. When the law "worked" it was improving the lot of farmers. And farmers were the constituents of the members of the Committee. "Works" was a very concrete, political standard of evaluation.

The standard was most prominently on display when the law did not work. According to its critics, cotton legislation passed in 1964 was a clear case in which the standard of "it works" was violated. A major change in the cotton program was passed in 1964. When the 1965 hearings took place opponents of the legislation were ready to assess the results.

> The Chairman. So that all of the estimates that were made last year that caused the Congress to enact this law failed, all the reasons advanced didn't come to pass.

> Witness. No, sir, I would not say that at all. I do not think there was anything in connection with the enactment of the legislation in 1964 that had any effect on the high yield per acre or the lower exports.
>
> The Chairman. But what caused Members of Congress, who were not interested in the cotton producer, to vote for this were the allegations by the proponents that it would reduce the surplus from 1,750,000 bales and that the cost would be $448 million, and that by equalizing the price to all purchasers of cotton both for domestic and foreign use, it would materially increase the consumption of cotton.
>
> Those were the three major points that were advanced as arguments in support of the program, and as I said, none of them came to pass.[18]
>
> Senator Eastland. Everything they said last year was wrong.
>
> The Chairman. How is that?
>
> Senator Eastland. Everything they predicted last year was wrong.
>
> The Chairman. Of course it was. There is no doubt about it.[19]

These are two brief excerpts from a long session in which proponents of the 1964 law were reminded of their predictions and the failure of those predictions to be realized. The upshot was another major change in the cotton program. The point here is the standard being employed. You claimed . . . That is not what happened! And the exercise of this standard, in the case of cotton, sent the Committee on a broad search for alternatives that would do a better job.

When provisions worked they were kept. In 1973 the Secretary of Agriculture tried to rid the agricultural program of production payments.[20] They are too costly, he said, and as agricultural income improves they are no longer necessary. Senator Dole pointed out how the wheat provision worked.

> Senator Dole. And I would suggest that the domestic certificate is the basic premise of the two price system, as Senator McGovern pointed out. We think the present program has a phaseout provision.
>
> If the market price goes up, the certificate value goes down. That was the intent of the act, and we think perhaps in the wheat area, we are ahead of the other commodities. We don't really see a need at this time to talk about the phasing out of certificates. That is really the effect of the program, and if the market price

remains relatively high, then the certificate program will cost less. I would hope that would be a consideration when we get into the bill itself.[21]

Senator Dole is calling attention to the homeostatic feature of the legislation—that it sets a lower limit on, thus protecting, farm income while varying the cost to the government depending on the market price.

But the important feature of the exchange for this section is the standard being employed by the Committee. "That was the intent of the act;" it works the way it is supposed to. And wheat farmers, Senator Dole's constituents, as well as taxpayers benefit from its working.

Improving farm income is an important version of "it did, or did not, work." Because this paper is about that feature of agricultural legislation the two illustrations were chosen to fit the subject of the paper. Both of these examples relate directly to the components of the law described in the paper and how the components are to be related to each other. But not everything about agricultural legislation can be reduced to improving farm income. In 1970 the specification of cotton quality "did not work." Some farmers were growing cotton that "qualified" for higher government support but the government could not sell it to the textile industry because it was too weak to be used easily in making cloth. That did not fit the committee's view of "works;" the committee did not want to produce government warehouses full of unusable cotton, and the definitions were changed. This example is included to illustrate the multi-faceted character of "it works." There is no simple definition of "works." What it means to work is context dependent, and if "works" was the focus of the paper a broad analysis of the thinking of the committee would be required. But the point of the section is calling attention to the one global criterion employed by the committee. "Works as claimed" can be made concrete by examining what was claimed.

If "working as claimed" is the standard of the Committee then claims made about the law can be assessed which the Committee did not review. Three of the claims are examined next.

One, when there is a substantial surplus the law sets a lower and an upper bound on the operation of the market. As the surplus declines agriculture returns to a freer market. These, at least, were the claims. The free market in agriculture is volatile; inelasticity of demand and of supply, within the production period, produces sharp swings in prices from year to year. If the claims about how the law

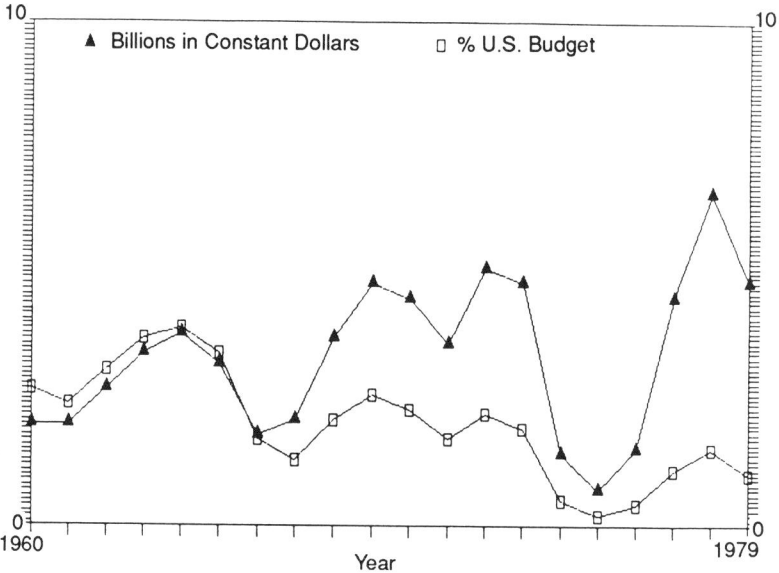

Figure 13.3. Agricultural expenditures 1960 to 1979

would work do characterize its operation then there should have been less volatility in prices during the 1960's and more volatility during the 1970's. And this is what occurred; the coefficient of variation for the 1970's is three times as large as in the 1960's.[22]

Two, the cost of the program will be higher during periods of surplus than in periods when agriculture is more prosperous. This was the claim. Figure 13.3 shows the cost of the farm price and income programs, in constant dollars, for the two decades of 1960–79. This claim did not prove to be true. The costs were greater during much of the 1970's though they were also more volatile reaching both the lowest and highest points during that decade. If one looks at these same numbers plotted as a proportion of the government's budget a different result is found. As a proportion of the total budget the agricultural programs cost less in the 1970's than in the 1960's. That may be the politically more important comparison.

Three, the "family farm" was the core concern of members of the committee as well as the linchpin of their appeal to society for the transfer of income into agriculture. Saving the family farm was what agricultural legislation was all about. However, saving the family farm meant something different to members of the committee than it does to observers outside the agricultural community. The committee knew that movement of population off the farm had been going on in this country for more than 150 years. They were not happy about losing constituents, but they viewed it as inevitable. Saving the family farm was, for the committee, making sure that those who stayed in farming were family farmers, and they believed the legislation would do this. The latest agricultural census shows that 97 percent of the farms in the U.S. are family farms (farms managed by a family) and 94 percent of the agricultural product is produced on family farms.[23] The number of family farms has dropped substantially since 1960 and the size of family farms has increased to keep tillable land in agricultural production. However, agriculture in the U.S. in the 1980s is still managed by families, and that will surely continue into the 1990s.

Conclusion

The development of U.S. agricultural policy between 1960 and 1973 has been described using, and elaborating, Herbert Simon's conception of bounded rationality. This leads to four conclusions:

1. The committee "bounds" their search for improvements to the law by operating under five constraints on what they will consider. This dramatically reduces the scope of their task by excluding many possibilities from consideration.
2. Policy and policy making interact in the development of the law. The law(t-1) plays the role of the computing equation for calculating how farmers will benefit from suggestions about how the law could be improved. This keeps the development of policy firmly tied to past law, and can be understood as a state dependent system which I argue goes to an equilibrium with the 1973 law which has been reproduced, largely intact, in each authorization bill since.
3. The procedural rationality of the committee can be seen operating through a global criterion of "worked as claimed." Claims are made for provisions in terms of improving farm income. When the claims are realized the provisions are kept. When the claims are not realized new provisions are sought and adopted.

4. The result of this style of decision making is a law which homeostatically sets a lower bound on farm income and adjusts government costs with the performance of the market.

Assessing policy can take many forms. The committee had their own procedure for assessing provisions of the law. In prospect: how would it work, integrated into the larger legislative program, relative to what was already in the law? In retrospect: did the provision work as claimed? By way of conclusion I would like to briefly lay out two other forms of assessment that might be employed.

A policy can be assessed by starting with the assumptions. The assumptions of this legislation—the five constraints—have been described in this paper. In assessing the current legislation one could go back to these assumptions and question one or more of them. In the 1980s, for example, there was a strong political push to move away from the international market. Two reasons were given for doing this. First, it would provide a mechanism for protecting the small family farmer by taking U.S. demand, carving it up between farmers then farming, and raising prices to consumers to make it possible for all of the farmers in business to survive. This is the policy of the Japanese government on rice production, and it leads Japanese consumers to pay 10 times the world market price for their rice. But it keeps the number of family farms constant. Second, it was argued by others that third world nations were becoming self-sufficient in agriculture, and the world market was "going away" for this reason. The agricultural self-sufficiency of third world nations was forced by the over-valued dollar, making U.S. agricultural products extremely expensive on the world market, and the rapidly growing third world debt. Whether that self-sufficiency can survive the comparative advantage U.S. farmers have in terms of soil and climate is not something that will be known for another decade—if the international economy "rights" itself. These two arguments did not gain enough "political clout" to be successful, but if they had U.S. agricultural policy would have moved in a very different direction.

I would like to make two points about this kind of assessment. First, for agriculture, where one would start is clear. The five constraints within which the committee operates could individually, or collectively, be challenged. Two, argument about the assumptions is only the starting point. There are hundreds of provisions in the legislation with strong interactions between them. It took a decade and a half to work out the interactions between the provisions when these five constraints were adopted. It would surely take as long to again work out the interactions between provisions if one or more of the assumptions were changed.

A second way to assess a policy is its survivability. Is the law adapted to historical conditions that may or have changed? Or is the law designed to adapt itself to changing conditions? I have argued throughout the paper that agricultural law, cum 1973, was adaptive to the boom and bust cycle of the agricultural economy. The middle 1980s were a period of "bust" for U.S. agriculture, and an authorization bill had to be passed right in the middle of that bust. The law survived—almost in tact. It is worth noting what the change was as a possible harbinger of things to come.

The combination of the nonrecourse loan and the target price (and the other provisions needed to work out this combination) spreads the cost of helping farmers survive bust between farmers and tax payers. Farmers must either repay the loan or turn their collateral over to the government which then sells it as demand and price improve. In the 1985 authorization act the repayment provision was changed for cotton and rice farmers; they must repay only what the crop sells for in the market. This change has two important consequences. First, the loan is no longer a lower bound on the market. Cotton and rice farmers now can sell their product no matter how low the market may fall since all they have to repay is what they can get in the market. This means that cotton and rice raised in other countries cannot take over the international market by selling just below the U.S. loan rate. Second, it means the total cost of assistance to cotton and rice farmers is borne by taxpayers. Taxpayers pay the deficiency payment; they also absorb the difference between the loan and market price. No surplus of U.S. commodities develops; the sale of these surpluses does not hold down future prices. The market clears each year—with substantial assistance from U.S. taxpayers.[24] Farmers will surely prefer this arrangement to the arrangement in which they have to share in the burden of bust. As demand improves the cost of the agricultural program will go down. At that point there will surely be a push from the other commodities to generalize this rule. Success in generalizing the rule will depend, in part, on taxpayers and their representatives understanding what is being done; on their ability to assess the consequences of what is being proposed.

Notes

1. Obviously, the Senate Agriculture Committee is not the only force in developing agricultural policy. They are important because there is less competition between the commodity representatives than in the House committee. They strongly oppose the policy recommendations of Republican Secretaries of Agriculture. And they are rather successful in the pursuit of their vision of what agricultural policy ought to be. They offer an important "window" onto the policy making process.
2. 'Equilibrium' is normally understood to be a property of systems of mathematical equations, but Ross Ashby showed that structure—rather than metric—is what is important for equilibrium. Search through a suitably defined space, whatever the metric, is the necessary condition for an equilibrium. This is the core argument of his *An Introduction to Cybernetics*. He also makes this point in a particularly explicit fashion in "The Mechanism of Habituation," in *N.P.L. Symposium on the Mechanism of Thought Process,* C. Cherry (ed.), London, pp. 1–21, 1959.
3. Herbert Simon, "Rationality in Psychology and Economics," *Journal of Business,* 1986, vol. 59, no. 4, pt. 2, pp. S209–224.
4. The processes reported in this paper are routines in a larger information processing model of the Senate Agriculture Committee. The model, computer program, is designed to accept recommendations from witnesses, argue with the witnesses about their recommendations, and use the information along with the (t-1) version of the law to write a bill. Preliminary results in producing provisions of legislation are reported in "Committee Law Making in the U.S. Congress," (paper presented at the 1987 meeting of the American Political Science Association) and G. R. Boynton and Chong Lim Kim, "Political Representation as Information Processing and Problem Solving," (paper presented at the 1987 meeting of the Southern Political Science Association). Preliminary results of the communication routines are reported in "Telling a Good Story: Models of Argument; Models of Understanding in the Senate Agriculture Committee," in Joseph W. Wenzel, ed., *Argument And Critical Practices,* Speech Communications Association, Annandale, Va., 1987. The two routines explicated here are intermediate routines in the program. Their output is passed to other routines which then produce an argument or a provision of the law. They are, however, very important routines in the overall operation of the model of the committee.
5. The principal legislation supporting sugar and tobacco are handled by the Finance Committee, and will not be discussed in this paper.
6. Herbert Simon, "A Comparison of Game Theory and Learning Theory," *Psychometrika* 21 no. 3 (1956), pp. 267–72.
7. Extension of Farm and Related Programs}, Hearings before the Committee On Agriculture and Forestry, United States Senate, Part i, (Washington: U.S. Government Printing Office, 1973) p. 88.
8. A nonrecourse loan was made by the government based on projected yield of the commodity. If the market price was higher than the value of the loan, when the crop was harvested, farmers sold their crops and repaid the loan. If the market price was less than the value of the loan, farmers turned their crop over to the Commodity Credit Corporation and did not repay the loan. It was called a nonrecourse loan because turning the collateral over to the government did not affect farmers' credit rating.
9. 1965 Hearing, p. 232.
10. R. G. F. Spitze has written a series of papers characterizing the authorization bills and the interpretation of continuing refinement given here is essentially the

same as he gives. He does not concentrate on the Senate Committee, and he gives a more standard economic treatment of the circumstances leading to the individual laws. See R. G. F Spitze, "Economic Redirections in Recent U.S. Agricultural Policy," *Journal of Agricultural Economics,* 1968, pp. 327–338, "Policy Direction and Economic Interpretations of the U.S. Agricultural Act of 1970," *Journal of Agricultural Economics,* No. 2, 1972, p. 99–108, "The Food and Agriculture Act of 1977: Issues and Decisions," *"American Journal of Agricultural Economics,* 1978, pp. 225–235, "The Agriculture and Food Act of 1981: Continued Policy Evolution," *North Central Journal of Agricultural Economics,* 1983, pp. 65–75.
11. 1965 Hearing, pp. 149–50.
12. The computation involved in this case is investigated in detail in G. R. Boynton, "Committee Lawmaking in the U.S. Congress."
13. 1965 Hearing, p. 207.
14. Even though they call it "price support payment," they are referring to a certificate based on production which was an income supplement and had no effect on the market price.
15. 1973 Hearing, p. 592.
16. Robert Wilensky, in *Planning and Understanding,* makes this point:

   Projector—The purpose of this component is to test plans by building hypothetical world models of what it would be like to execute these plans. Projecting the future requires considering other dynamics besides one's own plans, such as the probable actions of other planners or the course of natural events. Thus the Projector is actually a general purpose simulator capable of predicting a possible future from a current set of beliefs. In planning, this ability is used to debug current plans by simulating a future that may contain undesirable elements, thus enabling the goal detector to form new goals aimed at improving this situation.

   Wilensky does not have public policy in mind in his work. The concrete instantiation he works on is a routine which handles the interaction of computer users and computers. But he does find that planning by this program requires a simulator "capable of predicting a possible future from a current set of beliefs."

17. See "Historical Experience as a Source of Ideas in Committee Law Making; Incrementalism, Learning, and Planning," "Committee Law Making in the U.S. Congress," and "Telling a Good Story: Models of Argument; Models of Understanding in the Senate Agriculture Committee" in which historical experience is shown to figure quite prominently in the actions of the Committee.]
18. 1965 Hearing, pp. 679–80.
19. 1965 Hearings, p. 682.
20. "Production payments" are the certificate provisions that were transformed into the target price-deficiency payments in the 1973 law.
21. 1973 Hearing, p. 672.
22. R. G. F. Spitze and Marshall A. Martin, editors, *Analysis of Food and Agricultural Policies for the Eighties,* Agricultural Experiment Station, College of Agriculture, University of Illinois at Urbana-Champaign, pages. 8, 34, and 146.
23. Reported in *The Washington Post,* October 31, 1985, p. A17.
24. How this happened is a fascinating story of political bargaining which is too elaborate to be covered in this paper. The bargain was struck by Senator Dole, then majority leader of the Senate, in order to hold down the total cost of the agricultural act. From the perspective of this paper it was just the kind of combination of constraints that could move the law from one to another equilibrium point.